MW01155716

Casino Security and Gaming Surveillance

Casino Security and Gaming Surveillance

Derk J. Boss • Alan W. Zajic

CRC Press
Taylor & Francis Group
Boca Raton London New York

CRC Press is an imprint of the
Taylor & Francis Group, an **informa** business

Auerbach Publications
Taylor & Francis Group
6000 Broken Sound Parkway NW, Suite 300
Boca Raton, FL 33487-2742

© 2011 by Taylor and Francis Group, LLC
Auerbach Publications is an imprint of Taylor & Francis Group, an Informa business

No claim to original U.S. Government works

International Standard Book Number: 978-1-4200-8782-6 (Hardback)

This book contains information obtained from authentic and highly regarded sources. Reasonable efforts have been made to publish reliable data and information, but the author and publisher cannot assume responsibility for the valid-ity of all materials or the consequences of their use. The authors and publishers have attempted to trace the copyright holders of all material reproduced in this publication and apologize to copyright holders if permission to publish in this form has not been obtained. If any copyright material has not been acknowledged please write and let us know so we may rectify in any future reprint.

Except as permitted under U.S. Copyright Law, no part of this book may be reprinted, reproduced, transmitted, or uti-lized in any form by any electronic, mechanical, or other means, now known or hereafter invented, including photocopy-ing, microfilming, and recording, or in any information storage or retrieval system, without written permission from the publishers.

For permission to photocopy or use material electronically from this work, please access www.copyright.com (http://www.copyright.com/) or contact the Copyright Clearance Center, Inc. (CCC), 222 Rosewood Drive, Danvers, MA 01923, 978-750-8400. CCC is a not-for-profit organization that provides licenses and registration for a variety of users. For organizations that have been granted a photocopy license by the CCC, a separate system of payment has been arranged.

Trademark Notice: Product or corporate names may be trademarks or registered trademarks, and are used only for identification and explanation without intent to infringe.

Library of Congress Cataloging-in-Publication Data

Boss, Derk J.
   Casino security and gaming surveillance handbook / Derk J. Boss, Alan W. Zajic.
      p. cm.
   Includes index.
   ISBN 978-1-4200-8782-6 (hardcover : alk. paper) 1. Casinos--Security measures--Handbooks, manuals, etc. 2. Electronic surveillance--Handbooks, manuals, etc. 3. Gambling--Corrupt practices. I. Zajic, Alan W. II. Title.

   HV6711.B67 2011
   795.068'4--dc22
                                                       2010037026

Visit the Taylor & Francis Web site at
http://www.taylorandfrancis.com

and the Auerbach Web site at
http://www.auerbach-publications.com

To Ron Kohn, my mentor, you will never be forgotten. My family for always being there. And to my beautiful wife Cheri, whose love, support and assistance, made it all possible.

Derk J. Boss, CFE, CPP, CSP

I dedicate my portion of this book to the memory of my son who passed away in 2005.

Alan W. Zajic, CPP, CSP

CONTENTS

SECTION II　*Physical Security in Gaming Operations*

FOREWORD

Undoubtedly, two of the most important departments in the casino resort are security and surveillance. If the facility isn't safe and secure, it's not going to work for the customers, the employees, or the shareholders. Like an umpire or referee, however, it's best if they are not noticed, and if they're needed, they'd better be good.

That's what Al Zajic and Derk Boss have been throughout their careers. They've stepped in when necessary but, for the most part, they have designed and operated departments that were efficient, effective, and usually out of sight. Now, they're sharing their knowledge through this book.

When I first started in the gaming industry way back in 1979, I was a dealer in Atlantic City. One of the first things we were told during training was that the "eye in the sky" sees everything. We didn't doubt it. In those days, however, the cameras didn't really see everything, so there were catwalks from which surveillance officers watched over the important games. You could tell they were there because of the dust that floated down on the table as they walked overhead.

Today, the surveillance officer doesn't have to leave the control room. State-of-the-art cameras can pick up every nuance, move, and microscopic elements in any part of the casino resort. As a result, the focus is often on prevention rather than catching the bad guys in the act.

While security and surveillance have incorporated all the science and technology available today to allow those departments to stay on top of every threat, there is an art to their activities as well. Al and Derk reveal both sides of the equation in this book.

While in my mind, the importance of security and surveillance cannot be overstated, there is an unfortunate proclivity for casino executives to take these departments and their staffs for granted. Executives understand the need for security and surveillance departments, but are often reluctant to re-invest in increased staffing, new equipment, or updated training. Take one look at the extensive table of contents in this book and you will realize that the responsibilities of these departments extend far beyond safety and security. They also exist to protect the bottom line and the more attention and resources they receive, the better the job they can do.

In this economy, more attention must be paid to employee theft and internal fraud. When employees are squeezed by threats of layoffs or pay cuts, it becomes more likely that they may seek revenge upon the company and sometimes even a basically honest person can go wrong. The authors describe how to uncover the wrongdoing and how to handle it when it occurs.

For me, security and surveillance are among the most fascinating departments in a casino. As a writer, I covered gaming for nearly 10 years before I was permitted into a surveillance room to see exactly how it operates. In those days, the wall of video tape recorders took up most of the room. The room was kept very dark so officers could view the huge monitors without straining their eyes. It was kept very cool to protect the equipment.

During a recent visit, the HD monitors, relatively small computers, and bright, comfortable surroundings showed me just how much surveillance has changed in those 20 years.

What I like most about these departments is that they deal with the wide range of human nature in a way few other departments in the casino resort do. Executives and employees have to be tuned in to these factors and understand how to respond in a reasonable and nonemotional manner. It's professionals like Al and Derk who personify the professionalism that is crucial when establishing and operating modern casino security and surveillance departments. This book will quickly become the Bible for any security and surveillance officer.

Roger Gros, Publisher
Global Gaming Business Magazine

PREFACE

SURVEILLANCE IN THE CASINO

Casino surveillance has changed considerably in the years since I first started my career. Although I never had to walk the catwalks during my career, I certainly saw them and worked with guys who did. We've come a long way since then regarding equipment, personnel, our role, and our mission.

When I began my surveillance career in the late 1980s, we watched table games and specifically looked for card counters and card cheats. At that time, within the casino, the table games were everything and the casino shift manager was god. Our coverage and attention reflected that; we were constantly in the pit. Nothing else mattered.

Slowly over the next decade we saw surveillance change. Although the slot department was becoming much more important to the profit of all casinos, we in surveillance weren't really paying attention to that change. We were still watching the pit and using almost all of our resources to do so. Left alone, we probably would still be watching the games! However, one thing happened with technology that began the change: the use of multiplex recorder units.

Almost immediately surveillance operations changed. We went from recording only what was on our monitors to 100 percent recording. Surveillance was now a whole new world. Instead of saying "Sorry, we have no coverage of that area" or "Sorry, we weren't looking at that game," our response became "Hold on, we may have something."

For those of you who weren't around at that time, you probably can't understand what that meant to us and how it changed our world. It forced security to become a department that could contribute on a regular basis. It made other departments (and the general manager) take us seriously. Why? Because we could now provide information about events: thefts, cheating, who did what, where someone went and with whom, when games closed and opened, how long the casino shift manager spent in the pit, and so forth. These were areas we could never address before, or if we did address them, we provided the bare minimum of coverage.

We may have had 500 cameras placed in strategic locations, but because not all of the cameras were recording they couldn't provide any information as to what happened in a particular area. Multiplexes allowed those cameras to record, albeit not greatly, but record they did. Now we had all 500 cameras in strategic locations recording 24/7, and we became deadly.

I sincerely believe this is where surveillance took its first step to changing the world of the casino. The ability to record on all the cameras enabled the protection of the whole property, not just table games or even the casino. Managers would notice that there was something wrong in their area: an item or cash was missing, or maybe there was a report that an employee was using the area to sleep. Those managers began noticing cameras in their areas, and they made the call that changed our jobs forever. They called surveillance and asked if we had any coverage of their area, and for the first time we could say yes!

The ability to record everything changed all procedures within a casino. Now surveillance personnel had to learn about protecting slots, keno, sports books, bars, hotel, valet and parking lots. Essentially every area in the casino and on the property had some type of camera coverage, and we had to learn about every area and protect it.

This is where my career took off. I was, and am, a hotel casino guy. I started in slots as a change person and worked my way though the slots chain of command to slot shift supervisor, and then ultimately transferred to surveillance. I had learned a lot about casino departments and their operations. I learned a lot about the hotel and back of the house. I read everything I could get my hands on about casino operations and their security and protection. I knew enough to begin protecting the whole property.

My career has always been about protecting the entire hotel casino property, our employees, guests, and company assets. I've considered myself a specialist in loss prevention (or asset protection); although gaming surveillance is a very specialized type of loss prevention, it is still loss prevention. Looking at a surveillance director's role in the protection of the property took me (and now you, the new generation) to where we should be and what we need to do: a proactive surveillance operation that consistently detects crime, loss, and liability, and protects employees and guests from harm.

Section I of this book discusses how a surveillance department can improve its operation to attain that level of success. It is our intent to share with you the techniques and methods, the strategies and tactics used to protect the properties we worked for, and to develop and prepare the individuals who work in casinos for success and promotion.

The techniques contained within this book were gathered from different surveillance people and different surveillance rooms. We have always looked to see how our peers and colleagues in the industry were doing things and tried to use the best of the best techniques.

In this book we will discuss the core skills, essential knowledge, and vital techniques necessary for a surveillance room to be successful. You will learn about:

- IOU patrol
- Tri-shot coverage
- Conducting close watches
- Set-up and conducting surveillance audits
- Threat analysis
- Statistical review
- Basic strategy
- Card counting
- Game protection techniques
- Loss prevention
- Internal theft and fraud
- Players' club theft and fraud
- Surveillance standard operating procedures
- Surveillance training
- Surveillance investigation
- Security surveillance

As mentioned before, the information in this book is what a director of surveillance or an aspiring supervisor or investigator/agent will need to get on the right track and stay on track for the protection of the property.

The role of surveillance in the protection of today's casino property is an extremely important one. As mentioned previously, our responsibilities have grown tremendously since the day of table games only. I believe that if a casino property is to operate properly, be consistently profitable, have the ability to protect itself from constant litigation, and minimize losses to the greatest degree possible, the casino must have a proactive and effective surveillance room (as well as a proactive and effective security department). These departments are the foundation of any well-run and profitable property.

In this book you will learn about the costs associated with employee theft and fraud. They are sky-high and growing annually. I've spent most of my career fighting this internal problem and learned that we must continually be on the lookout for those employees who steal from the company. Internal theft and fraud, when left unchecked, will negatively affect your company's bottom line and could easily put your company out of business (or you out of a job).

Over the years, among all the scams I've witnessed, the internal scams cost the most. This will, more than likely, be true for your property. Yet, most surveillance rooms spend little, if any, time preventing or detecting internal scams.

Each department or area requires surveillance involvement and support. It's important to note that you can almost always expect that the department heads, managers, and supervisors have minimal, if any, training or experience in loss prevention. In fact, you may find that they have little training or experience in the operation of their department! This is why it is so important for you to take an active role in the protection of all departments. If not you, then who?

Almost all cheating, theft, fraud, or loss of any type can be detected through the deadly combination of surveillance audit observation and review of critical transactions or key statistical information. A proactive director who can field a team of well-trained and skilled investigators can consistently detect these activities using the techniques described in this book.

SURVEILLANCE VS. SECURITY

As a surveillance director I've worked with many security chiefs and security departments over the years. One of the best lessons I've learned from that experience is that it is much better for the property (and for the individuals involved) to get along and work together than not. It seems silly to even bring it up, but unless you make a concerted effort to work toward a solid and cooperative relationship between departments, that relationship can be ripped asunder by petty jealousy and rivalries.

I consider security and surveillance "brother" departments. In my opinion, we do the same things, only differently, and with a different focus. That sounds contradictory but not in the gaming world. We both protect the property from loss and liability; security does it physically and surveillance utilizes cameras. We both protect the property overall but security focuses on physical security (retail, hotel, parking lot, drunks, fights, etc.), while surveillance focuses on protecting the games, cash, and the casino floor. Again we do the same things, only differently. This why both departments are so close and yet, at times, can be so far apart. We always think that our department is better than the other guy's. There is nothing wrong with friendly competition as long as it doesn't turn into an out and out war, which I've seen happen.

As we've discussed here, the role of surveillance has increased over the past decade simply because more cameras are in more areas. More cameras increased surveillance involvement, often into areas traditionally in the realm of security (i.e., parking lots, back of the house, etc.). It is not hard to see that the opportunity exists to work together or to argue about whose case it is.

As I write this, one of my agents is in the monitor room complaining that he heard a security officer running down the surveillance department for some reason and our agent was, of course, unhappy about it. And our departments do get along! But left unchecked these feelings can get out of control.

Another reason for security and surveillance to be at odds is the overlap of responsibilities. For example, surveillance conducts an audit of the players' club and detects a clerk changing names on accounts to the names of her friends and robbing the accounts of their value. The clerk is taken to security holding to be interviewed. Who should interview the clerk? The security officer/investigator who does not have any training or knowledge of the players' club but knows how to interview, or the surveillance agent who knows exactly what happened and understands how the club operates but does not know how to properly interview suspects? In my opinion, the answer is both the security investigator and the surveillance agent should be involved. The departments must work together. There is a wealth of knowledge on both sides that must be used to protect the company.

As my colleague and coauthor said, it is important that the director of security and the director of surveillance meet on a regular basis not only to keep each other in the loop but to head off potential problems. Ideally, each director should attend the other's staff meeting for a few minutes to pass on new information and resolve any differences.

Personally, I also provide surveillance training to those security officers assigned to the security surveillance station. This helps both of these officers better perform their jobs, increases the effectiveness of the protection of the property, and establishes rapport and communication between vital departments.

When the security department and surveillance department work together to protect the gaming property, crime and loss will be reduced. That is our purpose and mission and it is our duty and responsibility to make it happen.

Derk J. Boss

SECURITY IN THE CASINO

The proliferation of legalized gaming in the culture of entertainment has progressed to legalized gambling in almost every state within the United States. In 1931, when gaming was first legalized in Nevada, the concept was deemed proprietary and lawmakers envisioned that Nevada would be the only state to ever legalize the business of gambling. As gaming became more popular, New Jersey became the next market for this lucrative business, and then the boom of land-based, riverboat, racetrack, and tribal operations flourished as it became clear that Americans were willing to spend disposable income at an amazing pace.

Along with this flurry of gambling money and various types of ancillary entertainment, there was the legal and moral duty to provide additional security to the important customers casinos were drawing in. The concept of large amounts of seemingly obtainable money and a chance to score the big jackpot also lured many undesirables into this cash mecca known today as gaming. These scam artists and criminals began preying on unsuspecting gamblers at alarming rates.

The role of security in the general sense is well documented in various professional security publications and within the various professional organizations related to security. Basic security functions utilized in all disciplines and environments are not detailed in this book. The role of the security officer in gaming environments specifically is not as well documented, and this void in the literature was one of the driving forces as we worked to produce this book from experiences that would be useful to the new or seasoned security and surveillance employee or manager.

The ideas, concepts, and strategies outlined in this book are from our experience and are not necessarily applicable to every security operation inside a gaming environment. Every location, demographic, and gaming operation has unique and different characteristics, and no one set of guidelines, standards, ideas, or concepts can be used by all casinos. Collectively, they need to be analyzed and applied appropriately. Having said this, our goal and hope is that the procedures, policies, guidelines, and real-world case studies that we present reflect the industry's best practices and that they will help you in your position and your environment.

The security section of this book is designed to help gaming security professionals develop operational proficiency by stimulating their thought processes and motivating them to improve their operations. It is also meant to be a helpful tool to those people interested in advancing from entry-level security positions into management, from the supervisor to the executive level manager.

We have attempted to summarize only the basic areas of security in a gaming environment and suggest solutions, or at least solutions that have historically worked for us, in a very general sense. We sincerely hope that proactive security professionals will find this book useful in their overall professional development.

Alan W. Zajic

ACKNOWLEDGMENTS

I would like to thank the many fine people I worked with and for over the years who've helped me get to where I am today and especially those who worked for me in all the surveillance rooms and bought into what I was trying to do.

Derk J. Boss, CFE, CPP, CSP

I would like to acknowledge the many employees who worked for me over the years ; they gave me the knowledge, the creativity, and the compassion to become a security professional. I learned more from them every day then I could ever teach them.

Alan W. Zajic, CPP, CSP

ABOUT THE AUTHORS

Derk Boss is a well-respected gaming protection operator and consultant with more than 28 years of experience within the gaming industry. He has served in executive positions in security, surveillance, and compliance capacities for American Casino and Entertainment Properties, Grand Casinos, Bally's, Aztar, Del Webb corporations, and Tropicana Entertainment. The surveillance teams trained and led by Boss have a proven track record of success in the detection of cheating, advantage play, both internal and external theft, and fraud. Boss has earned professional certification as a Certified Fraud Examiner (CFE), Certified Protection Professional (CPP), and Certified Surveillance Professional (CSP). Presently, Derk serves on the Gaming and Wagering Council for ASIS International and is a past chairman of the Council. He is currently the president of the International Association of Certified Surveillance Professionals (IACSP) and is one of its founding members. Derk is also a respected author, instructor, and speaker, specializing in the fields of surveillance training and methodology, gaming protection, loss prevention, and the detection of internal and external theft and fraud.

He has appeared as an expert on several television networks including the Travel Channel and his technical articles have appeared in dozens of professional journals, including *Security Management* magazine, which is published by ASIS International. ASIS International is the largest organization for security professionals with more than 36,000 members worldwide. As a speaker, he has been featured at several international conferences including the Global Gaming Exposition, Gaming Operation Summit, and Biometric Summit. Derk, his wife Cheri and their son Jason currently reside in Evansville, Indiana where Derk is the Director of Security and Surveillance for Casino Aztar.

Alan W. Zajic is a Nevada licensed independent security consultant specializing in hospitality, gaming and retail security environments primarily in Nevada. He has more than 30 years of practical hands-on experience in security and surveillance operations and served as security director for the Sahara Tahoe and High Sierra resorts in Lake Tahoe as well as corporate security for Del E. Webb, Corp. in Nevada.

Alan is a member of ASIS International where he holds the designation of Certified Protection Professional (CPP) and is currently the chairman of the Hospitality, Entertainment and Tourism Security Council as well as an active member of the Gaming and Wagering Protection Council. He is actively involved in the Northern Nevada and Las Vegas Chapters as well as the international security community. He is also a member of the International Association of Certified Surveillance Professionals (IACSP) where he holds the designation of Certified Surveillance Professional (CSP) and is a member of the International Association of Professional Security Consultants (IAPSC). He is a subject matter expert and track advisor for the American Gaming Association.

In addition, Alan is an instructor for the University of Nevada at Reno in the Gaming Management Program and at UNLV for the International Gaming Institute in security and surveillance applications. He is frequently requested to present sessions at international security conferences and for various organizations throughout the country. Further, he is frequently called upon to serve as a forensic security consultant (expert witness) in gaming, hospitality, retail, bars and nightclubs, and multi-unit housing environments nationally and in Nevada. His practice areas include forensic consulting, management consulting, major incident management, policy and procedure development as well as conducting tailored training programs for gaming operations.

Section I
Surveillance in Gaming Operations

1

Camera Operational Techniques

1.1 SURVEILLANCE PATROL

Surveillance personnel who want to be successful must use proven surveillance techniques. These are methods that, once learned, will assist the operator in the detection of policy or procedure violations or criminal activity. The surveillance patrol is one of those techniques. A thorough patrol, using cameras to search, monitor, and record routine and unusual activities occurring within the casino is a foundational surveillance procedure used to generate consistent detections. Detection of crime or the indicators that a crime is about to take place is probably the most important function of a surveillance department.

It's important to note that no matter how many scams you've seen or been involved with there will always be another new scam that you won't recognize or be prepared for. In fact, most old scams are often undetectable even when you're watching for them! Surveillance personnel must be trained in the techniques that will put them in the position to detect the scam.

Most new surveillance operators are not trained in the technique of proper patrol. Most, in fact, are trained to patrol randomly and not in a systematic manner. It is important to remember that "a random patrol equals random results." Random results will cost your casino money, a loss of efficiency, and will not deter crime.

Surveillance management should operate under the premise that crime is occurring somewhere within the casino or on the property each and every shift, every day. Why? Because it's true. Think about the last three crimes you've dealt with recently. How many were occurring before detection? And for how long? Did the crimes all occur within the casino or did one or two happen in a bar or restaurant, in the hotel, or in the parking area? What time did these crimes occur? During the day shift? Or did they occur at all different times?

I always cringe when I hear a surveillance director say that his or her property has little, if any, crime. I honestly don't think that's possible. To me, it means they're not looking in the right places. Usually, such surveillance operations are big on detecting procedure violations and making the lives of the other departments miserable.

I was involved with one property where the director of surveillance (DOS) said just that, and he sincerely believed it. I tried to discuss with him that every casino property has losses of some kind, but he was adamant. Unfortunately for him, after we began using proactive surveillance techniques, we found a significant internal theft in the gift shop. The DOS had overlooked many indicators that would have told him something was going on. I know he had to explain his mistakes to the general manager (GM), which didn't go over well. He left the industry shortly thereafter. Sad, because it didn't have to happen.

My point is that you never know where or when you're going to get hit or by whom. You just have to be ready to handle it when it happens. Operating under the premise that it can happen at any time and training your staff to think the same way will help you be prepared.

There has been a tremendous amount of research that has resulted in published studies and surveys that look at crime in an attempt to break it down into understandable components. Reports such as the Association of Certified Fraud Examiners Report to the Nation are invaluable tools for determining levels of crime. For example, the 2010 report states that the average U.S. business loses 7 percent of its annual revenues to occupational fraud. In other words, expect to lose revenue to your employees.

In another report, the University of Florida's 2008 National Retail Report, concerning shrinkage in the retail industry, estimates that about 1.54 percent of a company's annual sales revenue is lost to shoplifting, employee theft, and paper errors.

The research strongly indicates that theft and fraud occur in every industry on a frequent basis and most certainly negatively impact a company's bottom line. We will get into how loss affects the gaming industry later on. For now, it should be apparent that a gaming surveillance operation, or for that matter, any loss prevention program, if it wants to be successful, must work under the premise that crime and loss can and do occur at any time and in every department. Therefore, constant and systematic patrols of all areas will result in increased and consistent detections.

Most surveillance people do not look for or research such information. A lot of us work in a closed world and don't allow new information in. I hope that this book opens your eyes. There are a lot of loss prevention, security, and surveillance techniques out there that you can apply to your own situation.

1.2 IOU PATROL

I recommend the IOU patrol. IOU is an acronym for identify, observe, understand. This patrol was developed by a very experienced and accomplished surveillance person whom I met early in my career at a training class. She passed on this basic yet incredibly effective technique. These three components of a patrol accomplish everything that is needed for detection, response, investigation, and the gathering of evidence for any situation.

Each investigator is assigned to patrol a different area of the property. I suggest that you break down your patrols as follows: one investigator assigned to the pit and another to slots. Another setup is to assign one person to gaming and another to nongaming, or front of house and back of house. If you have more than two investigators you can break it down further.

Many properties have only one investigator on duty. The IOU patrol may and still should be carried out. The patrol is the most effective method to detect crime regardless of the number of investigators on duty. You will find that if the IOU patrol is done properly, it will consistently detect situations or individuals who should be followed through further observation and investigation.

An IOU patrol is conducted as follows: Begin the patrol at a standard reference point such as blackjack table number one or slot section number one. At the first table (or machine, or area):

Identify: Using your camera, identify each person at the table, including players and employees. Also include individuals standing next to the game or in the immediate area. It is necessary to identify the game number and the status of the game, such as the denominations and amounts of checks in the tray or the face of the slot machine (i.e., payout meters, etc.). When you have identified the game, company funds or property, employees and players, you can move on to the next step.

If you are performing the IOU patrol in the back of the house area or at a point of sale, use the same method by observing and recording all the employees in the area and the condition of the area at the time, or in the case of a point of sale located at a bar, you must record everything in and around the cash register and those seated at the bar, including the lounge area, bar backs, and waitresses in service areas. Again, everything should be recorded that may be important in the event you must review for a specific individual or incident that occurred or may occur in that area.

Observe: Observe the play or activity for indicators or tells of advantage play, cheating, or theft. These indicators include violation of internal controls, policies, or procedures. Remember, almost every case of cheating or internal theft (and frequently, advantage play, such as hole card play) is due directly or indirectly to a weak control or poorly trained employee, not to mention those employees deliberately ignoring or violating a control for their own purposes.

For example, in table games, also observe the play for size of wagers, players' knowledge of basic strategy and overall skill level, players' wins/losses, and so forth. This is the period of time you will use to establish your priorities. For example, while observing players at a particular game, you should be able to eliminate quickly those players who are losing small amounts, betting flat, or making consistent basic strategy mistakes. Doing so will help you quickly focus on higher action players moving their bets, playing strong basic strategy, or displaying tells of advantage play or cheating.

Understand: The final component of the IOU patrol is to "understand" the activity or action. What this means is that you must determine if it is legitimate play or if it is suspicious. If the play is legitimate (no violation of policy, procedure, controls by employees, no tells of advantage play, cheating or theft, etc.), the operator can move on to the next player, game, or area in the patrol. If the play or activity is suspicious for any reason, further observation and investigation are necessary and, in fact, required in order to protect the property properly. Think about it: you may have spent hours looking at normal activity and now you finally find something, no matter how small or insignificant, that is suspicious or outside normal parameters, you're in the right place at the right time!

An IOU patrol on a specific game is not complete until the investigator "understands" the action on the table or in the area. This often will mean that the investigator can confidently say that the activity is normal, the action is not unusual, and policy and procedures are being followed. I usually use the guideline in 21 of being able to predict the amount of a player's next wager. When you can correctly predict what a player will wager on an upcoming hand, you can safely say you understand his or her play and make the decision as to whether further observation is warranted. You can also apply this premise to any area—slots, point of sale (POS), warehouse—when you can "understand" that procedures are being followed and that the activity is normal, you can then move on.

By the way, understanding the game is often where investigators, especially new ones, get tripped up. They don't know when to say they "understand" and can often continue to look at a game longer than they need to. The same can be said of those investigators who haven't taken the time to learn the skills they need or they just don't care. Either one requires a supervisor to step in to help or discipline the investigator as needed.

Please note that an IOU patrol on a specific game, slot machine, or area may take anywhere from two minutes to eight hours. Of course, eight hours would be an extremely long period of time to evaluate a game or area; however, the point is that the operator, when he or she has determined the play is normal, should move on as quickly as possible. On the other hand, if the operator remains suspicious or uncomfortable with the play or the player(s), then this is the action to patrol and the place the operator should be and in fact is paid to be. The operator must stay with the action for as long as it takes until it is "understood" what the action is and what the proper response to it should be.

I can't stress enough the importance of speed, knowledge, and skill for an operator. You must always keep in mind that someone is out there on your property cheating, stealing, or otherwise harming your fellow employees or the guests of your property. If it is not occurring on the table, machine, or area that you're looking at, its occurring somewhere else, and you must detect (find out) where that is.

1.2.1 Case History

In one of my staff's first use of an IOU patrol in the slot area (which wasn't accepted well by the staff; they wanted to be in the pit, which is still true of most surveillance teams to this day), the investigator assigned found something unusual in the high action slot area. The investigator noted during his IOU patrol that two male slot player were sitting right next to each other (guys don't often do that) and that one of the players had an empty ashtray placed on the machine in front of him, although he wasn't smoking.

As he continued to observe (because he didn't understand this behavior) he also noted that the other player was constantly looking around and rubbernecking (see slot tells). Thinking all of these suspicious activities might indicate something was going on, he called over his supervisor for a look. Sure enough, something was going on. The supervisor recognized both players from a previous flyer reporting the two were using a device to cheat the slot machine. The device disrupted the optic reader in the machine so that it didn't count all of the coins it paid out. The ashtray was used to cover the coin pay-out meter because it would show that the machine was being cheated; the display of coins being paid, instead of operating smoothly, would actually hesitate and slow down due to coins not being counted. This indicator was extremely obvious and thus had to be covered. Security was alerted and the two were apprehended with the device in their possession. Because they played a $25 machine, the loss could have been significant. A great bust was due directly to a well-executed IOU patrol and a trained investigator.

Keep in mind that this bust would not have happened if we had not been proactive. Also keep in mind that, at the time, this cheating method and device were new. We had never seen it before but we caught it because we were looking and because our agent did not understand the play and was suspicious! He didn't say "Oh well, I don't think they're doing anything."

1.3 TRI-SHOT COVERAGE

During the IOU patrol the investigator will frequently find individuals or activities that appear suspicious. Upon detecting a suspicious or unusual situation, tri-shot coverage is placed to obtain the information necessary to make an informed decision about the event or activity or to gather appropriate evidence to prosecute individuals involved, if necessary.

You would think that this is something most surveillance personnel would do naturally. After all, we work with cameras all day long! But we often do not do this well. A lot of agents, when covering an incident or when trying to determine what's going on, will often use one camera only or will zoom in so tight that they can't see (and neither will a future jury) what is happening out of camera view, which usually turns out to be important.

The requirement of tri-shot coverage is critical for the success of a surveillance room. It really is all for nothing if you detect a crime and apprehend the suspect, only to later see him or her released based on a lack of evidence, not to mention the embarrassment.

Tri-shot coverage consists of a minimum of three specific camera angles or "shots." Each of these shots is important, allowing not only coverage of suspicious activity, but also providing the ability to gather necessary evidence in the event the suspicious activity becomes an actual incident. Tri-shot coverage consists of the following shots:

1. Overview: Camera overview of a game, such as a 21 game or a slot machine. Overview should provide an unobstructed view of the game device and related equipment used to play or operate the game. For example, a 21 game should be covered by an overview shot in the following manner:
   • View of layout to include the chip tray, card dealing shoe (if used), discard rack, and shuffle machine (if used)
   • Dealer's cards
   • Players' cards and bets
   • Players' hands
   • Table layout to at least the rail
2. Specific or bet shot: This shot is used to monitor a specific area of the game such as the wager, players' hands, or players' cards (or all of these at once). In the case of a slot machine, the specific shot should cover coin or credit meters and other displays on the front of the machine. This particular angle provides close-up observation and recording of a player's hands that he or she may use to alter or manipulate the cards or increase or decrease his or her bet or insert a device into a slot machine.
3. The identification or ID shot: This shot is placed to obtain identification of the players on the game, individuals on or around the game, and employees on or around the game or area. This shot shows "who did what" and who was present during, before, and after the activity.

Figure 1.1   Table game overview.

Figure 1.2   Table game ID shot.

Figure 1.3 Table game bet hand shot.

Figure 1.4 Slot overview.

Figure 1.5   Slot ID shot.

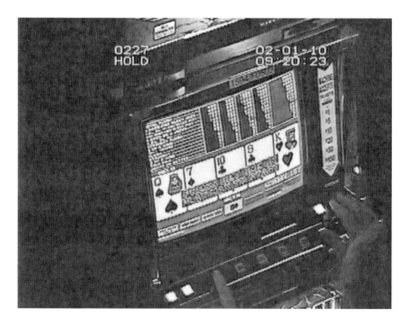

Figure 1.6   Slot machine screen shot.

Figure 1.7   Point of sale overview.

Figure 1.8   Point of sale register overview.

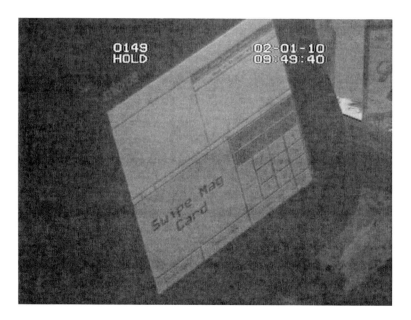

Figure 1.9 Point of sale register screen view.

Timely establishment of the identification shot, and in fact, establishment of the tri-shot at the onset of an event or suspicion nearly always provides the evidence or information necessary to appropriately stop the event or to investigate after the event.

Operators who place their cameras properly will not fall prey to the all too common situation of not having enough cameras in place prior to the player or suspect leaving the game or area. The tri-shot also works for those occasions when you initially thought a player was suspicious, set up a tri-shot, but later felt everything was okay and moved on in your patrol. Later, when you determine that your initial suspicion was correct, you can go back on the videotape and obtain quality video of the play, table conditions, and the all-important "ID" of the player. See the section on standard operating procedures for guidance on when to set up the tri-shot.

1.3.1 Case History

During an IOU patrol the agent observed a player jumping his bet from $100 to $2,000. He placed his tri-shot right away and began counting down the shoe, but the player continued to bet unusually; normally $100 but then suddenly table maximum, without paying attention to the count whatsoever. Yet, he was winning consistently and alarming those in the pit.

Pondering the situation, the agent looked over at the identification shot of the table he had placed. One of the individuals standing there seemed familiar. Checking the recent Griffin flyers, he got a hit. That person turned out to be a member of a shuffle tracking team. The person playing the game was a new member whom no one had seen yet. Needless to say the shuffle tracking activity was quickly disrupted.

1.3.2 Case History

The pit reported to the surveillance department that a $10,000 marker taken by a player earlier in the day and on another shift appeared to have a fraudulent signature. Investigation determined that the signature on the marker did not match the signature on file in the cage. Further investigation revealed that the player whose account the marker was drawn on was not on the property, having left several days previous. The floor person who conducted the transaction said that he had issued the marker to a man who had presented a players card to him as identification. The floor person had never seen the man before and had not asked for any photo identification. Upon receiving the $10,000 in checks, the man played briefly then left the table.

At this point it appeared that the casino was out $10,000. The money and the person who took it had left the property. Initial review of the tape showed the table layout and the marker being issued but nothing further. However, the surveillance department decided to review further. As it had happened on another shift, the surveillance logs for that time period were checked. The logs indicated that the agent on duty at that time had performed an IOU patrol of that pit and game about the time the marker was issued. Review of that tape provided a quick identification shot of the individual who was seated at the spot that received the marker. A photo was taken of the individual, shown to pit personnel, and the individual was recognized. He was the golf pro of the property's golf course. He was confronted by security and confessed to posing as the account owner. The real player had accidentally left his player's card behind after golfing one day and the pro picked it up. Most of the $10,000 taken was retrieved and the golf pro was terminated.

The photos presented in this chapter are typical tri-shot coverages for table games, slots, and a point of sale.

1.4 SURVEILLANCE AUDITS

One of the single most powerful weapons surveillance can use to detect and prevent crime is an operational audit. This technique catches more violations of controls, policies, procedures, theft, and cheating than any other technique I'm aware of.

I believe in audits strongly, as anyone who has ever worked for me will tell you. It is one of the reasons our teams were successful. I don't know why other surveillance directors don't use them. They always provide information or catch something somebody shouldn't be doing.

I recommend to you here that if you want to increase your department's detections and to operate proactively, set your team to doing audits. If your staff diligently performs the audit you've assigned, you will soon see a turnaround.

Most surveillance teams do not perform audits effectively for two reasons: (1) they don't use the information at hand to select the right area for audit and (2) personnel assigned to the task don't audit, they monitor.

Recently, I was assigned to assist in the turnaround of a surveillance department that over the years had not been able to catch crime events. It wasn't the fault of the agents, they wanted to succeed but they just hadn't been shown how to do it.

I would say here that in surveillance we often set up our surveillance rooms with all the equipment needed and then we expect the agents to catch things without providing the necessary guidance and training they need to succeed. Nowadays, with the proliferation of gaming across the country and around the world, we often have surveillance rooms staffed with personnel who've never been in a casino!

In the above case, my fix was to immediately set up an audit of the bars on the property. While we didn't catch any theft, we were able to report that not one bartender at any bar ever issued a receipt to any customer. This was significant information to both the general manager and the beverage director who were amazed. Not giving receipts can result in many forms of internal theft and is not a sound business practice.

We then did an audit of the snack bar. In about twenty-four hours we caught every employee working in the snack bar making food without paying for it, giving away food to other employees, and taking meats and product home, again without any payment. We also reported many health code violations. It was apparent that these activities had been going on for a long time and were certainly the primary reasons that the food costs in this area were always higher than they were supposed to be. The food and beverage director immediately made adjustments to personnel and to policy and procedure.

Of course, it amazed everyone that a quiet surveillance room was now catching things seemingly left and right. It also showed the surveillance personnel that they could catch thefts and they could be a force in the protection of the property. All this in about forty-eight hours of well-chosen and well-done audits by a team who had never done one before!

Let's take reason number one: not using the information at hand to select the right area. By information, I mean operating statistics, crime trends, exception reports, violations of internal controls, policies or procedures, and so forth. This type of information and more, when reviewed, will lead you to the proper area to audit. A thorough and consistent audit schedule will generate numerous leads and detections for the department and for the operator performing the audits.

Audits are used to monitor key areas, transactions, and processes used within the casino. Examples of key or critical areas, transactions, and processes are, but not limited to:

- Main cage
- Slot jackpots and fills
- Table game player rating cards
- Credit or "marker" transactions
- Points of sale

Surveillance audits are normally set up as described below:

1. The surveillance director selects an area or transaction type to monitor and establishes the audit's objective, for example, to detect criminal activity or ensure employees are following rules, policies, and procedures.
2. Information, documentation, controls, policies, and procedures used by the department or area to be audited or to complete the transaction are gathered. Personnel assigned to the audit, including supervision, should review all such information prior to commencing the audit.

3. Photos of employees, subjects of interest, or suspects may be included in the case file, as well as work schedules and any other pertinent information.
4. The parameters of the audit are established: time and date to start and end audit, who is assigned specifically to audit each shift, person responsible (case manager), types of notes to be made, who is authorized to know about the audit. This information is used to open the case file and is maintained in the case file at all times. Each person assigned to the audit must read this memo.
5. The audit is initiated as detailed in the case file.

A common audit instruction specifies that only exceptions to policy, procedure, or suspicious activity are logged into the case file. This prevents the file from becoming overloaded with unnecessary information and allows the case manager to quickly locate significant events.

1.4.1 Case History

The surveillance department was assigned by its director to audit player rating cards as completed and submitted by table games personnel. Surveillance personnel monitored and recorded green action and above for twenty-four hours to include for each shift. Upon completion of the observation period, surveillance obtained from the cage all rating cards submitted for the previous day. Cards listing action of $25 or more were located and distributed to investigators for review.

As the review of the players' ratings card progressed, it quickly became apparent that the information on almost all cards was inaccurate as to the amount the players bought in for, their average bets, and what they won or lost and their total time played was off as compared to the video. Something was very wrong.

Investigators also noted that a number of players were described as "refused name," meaning that apparently the player wanted to remain anonymous. Certainly this was odd!

Curious also was that a number of players listed as playing on a specific table at specific times were not located at that game. Often these players could not be located anywhere on the games records.

Obviously, the team had a lot of questions and a lot of investigation to complete. The team reviewed all pertinent paperwork and video. The findings of this audit were:

- Player rating cards were often inaccurate because floor personnel were not trained to complete the cards in a standard format. For example, each floor person used his or her own formula to compute a player's average bet instead of one formula used for all. As floor personnel were often watching more than four games, they could not keep up with the coming and goings of individual players, so they often just guessed about their playing time, wagers, and wins and losses. Many floor persons asked the dealer for this information!
- "Refused name" players were found to occur most often because individual floor persons did not want to approach players to introduce themselves and explain the rating program (so much for marketing!). Additionally any winning play that was missed by the floor person was attributed to a refused name player to cover the

floor person. So now we have unexplained losses on the table going to unidentified players (great way to cover theft and cheating!).

- Players not found on the games that they were listed as playing were the biggest problem. Investigators compared the names and addresses of these players to the employee database and got a number of hits. Some floor persons had signed up their friends and family members for a player's account. The floor person would then make up rating cards for those individuals who detailed large wagers for significant periods of time. Result: the floor person and his or her friends and family were able to obtain comps and cash back based on fraudulent play. A total of twelve fraudulent accounts were identified. Losses to the property were in the tens of thousands, if not more.

As a result of the audit performed by surveillance, table games were required to develop and implement controls, policies and procedures, and specific rating parameters for their player rating program. Floor personnel were required to approach every player who met the criteria for the rating program. Refused name players had to be reported to surveillance for evaluation.

Twelve floor persons were terminated for setting up fraudulent accounts. Those accounts and were removed from the system and the account owners were let go. The surveillance department began a daily review of a sampling of rating cards and conducted quarterly audits of the players rating program.

1.5 SURVEILLANCE CLOSE WATCHES

There are three basic observation techniques used by surveillance. We've discussed IOU patrols, surveillance audits, and the last one normally used is the surveillance close watch. This observation is usually performed because of a specific observation made or specific information received concerning suspicious or actual criminal activity perpetrated by specific individual(s) and/or occurring in a specific area. The close watch observation is used in these cases to specifically (in other words, closely) monitor the reported individuals' every move while on the property or any and all activity in the subject area.

A number of close watches are implemented at the request of a general manager, gaming enforcement agents, law enforcement, department heads, employees, or the director of surveillance. Such requests are almost always based on a tip from an employee or informant or generated by unexplained losses or consistently lower than expected win percentages.

Whatever the reason for the close watch, it has been my experience that such information received is usually pretty good. Almost all of it has some basis in fact and should always be developed as much as possible. Information received from employees is especially good. Remember, employees working with an individual or a group of individuals usually have at least an idea or suspicion of what's going on. Employees don't like to tell on other employees, but sometimes they do, and the information is usually right on the mark.

The key point about close watches is that when such information is received, make sure you follow it up. There is an excellent chance the information is solid and when investigated will result in an effective arrest. This is usually where surveillance rooms go wrong: they either discount the source of information or disregard it entirely; or because they don't watch the person or area long or well enough, they don't see the crime.

One property I worked at kept receiving anonymous calls reporting that the purchasing manager was up to something with a supplier. We did watch the individual a number of times, but never saw him do anything wrong. We later found that he was awarding contracts to the same supplier and was getting kickbacks. While we wouldn't have seen something on camera, a proper investigation would have located that information. In this case we dropped the ball too soon.

In another case, we received information from the payroll manager that one of her employees was suspected of stealing money from the purses of her fellow employees when they were out of the room. We set up a hidden camera over one employee's desk where her purse was kept, gave her money to put into the purse, and told her to leave both when she went on break. As we were waiting for things to develop, I went into my office and left the close watch in the hands of one of our agents with the explicit instructions "Don't take your eyes off that purse." I happened to glance up at the monitor in my office where the hidden camera was also displayed and immediately saw the suspect place her hand into the purse and take the cash.

I waited to hear the agent yell out something like "I caught her" or "She took it," but I heard nothing. I ran out to the room and saw the agent talking to one of the other agents. He had taken his eyes off the purse and missed the theft. By the time we dispatched security, the suspect had made it out to her car with the cash. Luckily she admitted to everything and gave up the money.

The above is a typical close watch situation. Unless you assign the right person with explicit instructions, it will fail.

1.5.1 Tips for Successful Close Watches

- Obtain as much of the necessary and relevant information to the case at the beginning. You may never get another chance. Get everything you can.
- Never, ever, take received information lightly, no matter how unlikely it seems. I have seen this type of information turn out to be correct more often than wrong.
- Assign close watches to your best people. You can't take the chance that the signature event will be missed.
- Take the time to put in writing the facts and beliefs of the case as you know them. Put this in a case file along with everything your investigators may need for the case. Include photos of suspects, schedules, pertinent policy and procedures, and so forth. Your people shouldn't have to hunt for anything. It should be at their fingertips.
- Assign a case manager to supervise the case. You need one person you can call and get updates from (and hold accountable).
- Ask for results daily. Close watches tend to start off strong, then, slowly lose momentum. Keep your people focused on this critical task.
- Be patient! Close watches are notorious for how long they can take. Don't get discouraged or let your people get discouraged. Usually you will find what you're looking for.

1.6 PROACTIVE OR REACTIVE?

Some surveillance departments catch more than others. In my opinion, this is not due to location or equipment. All gaming properties, in fact, almost all businesses, suffer losses from theft or fraud, whether it is perpetrated by internal (employees), external (guests, players, customers, vendors/suppliers) parties.

The reason some surveillance rooms catch more than others is due to their proactive approach to protecting the property from crime and loss and the level of buy-in to that premise by the department's management and staff. A surveillance team that knows that there is crime to catch and losses to detect tends to operate with that premise in mind and goes about every task expecting to catch something. If they can't find it in one location, they move to another. Such surveillance teams have the expectation they will succeed, and because they expect to, they do. Individuals who make up these teams are normally busy throughout their shift, positive about their work, and put their training and skills to maximum use.

A reactive team must wait until something is reported to them or until after the incident has occurred to go into action. Because they are reactive, they frequently do not have live or even good coverage of the incident. Their record of detections is low due to waiting for a report of an incident. As most of us know, not all incidents are reported or even found. In other words, if surveillance isn't looking for activity, no one else is either. A reactive team can be lethargic and unmotivated, sometimes needing prodding to do just the bare minimum to get by in their work.

What type of team would you want to lead or be a part of? A proactive team requires a proactive leader who teaches the fundamentals of surveillance operations (i.e., IOU patrol, tri-shots, audits,), recognizes that crime and loss occur routinely, and holds his or her people accountable for reducing or eliminating both.

I also think that surveillance personnel, especially those in leadership positions, must take losses personally. I know that when a loss occurs on any one of the properties I am responsible for, I don't like it. I do my best to determine what happened, who did it, and how it can be prevented in the future. I expect my staff to do the same. This mindset helps me to be proactive.

Let's discuss the differences between a proactive and a reactive approach. A typical situation in most casinos is a theft from a player or guest of a purse, coin bucket, or ticket voucher. The frequency of such thefts ranges from seldom to sometimes several times a day at some properties. The thefts usually occur in the slot areas and are usually perpetrated by opportunists or experienced street type or petty criminals.

Opportunists are individuals who enter the property not necessarily to commit a theft but will not shy away from taking the opportunity to commit a crime should the opportunity present itself. Opportunists may also be other players or guests who, while on your property, find a wallet, purse, or other valuable that they just "forget" to turn in.

Criminals enter the property for the purpose of committing a crime. These individuals mark a potential victim and cause the victim to be separated from his or her belongings. For example, a common theft technique is the "distract and grab." One or more individuals will identify a victim and the item to be taken, engage the victim in conversation, and while the victim is talking to one subject the other grabs the item and quickly exits the property. A reactive surveillance operator or team receiving the report of such a theft will base his or her response on whether the area where the theft occurred is being recorded and easily accessible. If the event was recorded, a review will be performed and security will be advised of the description of the suspect(s) and their direction of travel. An incident report will be filed describing the incident.

In the event that there is no readily available video of the area, response to the incident may consist of nothing at all. A quick call is made to security informing them of the lack of video, and the operator normally doesn't even have to write a report. And when all is said and done, surveillance has not put itself into a position to succeed by catching the bad guys.

Remember the purse and what was contained in it may not be important to you or me, and it certainly is no loss to the casino, but it sure is important to the lady it was stolen from. So, at the very least, we have an angry customer who will tell everyone she knows that she was ripped off in our casino. Also, people will think that our casino is not safe. And the worse part is that the person who stole the purse wasn't caught, so it will happen again.

Now let's take a look at a proactive surveillance room and how they would handle the same situation. Security reports the theft to surveillance. The operator on duty identifies that where the incident occurred there is no coverage available. The operator reviews the surrounding areas and aisles for possible suspects. He locates a possible suspect loitering in the general area at about the time the theft occurred. The operator reviews the tape of the entry and exit doors prior to and after the theft occurred. He finds the same possible suspect entering the property a few minutes prior to the incident and then exiting quickly a few minutes later. The operator is able to obtain a photo of the suspect. The operator reports to security the description of the suspect and provides a photo for their use should the suspect return. The operator places the cameras of the entryways and exits on his working monitors in order to spot the suspect the moment he enters the property. He briefs his relief about the incident, and shows her the video and photo of the suspect.

A few hours later the suspect returns and is immediately detected by the surveillance operator. Security is advised. The suspect is monitored by surveillance as he looks for another victim. After he has spotted a victim and takes the victim's purse, security rushes in and apprehends the thief. He is detained and held for the local police. This thief will not be active at least for the rest of the day, and he probably will not return to where he was caught.

Which team would you want to be a part of? Which team protects the property better? Yes, it is only a purse. However, I would venture to say that a team that can't stop a purse thief is also going to have a problem catching a professional cheat.

1.7 COVERT CAMERAS

Hidden or covert cameras are often used by surveillance and security departments to observe areas where surveillance cameras are not normally placed or even expected to be placed. Covert cameras are usually installed to detect illicit activities. Often these cameras are installed due to information received by the surveillance department.

The use of covert cameras may be limited or even prohibited in some countries, states, or by local government or other regulation. Their use may even be limited by industry, union contracts, or by the company you work for.

Before installing a covert camera, ensure you have checked that is legal to do so. I strongly encourage you to obtain legal counsel prior to using a covert camera. Even when it is legal to use a covert camera, there are certain areas that a covert camera should not be considered for: restrooms, locker rooms, private offices. Any place in which an individual may expect a reasonable right to privacy should not be considered as a place to install a covert camera.

You should also keep in mind the severity of the suspected or alleged criminal activity. Suspected marijuana use by one or two individuals may not trigger the placement of a covert camera in some areas, but the sale of narcotics to employees may. Employees hiding in a storage room to avoid work may not be serious enough to warrant the use of a covert camera, but theft of inventory from the storage room should. In essence, use of a covert camera may have to be justified to your superiors or even in defense to litigation. If you are unsure about whether you should use a covert camera or not, it is usually better to err on the side of caution and not to use one until you have received legal counsel.

1.7.1 Case History

The bar was an area of concern for the beverage manager. Sales were down and employees frequently disappeared into the storage area for undue lengths of time, affecting guest service. Of course whenever the manager went into the bar area, everything and everybody looked fine. The manager just couldn't shake the feeling that something wasn't right.

Finally, he asked the surveillance director for help. He was especially concerned about what the employees were doing where liquor was stored along with food that was to be served to the customers. The surveillance director agreed to help because he also suspected something was going on and wanted to get to the bottom of it.

A camera had not been installed in the storage area and the surveillance director instructed his technicians to install a covert camera as soon as possible. In this fashion, any activity that was occurring could be detected and recorded.

The camera paid off immediately. The employees treated the area like their private nightclub. Employees (bartenders, waitresses, bar backs, and even employees from other departments) were recorded drinking soft drinks, beer, and cocktails, as well helping themselves to the sandwiches meant for customers. Numerous health code violations were noted, including one instance where a bartender urinated into the drain located on the floor.

A total of eleven employees were terminated for their conduct in the storage room. Of course, the word spread like wildfire and the beverage sales returned to normal. Covert cameras used properly often provide quick and dramatic results.

2

Game Protection

2.1 SURVEILLANCE SKILLS

I think it is important that we discuss the skills utilized by surveillance personnel to do their job and protect the property. To do that, surveillance staff must possess the skills necessary to deter, detect, and respond to cheating, theft and fraud. The name of the game for the surveillance department is to protect the assets of the property through the detection of internal and external theft and fraud, cheating at gambling, and advantage play. The more you detect, the more you prevent, and the better you protect your property. The surveillance department can and should have a positive impact on the property and the bottom line.

Although we may all go about it a little differently, our mission is the same. In fact, regardless of the type of property or gaming jurisdiction, there are surveillance best practices and techniques that when used by surveillance personnel increase detection rates. Your surveillance team can benefit from these best practices. Using them properly can turn a team seldom heard from into a team that consistently and proactively protects the property.

Why is this important? Because in any gaming operation there are people who want to take your money. Whether they are outside agents, employees, or both working together, they exist. If you are not catching them on at least a fairly regular basis, you're getting ripped off, one way or another. It is a fact, count on it, it will occur.

So how do you go about detecting these scams, cheaters, and thieves? Maybe you have a new surveillance team or a relatively inexperienced one. How can your team detect and attack these sophisticated criminals and cheats?

The answer isn't as mysterious as you might think. Your surveillance operations can be formulated and directed to detect any type of scam or crime by using the right practices and techniques to put you in the right place at the right time, or failing that, as soon as possible after the crime begins in order to stop the activity and prevent your losses.

Detecting crime begins with knowing and applying the practices and techniques that provide you the best opportunity to do so. As we all know, once we know what's going on, we're deadly effective. The point is to get there. Here are three best practices you can put to work immediately:

2.1.1 Best Practice #1

Train, train, train: Surveillance personnel must be constantly trained in all aspects of gaming protection and loss prevention. To list just a few areas agents should be thoroughly trained in, the most prevalent are camera handling and patrol techniques; threat recognition, analysis, and response; monitor set-up and display; gaming regulations; the company's and each department's internal controls, policies, and procedures; game protection techniques; basic strategy; card counting; tells of cheating and advantage play; tells of internal theft and fraud.

As you can see there are multiple areas in which training must be done. The key is to identify your training needs and begin. In order to identify your training needs you must assess them. A good way to test your individual team members is to give them a basic strategy quiz. Each agent should be able to complete the quiz in less than three minutes (after all they use the information every day or should). Another method is to test their knowledge of each game type offered on your property. To test their camera handling, ask security to set off an alarm as a drill. These types of assessments will identify your training needs quickly. Your goal is for your surveillance team to be the most highly trained team on the property. Remember, the bad guys train every day; you must do the same!

2.1.2 Best Practice #2

Identify and prioritize your threats: Every casino, while sharing the same type of threats, can also have varying degrees of those threats or even threats that are unique to their particular situation or property. The key is to identify what threats you are exposed to and then determine how, when (if at all), and what resources you'll apply against them.

For example, almost every casino may be attacked by advantage players. In 21, you expect that card counters will visit your property and you should prepare accordingly. You should assign agents to monitor and patrol for that type of play and be ready to respond. You know the threat but you will have to determine how much time you allot to handle a particular advantage player or whether you should respond at all. This is where threat analysis comes in, for example: a regular player who counts but over three months is only beating you for $500 may not require a response at all. An unknown player winning $5,000 in a few hours may require an immediate response. The point is to put your resources where they will protect the property from the most harm.

Other examples are baccarat and mini-baccarat. These games, when compromised, can cost the casino tens of thousands in a matter of minutes. You can't afford not to continuously monitor these games, even when there is not a player on the game! The threat of collusion and a dealer not shuffling or false shuffling is such that you must know everything that occurs in the game, including the status of the game and its equipment prior to the arrival of players and during their play.

Know what your threats are and be prepared to adapt your operation to address them. Let's say recently there's been a rash of purse thefts on your property. No, the property isn't losing anything, but the property and your reputation are taking a big hit. Pretty soon, your boss will be asking you why you can't stop the thefts. In this instance, the threat level has changed. A relatively minor crime is now a significant threat. What do you do?

Apply the resources you need to stop the crime. If you treat the first theft as a crime to be solved and assign the personnel to locate the suspects who committed it, there likely will not be more than two thefts of this kind by the same individuals because you will catch them. Identify your threats and attack them. When you focus your resources, you will prevail.

2.1.3 Best Practice #3

Regularly review statistical information and exception reports: Being proactive means taking the time to look for negative trends and suspicious activity daily. You shouldn't do it with cameras alone. You have a wealth of leads just waiting for you when you choose to use them. Every casino, in fact every department you are protecting, maintains statistical information (both gaming and nongaming) and generates exception reports. These reports can normally be requested from the finance/accounting departments or may already be on your work computers.

Games statistical reports list valuable information such as openers and closers, handle, drop, credits, fills, win/loss, and win percentages. These reports are normally broken down by department (slots, table games, bingo, etc.), game type (21, craps, slot machine type), individual game, pit, shift, day, quarter to date, and year to date. With this information you can easily identify a losing game type. For example, if 21 is holding only 10 percent year to date for no apparent reason, an investigation by surveillance may be in order, or if blackjack table two is a consistent loser, you may want to apply your resources to determine why.

Exception reports are just that. The report is alerting you to an activity that is an exception to normal activity. An example is a void report. A void at the point of sale means that someone had to correct or delete a transaction. There are valid reasons for an employee to do this, and there are also reasons a dishonest employee would do this. If you knew that Joe the bartender had one hundred voids per week as opposed to Fred's five, who would you look at—Joe? You should, Joe has some explaining to do.

Use these reports and statistics to drive your team where it needs to go. If you review this type of information daily, you will often find anomalies and suspicious activity that help you find what's going on under the surface. You will also find that you may be the first person to even notice there is a problem. This is a good place to be for a surveillance director and the surveillance team!

Essential skills for a surveillance operator are, but not limited to, the following:

- Expert knowledge of all games, including slots, presented on the property, including how to play, how the games are properly dealt, correct payoffs and odds, and how to beat the games, internally and externally, through advantage play, theft, or cheating.
- Expert operational knowledge of all support departments such as the main cage, count teams and count room, food and beverage, hotel, warehouse/receiving, and their respective vulnerabilities and the loss prevention techniques used to deter and detect losses and shrinkage.
- Expert knowledge of all applicable laws, regulations, controls, and policies.

- Expert knowledge and the skills necessary to operate surveillance equipment properly in order to efficiently deter, detect, apprehend, prosecute, and recover losses and the individuals responsible for their occurrence.
- Strong investigative experience or knowledge, including investigative techniques, interviewing skills, evidence handling, report writing.
- Strong sense of curiosity and a willingness to ask questions.
- Self motivation.

There are others; however, these are, in my opinion, the most important. Surveillance personnel who take the time to develop and maintain these seven skills will be successful. Each of these skills interacts and is dependent upon the others.

A good surveillance agent will use all of these traits and skills in his or her observations and response to suspicious activity. You will have the knowledge to know when something is wrong because you already know what it looks like when it's right. When you sense something is wrong, you can apply the resources or experts you need to solve the problem, but someone has to question the activity in the first place. That is often, and should be, a surveillance agent.

Once an actual crime or prohibited activity is detected, investigative skill is critical. Usually not everything about the incident or who is involved is immediately apparent. In most cases, further investigation is necessary. The questions of who, what, where, when, how, and sometimes why must be asked and answered. The ability to conduct a thorough and conclusive investigation is extremely important to the successful prosecution of the case and to reduce any liability or opportunity for later litigation. We will discuss more about investigations in a later chapter.

Of course, in order for the skills to become second nature, constant study and daily practice are necessary. I highly recommend the daily practice of the following:

Basic strategy
Card counting
Critical index deviations
Craps payoffs
Tells of cheating and advantage play

Consistent daily practice of these skills will provide the strong foundation you need to be prepared when your property is attacked by advantage players or cheaters.

Each of the skills mentioned above will help new and older agents be more successful at their position. A lot of agents who've been around for a while do not know these skills as well as they should or haven't practiced them for a while. Recently, I was brought in to work with and train a surveillance team in the basic skills and I stressed the importance of practicing regularly. One member kept telling me how he had learned all those skills when he started as an agent (a number of years earlier) and didn't need to practice them anymore. Well, when we tested each person in basic strategy, he did the worst, by far, of anyone and he had been there the longest. Keep in mind that he always watched the pit and was evaluating players on a routine basis. And he didn't know basic strategy? No wonder the team wasn't detecting losses and needed training. This example is a reality in a lot of places. If you want to avoid this in your own operation, insist that your people practice daily and test them frequently.

Being an expert, or at least very knowledgeable, in basic strategy, critical index, and card counting will help you detect suspicious play or will help you eliminate the play as suspicious. Knowing the bets on craps and how they are paid and when they lose will let you know if something is amiss on the craps tables. And knowing the tells of cheating and advantage play will help you detect those behaviors immediately.

Nowadays, technology is moving faster than our ability to protect the property. While the surveillance skills we've already discussed remain critical, we must now also add computer and analytical skills. Why? Because computer technology is used against us by the bad guys. We must use technology to detect what they're doing and to stop the attack.

2.1.4 Computer Technology

Knowledge of computers is a requirement today. In fact, you can't walk into a surveillance room that doesn't have at least one computer. And almost all casino systems are now run by computer software. Think about player ratings in both table games and slots; how are they done? How about your points of sale (POS)? Aren't they run by computer applications?

Today, surveillance departments and their personnel must understand how to protect their property with technology. Fortunately, technology does of lot of this for us already. We just don't know it is there or fail to use it properly or at all.

For example, the software used to track player activity will also provide surveillance with the information as to who the players are, where they're from, their betting activity, their comp activity, the types of games they like to play, how often they come to the casino, and on and on. When you're conducting an investigation, this information is invaluable. You would be surprised how many people commit a crime before or after placing their players' cards in a slot machine.

The information tracked by a POS is just as good. You can identify employees who have too many voids, ring up "no sales," or work out of open drawers, allowing you to detect internal theft. You can track when a comp is redeemed and by whom to detect comp abuse by employees, players, or both working together.

One of the great things about this technology is you can monitor all this information at all times. You don't have to record it to have it. It's there already. You can even set alarm points that will notify you of certain activities.

2.1.5 Case History

A case I dealt with a number of years ago demonstrates the importance of surveillance skills and knowledge. A surveillance agent was patrolling through the poker room. The poker room was located within a casino property (riverboat) that had only been open for less than a year. As was the case with most new riverboats, it was located in a new gaming jurisdiction. The employees were drawn from a population base that knew relatively nothing about gaming. Most employees, including surveillance, were brand new to the field.

The surveillance agent patrolling had been trained in poker room operations and how the games were played. Luckily, this agent was serious about his career and studied his assignments diligently. As he patrolled through the three open games using his IOU patrol, he kept getting that feeling that something was wrong.

He kept patrolling because he didn't "understand" the game and based on IOU protocol he couldn't leave the poker area until he did. Finally he noticed that one of the dealers failed to take a rake from one of the pots. As he continued observing he noticed that the dealer did not take a rake from any of the pots!

He checked the dealers on the other two games and found the same thing. Not one of the dealers was collecting the rake as required. Obviously this initiated an immediate close watch of the poker room and a review of the table games reports for the poker room.

We quickly determined that dealers on all shifts did not and had not collected the house rake since the opening of the property. There was no theft or cheating involved. It was simply a training issue. Collection of the rake was not comprehended well by the trainer (who had no poker experience) and thus glossed over quickly. The poker room manager and supervisors had no experience either and didn't know the proper rake techniques. Actually, they thought they were doing well because they got so much play in their poker room as compared to others (I wonder why?).

Needless to say, the general manager wasn't happy with anyone, including surveillance. But at least consistent surveillance training along with an agent who applied the proper techniques paid off eventually. Otherwise the error may have continued to occur.

2.2 GAME PROTECTION

Protection of the games in the casino is the surveillance department's prime objective. Every game within the casino can be cheated or manipulated in some way by an employee or outsider or by both working together. Protection involves all table games, slots, keno, bingo, race and sports book, poker, and so forth. If it's exposed to play, it can be ripped off in one way or another, and often in more than one way.

Additionally, each game has its own type of cheater. This is an individual or group of individuals who dedicate most of their time, if not their lives, to developing one scam or move to beat a particular type of game. Such dedication allows the cheat to perfect his or her move to the point that it can't be detected unless you know exactly what to look for and even then you will probably miss it.

I have a friend who will tell you that he is going to switch cards in and out of a game and does it while you're watching. Even experienced surveillance personnel will not see the cards being switched. But the trained eye will see the tells, the behavior, the switch and that's what it is all about.

2.3 TELLS

Tells are indicators of the move to come or that a scam is in progress. For example, what you will normally see when a dice-sliding team is in action is: the slider takes possession of the dice, the bettor will place a large bet in the field, the distracter, positioned next to the stickman and at the opposite end of the craps table, will attempt to block the view of the stickman and box person or snap his or her fingers or otherwise distract the stickman and throw in a late bet just as the dice are released. As this move normally results in a sizable loss to the casino, once experienced, surveillance operators never forget what a dice slide looks like.

There are tells to every scam and cheating method that I know of. The move is normally so well practiced that you or I will not see it, even when we know it's coming. However, there is always a set-up move prior to the move or a clean-up move afterward.

Another example is card mucking. You won't see the card being mucked in or out of the game; the cheat is too well practiced for that. But the cheat must touch his or her cards twice: once to muck a card out, and again to muck a card in. How often do you see a player touch his or her cards or bet twice?

As mentioned earlier, knowing the tells of cheating and advantage play is extremely important. You must know this so well that you will know something is wrong even though you're not sure what it is. You just get that "gut feeling" that something is wrong and this will make you look deeper.

Some surveillance investigators evaluate a player for card counting, and if he's not counting, they figure the player is okay and move on. To me, if a player is consistently winning, then once I've eliminated card counting, that's just the beginning, not the end. I have to find out why the player is winning consistently, and looking for tells is part of figuring that out.

Listed below are tells to a number of common scams or indicators of advantage play used in blackjack.

Card Counting
  Bet variation
  Strategy variation
  Taking or not taking insurance at certain times
  Player watching all cards
  Nondrinker or doesn't drink beer or cocktail ordered
  Places bets after all cards picked up
Card Mucking
  Player touching cards or bets twice
  Player picking up cards with one hand, replacing with the other hand
  One or both hands going off the table
  Unusual hand movements
  Both hands handling the cards
  Distractions during the game
Card Switching
  Players sitting close together, arms in a folded position
  Hands on/off game
  Touching cards or bets twice
  Big money next to small money
  Distractions on game

Chip Cup
    Frequent buy-ins and/or color changes by same player(s)
    Dealer pays frequent attention to and manipulates checks in tray
    Player bets small denomination checks but has larger denomination checks in front or in pockets
    Ratholes checks
Computer Play
    Unusual hit/stand pattern
    Hesitation prior to strategy decisions
    Bet variations
    Unusual physical movements
Cooler Deck or Shoe
    Distraction during cut or placement of cards into shoe
    Player wearing jacket/coat
    Sudden increase in bets
    Game locked up
    Players receiving unusual number of naturals, double downs, splits, or strong hands not requiring a decision
    Dealer extends cards for cut farther than normal
    No cut of cards
Daubing
    Hands off game
    Minimum bets, maximum hands
    Hand movements to body, face, or hair
    Handles cards unusually, fingers may not touch all cards
    Rechecks cards frequently
Dealer/Agent
    Frequent player buy in and color changes
    Dealer favoring player
    Incorrect payoffs
    Payoff not clear
    Total of hands not clear
    Tipping hole card or flashing of top cards by dealer
    Unusual hit/stand pattern (receiving information)
    Dealer holding deck unusually
    Rubbernecking
Dealing Seconds
    Unusual deck hand movements (peeking moves)
    Audible snap of cards
    "Dead thumb"
Dealer Stealing Checks
    Hands moving/touching body, face without clearing hands
    Unusual physical movements
    Unusual pick up of checks

    Frequent manipulation of checks and/or straightening checks in the tray

    Rubbernecking

False Shuffle

    Incorrect house shuffle

    No squaring of deck

    Sudden increase in bets

    Game locked up

    Players receiving unusual number of naturals, double downs, splits, or strong hands not requiring a decision

    No cut of cards

Hole Card Play

    Unusual hit/stand pattern (receiving information)

    Placement of arm or device in a stationary position on the game

    Player(s) slumping

    Signal pattern from other player(s)

    Incorrect hole card placement by dealer

Marked Cards In Play

    Unusual hit/stand pattern (receiving information)

    Sudden increase in bets to table maximum

    Game locked up

    Signal pattern from other player(s)

    Big money next to small money

    Dealer not dealing as per procedure

Pinching/Pressing

    Movements to bets when dealer is facing away

    Touching cards or bet twice

    Hands moving over bet

    Hands close to bet

    Distractions on game

Shuffle Tracking

    Large bets at top of shoe

    Large bets from outside game

    Sudden increase in bets

    When offered cut player takes a long time placing cut card

    Players at game often refuse cut, allowing one specific player to cut cards

Common to Most or Cause for Further Investigation

    Procedure break or violation (intentional or not)

    Unusual hit/stand pattern

    Larger or maximum bets (follow the money)

    Rubbernecking

    Distractions during the game

    Listed below are tells indicative of slot cheating, slot advantage play, or employee theft:

Cashier/Floor Theft
  Unauthorized countdown of bank or other funds
  Constantly manipulating funds or paperwork
  Rolls of coin or tokens short, cashier handles rolls frequently
  Removes coins from coin bags, bags not weighed
  Straps of currency short, positioned in back of drawer so as not to be verified
  Offgoing cashier enters amount of funds counted by oncoming cashier
Counterfeit Bills Placed in Validator Units
  Frequent input of cash, frequent cash out of credits
  Minimal or brief play
  Player or associate continuously cashes out
  Unknown or new players
  Rubbernecking
  Bills rejected often, suspect tries same bill repeatedly
  Counterfeit and good money kept separate, bills into validator from one location
    and from cash-out to another
Counterfeit Tokens
  Maximum coins in, then cash-out of credits
  Minimal play
  On and off play
  Unknown or new players
  Rubbernecking
Devices Used to Disrupt Coin Readers
  Coin payout meter does not match coin paid out
  Payout does not match symbols on reels or on screen
  Player reaches into payout chute or other area of machine to place and retrieve
    device
  Hoppers found empty or near empty without players present
  Rubbernecking
  Usually occurs on higher denomination machines
  Player may sit with legs up on each side of machine
  Unknown or new players
Distract and Grabs (Purse/Coin Bucket/TITO Theft)
  Individuals who enter casino together, then split up and move about in different
    directions in slot area
  Individual(s) roam slot areas without playing
  Often carrying coin, wallet, purse, or TITO (ticket in, ticket out) ticket to throw on
    floor
  Individual approaches slot players and engages them in conversation or tosses an
    item on the floor
Drop Door Breaking/Entering—Theft of Drop Bucket/Bill Validator
  Illegal drop door or drop door open signal or alarm at unusual time of day and/
    or without prior notification
  Suspicious individuals loitering about during drop or during quiet periods

Unsecured and/or broken drop door or lock (internal collusion)
Drop crew leaves behind drop bucket or validator (internal collusion)
False Hopper Fills
    Required number of employees not present at fill
    Fill not located at machine listed on slot system and/or paperwork
    Signatures of verifying personnel not legible or identifiable
    Fill slip not signed at location of fill
    Coin for fill not placed directly into hopper
    Fill bag opened prior to arrival at machine
False Jackpots
    Required number of employees not present at jackpot
    Jackpot not located at machine listed on slot system and/or paperwork
    Signatures of verifying employees not legible or identifiable
    Jackpot paperwork not signed at location of jackpot
Injecting Slot Machine RAM with False Information
    Unknown or new players
    Blockers/distracters in use, blocking camera angles (usually must open machine to access RAM (random access memory)
    Playing machine or linked machines for substantial jackpot (usually a progressive) for cash or high value prizes (cars, boats, etc.)
Manipulation of Machine or Malfunction
    Rubbernecking
    Player attempting to disguise/camouflage, or cover up method of play or readouts of the machine
    Payout does not match combination or display on machine or screen
    Wins consistently and cashes out frequently
    Machine in constant play by individuals using same method of play
    Abnormal number of fills
    Unusual and consistent method of play
    Expert input of coin or use of play/credit buttons
    Items observed that could be used as tools such as bobby pins, drink or cocktail straws, etc.
Professional/Advantage Players
    All machines of type in constant play
    Players are extremely adept playing machines
    Players familiar with casino rules, procedures, and operations
    Players appear to be locals
Shaved Tokens/$2 Tokens
    Player continuously sorting coin
    Rubbernecking
    Coins frequently fall through to tray
    Blockers/distracters in place
    Coin out doesn't match win meter
    Frequent cash-out of credits

Shaved tokens/$2 tokens found in drop during weigh/wrap

Player catches tokens as they are paid out and before they hit the tray

Shorting Players

Cashier/change person does not empty all coins/tokens from bucket

Cashier/change person does not run all coin/tokens through coin counter, sets aside some in tray

Short rolls, cashier/change person handles frequently

Unauthorized countdown of bank

Hands to body without clearing hands

Slot/Casino Employee Impersonator

Dresses as or similar to a slot or other casino employee

Roams slot areas without playing

Approaches players, obtains cash (pretending he or she will get change for them), and immediately leaves the property

Theft from Slot Machine

Floor person or slot technician enters machine for no apparent reason and/or a player not present

Hands to body without clearing hands after entering machine

Does not sign entry card and/or use card system

2.3.1 Case History

The 21 game was getting beat badly. The game had already lost over $20,000 and both surveillance and the pit were nervous. All the tells that something was going on were there, but we couldn't find what was being done. The game was locked up. The players hit/stand pattern strongly indicated the players were receiving information. Their wagers had gone from minimum to table max. All indicators of marked cards were in play. But this game was dealt from a shoe and players did not touch the cards. So what was going on? (See Figures 2.1 and 2.2.)

We sat there for a while and watched the game lose while we racked our brains for answers. The cards had to be marked, but how? Finally, we got it. A review of the activity on the game prior to the increased wagers located suspicious activity. The answer was so obvious; we couldn't see it right in front of us. One of the players continuously reached out with a check and tapped on a card. It looked like he was just asking for change. A more thorough review of his activity determined he needed a lot of change and that there was a definite pattern to the cards he was striking. The player struck the cards in such a fashion that it left a mark that could be read by all the players on the game. Knowing what they had done allowed us to respond appropriately and the gang was shortly detained and the cards retained as evidence.

2.3.2 Summation

Knowing the tells to common scams and cheating is extremely important for the protection of the casino and your personal success. Some surveillance people are extremely good at spotting and recognizing bad guys and advantage players based on having seen the

Figure 2.1 An illustration of the bottom flash technique. (With permission. Courtesy of Michael A. Joseph, International Gaming Specialist, TrainingInGaming.com, Las Vegas, NV.)

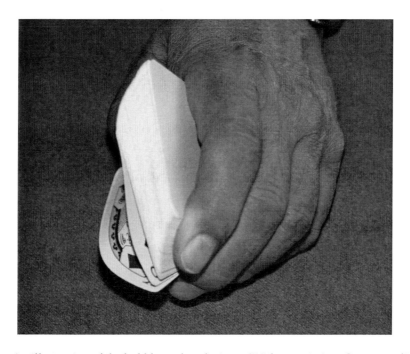

Figure 2.2 An illustration of the bubble peak technique. (With permission. Courtesy of Michael A. Joseph, International Gaming Specialist, TrainingInGaming.com, Las Vegas, NV.)

person or their picture before. This is great if you can do it; some people have that ability. In most cases, once you recognize the person, you also know what he or she will try to do to you, and you can get prepared for the scam with proper personnel and camera angles in place.

If you don't recognize faces, you have to recognize the play or the set up first. This is where knowing your tells backward and forward comes in handy. When you spot a tell that you recognize, you are ahead of the game too; you don't have to wait until you're beat or keep losing more money to respond with your prepared countermeasures. Whichever way you're best at is what you should do. However, you should be able to do both. Practice by drilling yourself in face recognition (study of video and photos) and memorization of tells.

I know that there are many fee-based reporting services out there as well as free surveillance associations that provide or share photos and information. You should subscribe and belong to any and all of these. However, use these as information sources only; you *must* perform your own evaluation prior to detaining or backing anyone off. You or your staff can easily accidentally misidentify someone or you can even actually correctly identify an actual bad guy, but if he isn't committing a crime when you grab him, you may be in some trouble. Always, always evaluate before response.

2.3.3 Case History

A rookie surveillance agent was working alone on a swing shift at a small property. He was contacted by one of the security officers who informed the agent that he had recognized a female subject as a suspect in some purse thefts that had been occurring. The officer stated the suspect was playing a slot machine and requested camera coverage.

The agent placed the coverage and began his observation of the area. The officer had decided that to catch the suspect in the act he would place a wallet with some cash in it next to her and see if the suspect took the wallet, whereupon she would be taken into custody.

This was done and the agent began watching the suspect and the wallet; however, the agent had to answer phone calls and looked away from the monitor on several occasions. Suddenly, the security officer reported via radio saying he had taken the suspect into custody because the wallet was gone. The agent didn't know if the suspect had taken the wallet, but assumed she did and only told the officer that he would get the tape ready.

As the agent reviewed the videotape (which he should have done in the first place), he couldn't find where the wallet had been taken by the suspect. Other players had moved into the scene, and his view of the wallet was frequently obscured. After review he could only say the wallet was gone, but he could not say that the suspect already in custody had it.

More bad news followed. The suspect didn't have the wallet. She said she didn't take it and after a search of her person, it was found she didn't. Frustrated, the security officers had the female suspect remove her clothing (yes, I know, an extremely bad move!) and still no wallet. The suspect was released with profuse apologies. Surprisingly, she left without a word. I don't know if she ever sued that property, but she could have.

So what happened in the case of the disappearing wallet? Who took the wallet? Upon further diligent review the agent finally realized that a hotel porter entered the area immediately after the wallet was placed by the officer. The porter, seeing the wallet, took it and left the area. No one noticed, not security, not surveillance, certainly not the suspected female. Have you ever noticed that porters and maids tend to be overlooked? They are so obvious we tend to discount them.

The point in all of this is that the surveillance agent accepted information as accurate that he should have weighed with a grain of salt. He accepted that the security officer knew what he was doing (he didn't, and the agent should not have joined him in his plan) and that the female was indeed the suspect and failed to consider anything else. He did not perform his own investigation. He should have watched the wallet and not taken his eyes off of it. When he realized that he couldn't say where it was, he should have stopped everything. The review should have been done before the suspect was detained. This incident was certainly a comedy of serious errors, all stemming from a case of mistaken identity. It is an extreme example of why you must perform your own evaluation or conduct your own investigation before making an accusation.

2.4 BASIC STRATEGY

In order to protect the game of 21, you must know its basic strategy. Every professional or student of the game, to have any success at the game, whether that be playing, cheating, or protecting the game, must be an expert at basic strategy.

Essentially, basic strategy is the correct way to play: making strategic decisions concerning whether to hit, stand, surrender, split, or double down based on the two cards you have against what the dealer is showing as an up card.

Basic strategy was derived using computer models that played millions upon millions of hands of 21 and used the results to calculate the best decision to make given any two-card combination of a player's hand against every possible dealer's up card. This information was then placed into a chart and called a "basic strategy chart."

Basic strategy is dependent on the rules and the number of decks used in a particular 21 game. You should use the basic strategy chart for the specific game it is designed for. For example, for a six-deck, strip rules game you should use a six-deck, strip rules basic strategy chart.

Learning basic strategy is really the first step to becoming a good 21 player. The next steps are, of course, money management and card counting. Basic strategy is probably one of the most important thing you will learn as a surveillance agent and the one thing you will use the most often. Surveillance agents tend to spend most of their time watching 21 games (we'll discuss this issue in more detail later), thus basic strategy can and should be used frequently.

Why is it so important for surveillance to know basic strategy? There are a number of reasons:

- To identify a good player from a bad player
- To determine a player's level of skill and threat level
- Assess level of time or attention the player requires from surveillance, if any
- To determine if the player is receiving information

An agent can usually look at a player and game and quickly determine if there is anything going on that warrants his or her attention. For example, if the players in the game are betting small action and show a minimal knowledge of basic strategy, the agent can and should move on. On the other hand, a player or players displaying knowledge of basic strategy should be evaluated even if only small action is on the game. Why? Remember your tells; what if the cards are being marked? *Even though it is small action now, it may escalate later. Cheaters know basic strategy and follow it unless they are receiving information!*

Table 2.1 is a typical basic strategy chart for six decks. Table 2.2 is a basic strategy study guide. Remember 21 games have different rules in different gaming jurisdictions that will affect what basic strategy you will use, as well as the number of decks used. *Use the correct basic strategy for your property!*

2.5 CARD COUNTING

Another critical skill each surveillance agent must possess and be an expert at is card counting. Along with basic strategy, this skill should be practiced daily so that when you need to do it under pressure you are ready.

A player will use the count for three reasons: to make betting decisions, to make correct insurance and surrender decisions, and to make correct playing decisions.

You should be able to count cards and maintain a side count of aces and fives, monitor a player's basic strategy and bet movements, while observing the dealer for violations of procedure and indications or tells of cheating, theft, or advantage play by anyone in the game including the dealer and floor person. Chart the play by hand if necessary! Believe it or not, this can be done with practice and is the mark of a highly trained and skilled surveillance agent.

All of the above are important when you are evaluating a player, especially an unknown player who is winning a lot of money quickly and no one knows why. Evaluating the player as described will begin to isolate what the player is or isn't doing and help you to focus on what tells you are seeing.

For example, surveillance is notified that a player is on blackjack table six, betting heavily and at this point is ahead several thousand. You place your cameras on the game and on the player. He is unknown to you. As you begin to monitor his play, you receive another call from the pit boss, who is now worried; the player is now up over ten thousand "What is he doing to me?"

Your job is to gather and provide accurate information as quickly as possible in order that an informed decision can be made. First, you begin attempting to identify the player by using your databases and alerts. The player does not show up anywhere. You then evaluate the player's money management, basic strategy, and count the player down. You determine that he is a win progressive player, plays average basic strategy, and is not counting. You can now focus on indicators or tells. You are unable to locate any tells by the player, other players in the game, or the dealer or floor. In other words, the player is okay, is a normal player, and is just winning at this point in time. This is what you report: the player is a win pro, he has an average knowledge of basic strategy, he is not betting with the count, and you cannot locate any indicators of illicit activity at this point.

Table 2.1 Basic Strategy: Six Decks, S17, DA2, DAS, No Surrender

	2	3	4	5	6	7	8	9	T	A
Splitting Pairs										
(A,A)	Y	Y	Y	Y	Y	Y	Y	Y	Y	Y
(T,T)	N	N	N	N	N	N	N	N	N	N
(9,9)	Y	Y	Y	Y	Y	N	Y	Y	N	N
(8,8)	Y	Y	Y	Y	Y	Y	Y	Y	Y	Y
(7,7)	Y	Y	Y	Y	Y	Y	N	N	N	N
(6,6)	Y	Y	Y	Y	Y	N	N	N	N	N
(5,5)	N	N	N	N	N	N	N	N	N	N
(4,4)	N	N	N	Y	Y	N	N	N	N	N
(3,3)	Y	Y	Y	Y	Y	Y	N	N	N	N
(2,2)	Y	Y	Y	Y	Y	Y	N	N	N	N
Soft Totals										
(A,9)	S	S	S	S	S	S	S	S	S	S
(A,8)	S	S	S	S	S	S	S	S	S	S
(A,7)	S	Ds	Ds	Ds	Ds	S	S	H	H	H
(A,6)	H	D	D	D	D	H	H	H	H	H
(A,5)	H	H	D	D	D	H	H	H	H	H
(A,4)	H	H	D	D	D	H	H	H	H	H
(A,3)	H	H	H	D	D	H	H	H	H	H
(A,2)	H	H	H	D	D	H	H	H	H	H
Hard Totals										
17	S	S	S	S	S	S	S	S	S	S
16	S	S	S	S	S	H	H	H	H	H
15	S	S	S	S	S	H	H	H	H	H
14	S	S	S	S	S	H	H	H	H	H
13	S	S	S	S	S	H	H	H	H	H
12	H	H	S	S	S	H	H	H	H	H
11	D	D	D	D	D	D	D	D	D	H
10	D	D	D	D	D	D	D	D	H	H
9	H	D	D	D	D	H	H	H	H	H
8	H	H	H	H	H	H	H	H	H	H

Note: Y = Yes, split the pair; N = No, don't split the pair; H = Hit; S = Stand; D = Double; if unable, Hit; Ds = Double; if unable, Stand.

Table 2.2 Basic Strategy Chart

Player's Hand	Decisions
5–8	Always Hit
9	Double 3–6, o/w hit
10	Double 2–9, o/w hit
11	Double 2–10, o/w hit
12	Stand 4–6, o/w hit
13–16	Stand 2–6, o/w hit
17 or higher	Always stand
A,2	Double vs. 5 and 6, o/w hit
A,3	Double vs. 5 and 6, o/w hit
A,4	Double vs. 4–6, o/w hit
A,5	Double vs. 4–6, o/w hit
A,6	Double vs. 3–6, o/w hit
A,7	Double 3–6, stand vs. 2, 7, 8 hit vs. 9, 10, A
A,8–A,9	Always stand
2,2	Split 2–7, o/w hit
3,3	Split 2–7, o/w hit
4,4	Split vs. 5 and 6, o/w hit
5,5	Never split, treat as 10
6,6	Split 2–6, o/w hit
7,7	Split 2–7, o/w hit
8,8	Always split
9,9	Split 2–9 except 7; o/w stand
10,10	Never split
A,A	Always split

It is always good to provide specific examples of the player's basic strategy and card counting knowledge, such as the player failed to double down on an ace four against a dealer's five and he dropped his bet to one unit on a strong plus count. This report leaves no doubt that you checked the player thoroughly and gives information the pit can work with.

Because the player has checked out okay at this point, you can move on. You have determined that the player is not a threat and you should move on looking for threats that do exist. I would recommend that you keep cameras on this player in case the play changes or the pit requests further assistance. We will talk about the techniques for player evaluations in detail later on.

In summary, card counting is an important skill, along with basic strategy, for all surveillance personnel. What count system should you study and use? I recommend the simple plus–minus system. It is simple to learn and use, it is almost as accurate as any other counting system (within hundredths of a percentage point), and you can use it while you're watching all of the other things you have to watch for. As mentioned earlier you can also keep a side count of fives and aces, if necessary. The simple plus–minus system is implemented as follows:

Count always begins at zero, also called even.

2–6	(count as + 1)
7–9	(neutral, no value)
10s and face cards	(count as – 1)

Thus, cards 2 and 3 would be counted as plus two. Cards 7 and 8 would be zero. Cards 10 and face cards would be minus two. Cards 2 and 10 are zero (they neutralize each other). Cards 2, 10, 3 are counted as plus one (2 and 10 cancel each other out, the 3 remaining is plus one).

Practice counting the cards with a single deck until you can count the deck in less than thirty seconds (the deck should end up even when you're done). By all means, count by pulling two or more cards off the deck at a time. The more cards you can count at a glance, the more time you'll have available to see what else is going on in the game.

The count you obtain from the above process is called the running count. The running count does not account for the number of cards dealt. A strong count either plus or minus is much more impactful two-thirds into the deck that it is in the first third. You can calculate this impact by converting the running count to a true count.

The "true count" is the actual count or value of the deck at the point of the player's decision. (*Card Counting for the Casino Executive,* Zender, 1990, p. 52)

The formula for true count conversion is as follows:

$$RC/N = TC$$

RC = Running count
N = Number of decks remaining
TC = True count

I advise most surveillance personnel to use a running count as they perform their IOU patrol through the pit and to evaluate players who are trying to "understand" their play. Doing so will aid you in moving quickly through your patrol. You don't want to get tied up spending time fully evaluating players who don't require such focus.

If you are using the running count and you detect a player who seems to be following the count, then begin a thorough evaluation. The more you see the player bet with the count, the more you want to convert the running count to a true count and incorporate your knowledge of the critical index. This will help you determine the skill level and thus the threat level of the player.

Of course, I believe you should not have to waste too much time on card counters. Once you have determined what they are doing, you should apply countermeasures such as shuffling up, limiting to a flat bet, and so forth. Your property should have some basic response to card counters, including telling them they can play anything else but 21 (check the regulations in your jurisdiction for what you can or can't do). Card counters are normally not a major threat unless you let them become one. Detect their play through IOU patrol or reporting parameters and limit or stop their win through proper response, so they move on.

One countermeasure that you can use with known advantage players is to page them overhead using their real name or known alias, or have a floor person use their names when speaking to the players. That sends the message that we know who they are and the players will often leave on their own volition.

If you really are concerned about counting, shuffle tracking, or hole card play or you are getting hit frequently (or it is believed that you are by the general manager [GM] or the pit) the best thing you can do is purchase and use the blackjack survey program developed by Oliver Schubert of Casino Software (www.casinosoftware.com). His 21 evaluation program provides all the critical information you need to make an informed decision and can be used regardless of your agents' experience level.

2.6 MONEY MANAGEMENT

We tend to gloss over the player's management of his or her money as not as important as the other components of skill. However, it is a mistake to think that way. Money management is critical to player success, and his or her lack of skill in this area can improve the house edge against that player. Of course, the more skilled a player is in money management, the better opportunity for him or her to beat the house.

A professional player who bets his entire bankroll on a plus-three count may not be a professional for long. On the other hand, the player who wagers within the limits and only risks more when the advantage has increased in his or her favor will usually live to bet another day.

In my experience we lose the most to the money management player. Usually, this type of player is a wealthy individual who is intelligent and plays intuitively well. Such a player just seems to know when to bet conservatively and when to go for blood. Additionally, this player has the resources (more cash or the ability to obtain credit/markers) to ride out a negative turn of the cards or the discipline to walk away.

There are many types of money management systems. I recommend that you familiarize yourself with the ones used most commonly in order to recognize them when one is used by a player. You need to be able to identify the type of system used by the player to determine his or her threat level, if any.

For example, a player who is playing a win progressive system (adds to the bet a portion or all of his or her winnings from the previous wager when it wins or starts over again with a minimal bet after a loss) often looks like a card counter while he or she is winning. If you don't recognize the system, you may mistakenly identify a player as a counter and lose a customer.

I don't know of one money management system that is foolproof and allows the player to win all the time. I think the dangerous system is the one that beats you consistently at the time. You can and should learn about money management systems to the extent that you know when one is used by a player. At least know where to find the information should you need to do so. Knowing this will help you isolate those players requiring further evaluation or response as opposed to those you can safely pass by in your patrol.

Some of more popular money management systems you'll see are:

Win or Positive Progression: Player adds unit(s) after each win or the bet is parlayed. When the bet loses, the wager is returned to the original amount. A good system, it can look like the player is counting. Don't jump the gun, watch the player through positive and negative decks/shoes.

Loss or Negative Progression: Player adds unit(s) after each loss or the bet is parlayed. After a win, the wager is returned to its original amount. A good system, table limits are our major countermeasures against this system.

Flat Betting: Player bets the same amount, no variation.

Hunch Betting: No apparent rhyme or reason for the player's wagers. This type of play is often based on player superstition or "gut feeling." Asian players often play this way and they are exceptionally good players.

Kelly Criterion: Player places bets bases on the player's advantage in proportion to the size of his or her bankroll. After each win or loss the bankroll and advantage are recalculated.

Martingale: Doubles the bet after every loss. As stated earlier, table limits are in place to counter this system

I don't personally know a money management system that works perfectly or even at all. I think that each system faces its own worst enemy: the house edge. The edge always prevails in an honest game.

Over the years I have seen that some players who can combine basic strategy and a win progression system seem to have more success, but that isn't an opinion based on any mathematical theory, just my own observation.

2.7 CRITICAL INDEX

Table 2.3 presents the "illustrious eighteen" or critical index numbers. These numbers represent the points where a card counter should deviate from basic strategy.

Table 2.3 Critical Index Chart

	2	3	4	5	6	7	8	9	T	A
16								+5	0	
15									+4	
14										
13	−1	−2								
12	+3	+2	0	−2	−1					
11										+1
10									+4	+4
9	+1					+3				
TT				+5	+4					

Note: Insurance should be taken at a true count of +3 or higher.

2.8 EVALUATING PLAYERS

Players must be evaluated to ascertain their potential threat level, if any, to the casino. Players can pose a threat to any game, not just 21. There is significant risk in slots, baccarat, bingo, race and sports book, and poker, to name just a few. Surveillance must be prepared to evaluate a player's skill level in any area.

Evaluating players is all about determining their knowledge of the game. Every game offered for play in the casino has an optimal way to play. As we know, in blackjack, basic strategy is the key to understanding an individual's play. Other table games such as Caribbean stud, three card, and the many variations of 21 have their own basic strategies for optimal play.

Another example is in slots. There is an optimal strategy for playing video poker machines. Slot professionals and advantage players are experts in using this strategy to increase their chances of hitting the royal flush.

Surveillance personnel should develop their knowledge of optimal play for each game for the simple reason that doing so allows you to quickly assess a player's threat potential. Once known, a player's threat potential determines your response, whether it is no action, further evaluation, or immediate response. It really is about recognizing, responding to, and resolving an observed condition that falls into previously defined parameters. What that means is that you can't evaluate each and every player in the casino. There are just too many people to look at. But you can look at all players falling into certain categories based on amounts of wagers, amounts won, or unusual activity or tells. Let's look at this in practice.

You are performing an IOU patrol of pit one. You begin at blackjack table one. You do not recognize any player in the game, and it is all $5 action. You do not observe any unusual play. You move on to blackjack table two.

At blackjack table two you observe a player wagering $500 a hand. Because this level of wager falls under your evaluation parameters (wagers of $100 or more), you set your tri-shot and begin your evaluation. Most surveillance personnel begin counting down the player immediately. While this is a way to get started, it doesn't take into account that the player may be cheating or working in collusion with the dealer. Further, the player may not even warrant attention based on the basic strategy play or money management.

Ideally, you should be looking at all and for all things at once. However, this takes daily practice and years of experience. In the meantime, I recommend the following steps:

Establish a tri-shot on the player to be evaluated.

Attempt to identify the player: Have you seen him before? Is he a known player? If he's known, you or someone else in surveillance may have already evaluated him and a record exists that can be checked. If you can identify the individual as a known player with an existing evaluation and win/loss history, you may be able to eliminate him as a threat without performing an evaluation. An unknown player must be evaluated. However, you should first check your alerts and databases of cheaters and advantage players to see if your player is listed there. If he is in the database, his activity (counter, card marker, etc.) will also be listed and you can observe for that specific activity. Also, at this time, you should see who else is in the game. Many scams are done using a big player to make the wagers and play the hands but the actual dirty work and signaling is done by other members of the team (for example, hole carding, marked cards, camera/computer play). Other players in the game should be considered as potential or existing threats. If you cannot identify the player or there is no record of his play, you must evaluate his skill level.

Evaluate the player: First, observe how the player bets and plays his cards. Just watching for a few minutes will tell you a lot. For example, if he's flat betting and not using basic strategy, that may indicate that he is an unskilled player. Or if the player continually checks his cards and bets, you might consider potential bet pressing or pinching (or other scams!). In either case, counting the player down may have taken time away from detecting the actual threat. It is wise to spend a few minutes up front just observing the player's actions.

Count the player down: Spend enough time to ensure you see enough hands to be able to convincingly state that the player is or is not counting. You don't want to label someone a card counter unless you are sure. Based on your information the player may be asked to stop play or leave the casino, not to mention having his picture sent around the world and being described as a counter! Another reason to be absolutely positive is your credibility with the pit. You make a wrong call on a player and it will take years to forget. Not only your credibility, but the department's will suffer as well. Remember, this cuts both ways. Saying someone is a counter and he isn't or saying someone is not a counter and he is can damage your credibility and cost the company. In other words, take the time to count the player down thoroughly. When counting a player you must (1) count down the deck(s) or shoe; (2) evaluate the player's basic strategy; and (3) monitor his money management to the count.

The more hands you can see, the better evaluation you can provide. One hundred hands are good but often unattainable. Usually you have to make the call with what you have. I seriously recommend you use a hand chart to list the play hand by hand. The chart should list, at a minimum, the player's identifying information, the player's bet, the dealer's up card, the cards dealt to player, the running count at the beginning of the hand, and the player's hit cards. Some charts also list an ace count, five count, or both.

When the player's session is complete, what you have is a detailed history of the play. Use the list to review how the player bets to the count. This step increases your accuracy because you won't be able to remember every turn of the card. Having to go back on the video to prove your point is an incredible waste of time. Remember time is of the essence. As discussed previously, identifying specific hands or plays to base your evaluation of whether a player is counting cards or not establishes your credibility with fellow agents and the pit.

There is an excellent software application developed for surveillance and table games departments to evaluate 21 players. The program is called *BJ Survey* and every surveillance room should have it. The program tracks each card and wager for each player on the game, including the dealer's hand. It does so through input by an individual through voice or text input. The program analyzes a player's basic strategy, money management, and card-counting skills (along with many others, such as knowledge of hole card, shuffle tracking, etc.) and provides statistical information that is used to specifically identify a players skill level. Probably the best information it provides is the casino advantage against the player. This is the advantage or disadvantage expressed in a statistical number that a casino has against a specific player. The number is created from the player's play information input into the program so that it is an extremely thorough analysis of player's skill level.

Please note that some players, though they are not advantage players or cheaters, are so skilled that the casino will have a very small advantage against them. These are usually the players who seem to always beat the house and the pit is screaming that the player is doing something yet you can't find an indication of anything. Sound familiar? These are the players you may not want to deal to because of their skill level. Not only are they great players, they usually know when to stop when the hands are going against them. Also, such players are normally comped at a high level and so, to add insult to injury, you're paying them to beat you!

The *BJ Survey* program will help you identify such players and assist you in explaining what they are doing or not doing to the casino manager and the GM. For some reason, although they will argue with you about the results of your evaluation, they will not argue with the computer analysis.

2.8.1 Case History

At a property where we used *BJ Survey* a player for some reason beat us consistently for hundreds of thousands of dollars. He was loved by the dealers because he toked them extremely well. Of course, since he won so often, the casino manager thought something was going on. He asked me to investigate the play to see what the player was doing.

Using *BJ Survey* I evaluated that player and his play for many hours and probably thousands of hands. He was probably the most evaluated player on earth (probably still is). I called in Oliver Schubert, who invented and designed *BJ Survey*, and we reviewed together the results of the analysis. The final line: The player was not doing anything, he was just a normal player but had deep pockets. The survey said that the casino had an advantage against the player and in essence said that we would beat him. I completely believed that to be true and reported the same to the casino manager.

Unfortunately, he didn't believe the findings in this case. He thanked me and later backed off the player because he kept winning. That player left and went to another property. Eventually his luck turned, as luck always does, and he lost over $1 million at that property. *BJ Survey* was right, as I've always found it to be.

2.8.2 Threat Level

Now that you've completed your evaluation, then what? It all comes down to a player's level of threat to the casino. Your decision, based on your evaluation, determines how that player will be handled by the pit or by law enforcement, if necessary, or if you will respond at all.

A player's threat level can be looked at in two ways: potential loss of money or potential violation of law. Each one must be handled differently. A player who is counting cards is not violating the law, but he could win a lot of money! Or none at all!

To me, if the player is skilled or an advantage player, I would first look at the amount of money at risk. A $5 player should not get much attention. However, a $100 player should.

Another way to look at a player is by career wins versus losses. A card counter who has won $1,000 over a year's time really isn't much of a threat. A player who isn't card counting but has won $100,000 over a year's time warrants your attention. Even though he may not be counting, this is the type of player who will drive the pit and your GM crazy and thus, you too.

Set your parameters for evaluation, evaluate the player, determine the threat level, and report the information to the pit consistently and accurately. Parameters are set based on your casino and your player wager levels and types. It must work for your property and for your surveillance team. Typical parameter levels the warrant player evaluation are:

- $100 wager or more
- Win of $2,500 or more
- Apparent knowledge of basic strategy
- Indicator or tell of cheating or advantage play
- Any suspicious or unusual activity

In essence, what you do is ensure that your people evaluate any player who falls into your established parameters. Of course, once evaluated, the player should be placed into a database that allows you to locate the player immediately when necessary. Yes (and especially so), even the players who are not advantage players or cheaters should be placed into the database. Why should swing shift evaluate the player if day shift already has? (Please note that you should always ensure a player is playing as described in the database. Players do camouflage their play or change tactics. Perform an initial check and move on if all is okay. If there is any question or the player is winning more than normal, evaluate.)

2.9 SUSPICIOUS ACTIVITY, ADVANTAGE PLAY, AND CHEATING AT GAMING

It is important for you to remember that once you determine (or believe you have) a player is not counting, you should continue evaluation if the player is winning consistently. Too many surveillance agents stop evaluating the moment they feel the player is not betting with the count. Not so; your job has just begun. Why is the player winning consistently? There are many ways a casino can be beat and card counting is just the easiest to detect.

Player evaluation will detect suspicious activity or what appears to be advantage play or cheating at gaming. Proper evaluation is critical to your response and must be done as quickly as possible to protect the property from unnecessary loss. Your response should be as follows:

Upon detection of suspicious activity, tells, or indicators of advantage play or cheating, immediately establish tri-shot coverage.

Alert necessary personnel and obtain assistance from other agents. You need to focus on what's occurring and not on answering the phone.

Attempt to identify the player(s) if at all possible, especially if you can't determine what's going on. If you can identify the player(s) through the database, you can, more than likely, also find the scam or move that they are known for. Knowing that, you can look specifically for the tells for that move or scam and apply the appropriate response. If you can't identify the player and/or his associates, go through your list of tells for the various scams and moves appropriate for the game type. For example, if the players are in a handheld 21 game, the fact that they handle the cards exposes you to a number of things. Marking the cards and card switching come to mind. Yes, the cheaters will hide their activity from you and they are good at it. But you have weapons too. Let's start with card marking. What are the tells to card marking? Actually there are two different situations. One, the cards are being marked as you monitor the game, or two, the cards are already marked and are in play.

What are you seeing in the game? Is the game locked up (all spots being played)? Are the player's taking every opportunity to hit, split, double down, play as many hands as possible? Are one or more of the players handling the cards unusually? These are common tells that the cards may be in the process of being marked. Respond accordingly. Or are you seeing players playing with unusual hit/stand patterns, not following basic strategy? Do you see a signal pattern from one of the players? It's possible the cards are already marked and are in play. The players are receiving the information they wanted and are using it. Respond accordingly. The objective in evaluating the player who is winning consistently is to find out why—luck, skill, or cheating—and respond accordingly and appropriately. Do not stop at card counting or you will get burned.

Follow the money: There are always new scams and ways to cheat. There are always new people committing the scams, both old and new. There may not be a known tell to what's being done to your game. Remember, when all else fails and you can't determine how the player is beating you, follow the money. It should lead you to what you want to know. Advantage players and cheats do not put their money up lightly. They only risk their money when they have the advantage or when the fix is in. The card counter risks his bankroll when the count is in his favor and lowers his risk when it is not. The shuffle tracker risks his money when the group of cards he wants are coming out and drops his wager when the group is gone. The cheater risks his money when the fix is in or when all parts of his scam are in place and he is prepared to strike. When the cards are being marked you will usually see minimal play. As soon as the cards are marked, bets increase, often to table maximum. My point is that when you follow the money to where the bet increases or where the money is won, you can often determine what is occurring by investigating and analyzing the game conditions and activity at that specific time. By the way, the same case is true with distractions occurring during the game; if you look at what's going on in a game at the moment of distraction (spilled drink, fight, bared female breasts) you may find a clue to which scam is being used.

2.9.1 Putting It All Together

- Locate or isolate player to evaluate based on your established parameters.
- Place tri-shot camera coverage.
- Begin evaluating skill of player.
- Monitor game for violations of policy or procedure.
- Monitor game or player for dealer/agent collusion.
- Monitor game or player for tells of table game cheating and/or advantage play.
- When you *understand* that the game is normal, move on.
- As long as you remain suspicious, keep looking!
- Resolve! You must "understand" the play or activity and ensure it is resolved.

2.9.2 Case History

As often happens in a lot of casinos, we get used to our players who visit us regularly and often allow them more latitude than we would newer players. In this case a player lulled the casino by toking very well and being very friendly with floor personnel.

A surveillance director asked for and received from the pit a list of the top fifty winning players. These players should be evaluated on a regular basis because, based on our "follow the money" rule, players who win consistently will show up in our database. If a player is winning consistently, we need to know why!

At this property, the surveillance director had just been brought in and this was the first time the winners list was reviewed. Almost all of the players on the list were well known to surveillance but had not been thoroughly evaluated in a long time. Almost all the players checked out as normal players who posed little, if any, threat. Eventually, their winning streak would end (this ultimately would prove to be the case).

There was one player who stood out. Evaluation of his play determined he was counting cards. He was a lifetime winner of over $50,000 and it didn't look like we would stop him anytime soon. He was too good at managing his money; if he wasn't winning he wasn't playing!

Of course the player's skill level was duly reported to casino management. The vice president of table games, of course, was angry. Floor personnel (most of you will guess what they said) said they knew he was counting, but that he was not very good and he did take care of the dealers. Of course, it's not their money that's being lost to an advantage player and being used to toke the dealers! Surveillance ultimately prevailed and the counter was backed off. The pit was sad, but surveillance plugged a substantial leak.

REFERENCE

Zender, Bill. 1990. *Card Counting for the Casino Executive*, p. 52.

3

Internal Theft and Fraud

3.1 WHAT IS INTERNAL THEFT AND FRAUD?

The term *occupational fraud* may be defined as "[t]he use of one's occupation for personal enrichment through the deliberate misuse or misapplication of the employing organization's resources or assets" (Association of Certified Fraud Examiners 2010 Report to the Nation).

The Association of Certified Fraud Examiners (ACFE) in the 2010 Report to the Nation stated that approximately 7 percent of a company's gross annual revenue is lost to occupational theft and fraud. The survey used to compile the report was conducted nationwide and represents all business types, including the gaming industry.

Internal or occupational theft and fraud are employee theft and fraud! Such activity includes, but is not limited to, time fraud, petty theft, asset theft and misappropriation, corruption, bribery, and embezzlement.

Employee theft and fraud occur in every organization and certainly within the gaming industry. In fact, I believe we have more employee theft and fraud than most businesses. Think about it: we work in a cash rich environment, our cash and checks are constantly handled by employees, we don't know how much money we have at any given point until it is counted for the day, we issue comps and give away rooms, liquor, and food and constantly run promotions with free giveaways.

Think about recent gaming scams from the headlines or that occurred at another property. You will find that a good number, if not the majority, of scams involved employees acting independently or working in collusion with others.

Another important fact to know about employee theft in the gaming industry is that it doesn't just happen in the gaming areas. It happens in all areas. In my experience, I have not found an area left untouched by internal theft. From human resources to warehouse/receiving, I've seen internal theft occur. Knowing that internal theft and fraud exist, you as a surveillance manager must prepare to deter and detect it before it costs your company thousands or millions of dollars. The key premise you should operate by is that internal theft exists on all properties and in all departments, and you must find it!

3.2 WHY IS INTERNAL THEFT AND FRAUD SO COSTLY?

Remember, employees who are stealing will hide it from you. It is not easy to catch them. In fact, the reason so many internal theft scams grow so large and cost so much is that they remained hidden for long periods of time. The 2010 Report to the Nation states that the average fraud continues for two years prior to detection.

Not only do employees hide theft, they know how to do it without getting caught (at least for a while). Who knows more about a specific job or transaction and about the controls, policies, and procedures involved in a specific job or transaction (and how to avoid them) than the employee who does it every day?

Let's look at a specific example. An employee assigned as a cashier at a casino gift shop knows exactly how items must be entered into the cash register to complete a valid sale. The cashier also knows exactly how to void a sale when necessary for legitimate reasons. The cashier knows that to make change at a customer's request, the No Sale key can be used to open the register without entering a transaction. The cashier may also know that the gift shop manager doesn't pay particular attention to voids or no sales and rarely performs an inventory. Maybe the manager is too busy or just doesn't care. Whatever the case may be, the cashier knows that the manager isn't likely to catch mistakes, intentional or not.

What we have is the potential for internal theft to occur. As long as the employee remains honest, no theft will occur. The minute that cashier becomes dishonest (for reasons we'll discuss later), the company is at risk for employee theft. Let's say the cashier decides not to ring up items properly and enters an item as a no sale. The cashier can now pocket the money received from the customer without fear of detection. Unfortunately, you won't know it because the cashier can make it look like normal sales activity (unless you know what to look for), and the person who should catch it isn't even looking for the indicators that it's going on!

By the way, when I say employees, I mean every employee, including supervisors, managers, directors, and CEOs. I've dealt with employee theft at all levels and so will you. In fact, the largest and most costly cases occur at the top levels. This is because supervisors and their superiors are entrusted with more responsibility and have much more access to company funds and assets than the line employee. An employee can steal a case of lobster; a manager can steal hundreds of cases.

3.3 WHY DO EMPLOYEES STEAL?

Unfortunately, employees steal for many reasons. It usually boils down to a need for the money for some reason, although that's not always the reason. Motivators for committing internal theft range from being passed over for promotion to a divorce or an ill family member.

In the gaming industry, one of the primary reasons employees commit theft is due to a gambling problem. Employees who gamble will lose consistently and constantly. I think we can all agree that the house edge will beat anyone over time (unless there is cheating involved, and that's another issue).

What happens to the employee who gambles constantly is that money needed to pay bills is gambled away. The bills must be paid, so eventually the employee must find additional funds to pay the bills and gamble, not necessarily in that order. Perhaps he can borrow some money from parents or friends. However, that won't last long and those funds must be paid back too.

If the gambling isn't stopped, eventually the employee must turn to other means. In too many cases, that means stealing from where the employee works. The employee already knows how to do it (see our cashier discussed above; the cashier now has a motivator to steal and can begin immediately).

Remember, we are discussing one cashier at one location in the example. How many cashiers and how many locations do you have? What about bartenders and dealers? How about slot floor personnel? What about the warehouse clerk? Race and sports book? The purchasing manager?

3.3.1 Case History

While patrolling through the ticketing area, the investigator noticed one of the clerks pocket some cash from the register. Not knowing if the money was from a tip or if it was stolen money, the investigator reported the observation to his supervisor. They decided to establish a close watch on the employee the next day.

Upon the employee's arrival for duty the next day, he was placed under observation. It soon became apparent that the employee was stealing. Wrist bracelets that allowed unlimited access to the attractions were being sold, but the transactions were not entered into the register. It was later determined that these bracelets were never inventoried (which was known by the employees who sold them) so no one in management knew how many had been sold or should be left in stock.

Investigators also observed that discounts given by the clerk were not authorized. A family from Japan unknowingly received a local's discount. A young man was given a senior citizen discount. Of course they didn't actually receive the discounts, the difference was pocketed by the employee. When the employee was interviewed about this he said he was taught to steal by another employee and that they were each stealing about $600 a day. No small potatoes!

You must prepare and monitor for employee theft in all areas. How do you do it?

3.4 DETECTING INTERNAL THEFT AND FRAUD

- Identify and audit critical areas and key transactions regularly
- Review exception reports
- Review pertinent statistical information

3.4.1 Identifying Critical Areas and Key Transactions

There are critical areas and departments that must be identified. Table games and the slot department come to mind. Within each are key transactions: fills and credits, markers for

Table 3.1 Areas and Transactions for Scheduled Audits

Credit transactions markers and redemptions	Slot jackpots
Table fills/credits	TITO (ticket in, ticket out) redemptions
Bingo/keno payouts	Points of sales
Voids	No sales
Receiving/warehouse	Lost and found
Player ratings	Players' club
Sports book	Bars
Meat cooler/storage	Kitchens
Recycling dock	Top player list

table games, jackpots, overrides for slots, to name a few. Each area, department, and key transaction should be audited by surveillance on a regular basis. A surveillance director should put together an audit schedule for the property that will include these areas.

Table 3.1 lists the critical areas and key transactions that are common to most, if not all, casinos. These areas and transactions should be scheduled and audited on a regular basis. They are representative of what should normally be checked. In actuality, every type of transaction should be audited. It's amazing what you can find when you observe routine transactions and employee activity. I'm surprised that more surveillance rooms don't use this technique! They would be more successful if they did.

3.4.2 Exception Reports

Exception reports are just that; reports of exceptions to normal operation, controls, policies, or procedures. The reports are normally generated automatically by a computer application or system or can be manually generated by the audit staff.

An example of an exception report is a "void report." This report lists voids that are performed at a point of sale (POS) in a specific location (bar, restaurant) or for a specific department (food and beverage), or for the property as a whole. Such information is invaluable when attempting to detect internal theft. Because voiding a transaction is one method of committing theft at the POS, reviewing such activity can identify employees who are stealing through the use of the void function. Other examples of exception reports are:

- "No Sale" report
- Personal identification number (PIN) change
- Name change
- Invalid signatures or insufficient signatures
- Cash variance reports

Using exception reports in conjunction with video is particularly effective. For example, recording a POS and the employee assigned to that POS as he or she performs sales transactions provides an excellent video record. The video record compared to the void sheet will tell you whether the void was legitimate or not. A bartender who sells a beer, receives cash, enters the transaction into the POS, and then voids the transaction may then pocket the cost of the beer. However, reviewing the video will quickly identify the void as an improper transaction and generate the appropriate response to the theft.

3.4.3 Statistical Information

Another method to identify and combat internal theft and fraud is reviewing statistical information. All casinos maintain statistics of game performance. Such statistics are broken down by game type, pit and table number, shift, day, week, month, and year, at a minimum. Included in these reports are openers and closers, fills and credits, credit transactions (markers/buybacks), drop amount, and win/loss.

The slot and other gaming departments maintain the same information albeit pertaining to the specific department. Additionally, departments, such as food and beverage and catering, maintain their own statistics that provide operational and financial details.

Reviewing statistical information on a regular basis provides solid indicators of areas that are losing or not holding as well as they should, for whatever reason. Identifying these areas is an essential requirement for the protection of the property.

For example, reviewing a daily table game report may tell you that blackjack table six (a six-deck game) held only 8 percent the previous day. Based on the game type that means the game lost about 6–7 percent more than it should have. For convenience sake, let's say that in this case this table lost $1,000 more that it should have. You can, and should, review the report specifically for this table in an effort to determine what, if anything, may have occurred and what happened to that money. First, check for win(s) that may account for the loss paid to one player or several. Such play, if it occurred, may not have been observed or rated by the floor person or observed by surveillance. A comparison of the table games win sheet and the surveillance daily activity log might locate an action not seen by surveillance. Play that is on the win sheet but not in the log may indicate it wasn't reported to or detected by surveillance, or it didn't occur at all. It may be that the win was a player who may have won more than stated.

Next, review the video. If you find the play, evaluate it to ensure it was a legitimate win and nothing suspicious occurred (obviously if you find something wrong, respond as necessary). You should also look into why your team wasn't aware of the action and correct anything that needs to be corrected in your table patrols and notification requirements.

In the event you cannot locate the play on video, check to ensure the openers/closers, fills and credits, and any credit transactions were done as stated and are accurate. You do this by comparing the stiff sheet to the video. You will usually find the mistake here. A fill that was listed incorrectly or posted to the wrong game or a marker that was taken on another game but listed to blackjack table six will throw off the numbers for that game.

Again, if you find the $1,000 loss here you can get it resolved and move on. Ensure that the reason for the false win is corrected. Note that if the surveillance team or table game doesn't catch the mistake at this point, it won't, more than likely, be caught. It will become part of yesterday's numbers and forgotten (unless a scam is perpetrated whereupon one day the $1,000 will come back to haunt you). I can't tell you the number of times we called the accounting office to report the numbers were off because of an error in the fills or credits. Otherwise they would not be corrected.

After all this, you haven't found the $1,000. Now you must consider that there might be something going on. You must investigate further and more intensively. You may be getting ripped off, and this is where you need to focus your efforts until you can explain what happened to the missing $1,000.

There are a number of things you must do now to solve the mystery. First, you need to determine if the cash stated as being in the drop box is actually there. You should review the video to check (to the best of your ability) how the number and denominations of bills were placed into the drop as compared to what is shown on the stiff sheet for the game.

It is tough to do, but you can identify most of the bills, especially the $100 bills. You can also identify a lot of $20 bills. The purpose of this exercise is as mentioned above: to see if what was placed into the drop box arrived at soft count. At this point, if you see it go into the box, the only answers are that soft count miscounted the contents of the box or applied it incorrectly to another table, or someone in the count room stole the contents or portions therein.

The above is representative of what you can do to investigate a variance or potential loss. There are other ways and methods to conduct the review, but the point is, conduct the review. This is what you're paid for.

Gaming statistics also will tell you that a game or game type is holding lower than expected. For example, if 21 is holding 10 percent for the past ninety days, something is wrong that you need to investigate. To perform a review to locate the reason the 21 hold is down overall requires a different perspective and different questions.

First, identify approximately what 21 should have held over the ninety days and subtract what you did hold. This gives you a number that approximates your assumed loss amount. This is the number we're looking for. Let's say it's $50,000. Our formula would look like this:

$1,000,000 (total handle) × 15% (expected hold) = $150,000. Subtract $100,000 (actual hold amount) to obtain your approximate loss amount of $50,000.

Now we have to find out where that $50,000 went and account for its loss. The first thing that should be done is to check all the player wins for the subject time period. It is extremely possible that one player (or a combination of a number of players) won a total of $50,000 legitimately. The $50K win may be an unusually high amount for a particular property, and if the player(s) left with money without putting it back into action, this win would account for the drop in the hold percentage. Now if you don't have any large player wins to account for the loss, you must investigate further. Some things to check would include:

- Recent game or rule changes
- New promotional coupons or old coupons suddenly used more often
- Side bets
- New marketing strategy (buy $10,000 in checks, receive $11,000)

These actions, of course, represent the basics. You should check anything you feel may affect your numbers.

If you find the loss is caused by any of the circumstances above or something similar to them, meet with the person responsible for the program and have it corrected, if possible. If you are unable to convince the person that the program or the change that was made is affecting the games, you must go to the general manager (GM) to resolve the issue.

Remember, it is your duty to determine the reason for the loss and you should ensure the GM is aware of it and let him or her take care of it. You've done your job. However, if the activity is criminal, there are other ways it must be handled. We will discuss this further in Chapter 6.

In the event you cannot attribute the loss to play, rule changes, or marketing programs, you must continue your search. As described earlier, you must look deeper into the numbers. For example, when did the $50,000 loss occur? Was it in a lump sum or over a period of time? On what game or games did it occur? What shift or shifts? Who were the personnel involved? Were there any problems with fills or credits, markers, or buybacks? There is a wealth of information available through paperwork alone. If you have video available, that is even better.

3.5 LOSS PREVENTION PROGRAMS

Detecting and reducing thefts and losses require a proactive loss prevention program that is consistently applied. Most businesses fail to design and install a loss prevention program. Many programs are developed and placed into action after a loss has occurred (too late!). The departments responsible for operating the program (security, surveillance, risk management, etc.) often don't even work together for the common goal! In order to consistently detect and reduce employee theft and loss you must:

• Initiate a preemployment screening and background check program
• Install a confidential employee hotline
• Develop and implement an overall company loss prevention program
• Identify the threats and risks for the business
• Develop measures to counter and mitigate those threats and risks
• Obtain a buy-in program from top management and program partners
• Determine program objectives
• Train program participants to operate the program
• Perform daily analytics
• Implement program
• Monitor program
• Evaluate results of program

Let's discuss the basic components of a loss prevention program. We all know that not everyone is honest. This is also true of your employees. It is important to note that most of your employees are honest, hardworking, dedicated, and loyal. However, there are those employees who are dishonest and will steal from your business. It is also possible that honest employees can turn to theft due to traumatic events in their lives (illness or death in family, divorce, etc.) or tremendous financial pressure (gambling, drugs, alcohol, etc.).

How does any business, especially a small business or a start-up business, protect itself from dishonesty in the workplace?

3.5.1 Prescreening Techniques

A lot of businesses hire people without taking the time to learn as much about them as they legally can. These are people the business wants to hire to handle their cash, goods, and services. If you aren't careful about whom you hire in your business, you are vulnerable to potential loss and litigation.

Implementing a preemployment screening program is critical in today's world. The program doesn't have to be expensive, but it must be effective. Many large companies have such a program and usually a department to run it, but too often, the program isn't monitored and the information it generates isn't analyzed or used to make informed decisions.

For example, how many times have you heard "I fired an employee for stealing the other day and found out today that he had been fired by his boss before me for the same thing." Sound familiar? While a good program won't eliminate theft and other issues completely, it should eliminate incident such as that described.

3.5.2 Basic Prescreening Program Components

Require prospective employees to complete an application. Do not rely on a résumé. The application provides a wealth of information and is your first step in ascertaining who the person is. Also, there should be a place for the candidate to place his or her signature to attest that what he or she listed on the application is honest and true. Important, if you find out otherwise later.

Interview prospective employees in person. Go over the application in detail with your candidate. Obtain answers for gaps in employment, reasons for leaving last jobs, and so forth. The information you elicit at this point should eliminate or highlight concerns you may have.

Check references. Too many employers do not check references and later wish they had. Check references for at least five to ten years. Even though some employers will not give any details, ask the questions and document your efforts. Check for discrepancies between information developed and what the applicant reported in the application (dates, title, salary, reason for leaving, etc.).

Perform a background check. It is well worth the investment to perform background checks of those candidates you wish to hire. Wouldn't it be nice to know that your candidate had been convicted of a crime such as fraud or embezzlement before he or she handles your cash and products? It is recommended that you use a background screening professional to do so. The cost is relatively low as compared to the cost of one incident of theft or fraud or having to replace a terminated employee. You can also perform different levels of background checks for different levels of employees. A dishwasher may not need to have a credit check or educational verification, but your bookkeeper probably should.

Install a confidential employee hotline. Most internal thefts are caught by tips. This is a well-supported fact (see the ACFE 2008 Report to the Nation). Tips come from employees, vendors, and customers to name a few. Remember, although we may not know what's happening on the gaming floor or within the various departments, there are people who do know. Just think about what you usually hear after someone's caught stealing: "I thought he was up to something," "I always wondered where she got all that money to gamble with," or "I wondered why he got all the bids."

People know what's going on and they want to tell you. We make it difficult for them to do so. We have an "open door policy" and a "chain of command." What happens if it's their supervisor or manager they want to report? Employees are afraid of repercussions. There is also, of course, concern for retribution from the persons reported if they find out who reported them. Not unlikely in today's world of workplace violence.

I've found employee hotlines work very well. Yes, you will get a lot of calls about employee's supervisors and how they mistreat their employees. In fact, most of your calls will be human resources related and should be turned over to them. However, you will get two to three calls a year that will lead you directly to major cases of internal theft and fraud or collusion with outside agents. Well worth the time and effort.

I would suggest you outsource your hotline to a third party who can monitor the line 24/7 and provide professional interviewers to talk to the callers. They will obtain the necessary information. Most hotlines provide immediate reporting to you through e-mail notification so you can get right to work on the case!

3.6 THREAT AND RISK ASSESSMENT

Establishing a threat/risk assessment program for your property or business is one of the most effective things you can do, and it doesn't have to cost a lot of money. Another advantage to developing such a program is that taking the time to identify potential threats or risks allows you to proactively protect your property rather than wait for the news that you've been hit with a substantial loss.

All businesses are vulnerable to loss. You can expect to be hit. Knowing that, you can certainly prevent or detect potential and existing losses or at least reduce the amount and impact of those losses.

While developing and implementing a loss prevention program is a significant undertaking, sometimes requiring outside professional assistance, here are a few tips to get you thinking and point you in the right direction.

3.6.1 Identify Your Vulnerabilities, Risks, and Threats

Where are you exposed to loss and to what type of theft or scam? You need to identify these areas in order to protect them. For example, in gaming, we know that baccarat and blackjack are vulnerable to cheating and advantage play. Because we know that, we should prepare for a potential attack and be prepared to detect and counterattack or prevent the event.

An example of vulnerability for a POS is the Void key on the cash register. An employee can easily use that key to skim cash from sales and, in fact, this method has been used over and over again by dishonest employees. Again, this can be identified as a potential threat and should be prepared for.

Yes, there may be many areas to identify and protect, but they usually have to do with the company's (or your) money or property. First, look for those areas or inventories that have high value and that would significantly impact your business if taken. Another way to identify these areas or transactions is by amount: losing $20 to theft in one area or $1,000 in another may indicate to you where and what should be monitored. Critical areas and key transactions are good places to start—where you have the most to lose and that are the most vulnerable to internal theft.

Every property is different yet the same. We all have the same basic games, operations, support departments, as well as controls, policies, and procedures. It is also true that we will tend to get ripped off in the same areas. I can't emphasize enough that you must take the time to identify where you expect to be hit and plan your response. Doing this alone will reduce your exposure to internal loss.

A good way to get started is to ask each department head (include each department on the property, no matter how small) to provide you with a list of threats or risks that he or she is aware of and any tells, indicators, controls, or reports that could be used to identify risks. Don't be frustrated if you don't get what you want the first time you ask for it! Remember, they may not have ever thought of putting such a list together. They, more than likely, may not even know that loss prevention is part of their responsibility too.

Keep asking and eventually you will have for each department a list that details expected methods an employee could use to steal from that particular department. That list tells you a number of things:

1. The items or assets exposed to loss
2. The type of theft/fraud that may occur in that department
3. The controls presently in place to prevent the loss
4. The controls presently in place to detect the loss

This is a revealing exercise for all. Many department heads have never been asked to think in this fashion or even know that it is necessary to protect their departments. A lot of department heads don't know why specific controls are in place and (even worse) do not review their daily reports, statistics, or exception reports to identify losses. As a proactive surveillance director you can point out what the department head can do to protect his or her department and how to work with you should a loss occur.

3.6.2 Case History

A surveillance investigator, while patrolling through the gift shop, noticed that a cashier was only ringing up every other item for a particular customer. The items not entered into the register ranged from candy bars to cigarettes to T-shirts. Obviously something was not right, so the investigator reported the activity to his director.

The director instructed that an audit of the cashier be initiated. As the audit progressed, the investigator noticed that the same customer came in every few days and always received some merchandise without payment. This customer was always served by the same cashier.

The general manager and the vice president of finance (who had responsibility for the gift shop) were contacted and informed. They decided to inform the gift shop manager (whom we all knew and trusted) in order to obtain her assistance in the investigation. Of course, the manager was extremely concerned that one of her employees might have been involved in theft, but she agreed to help. We started with comparing the register reports to the video from the audit and quickly determined that the cashier and the customer were colluding to steal items from the store. The customer would bring up to the counter a number of items as well as ask for several packs of cigarettes. It was clear that most of the items were not entered into the register or paid for.

While we were sure that we had enough evidence to confront the cashier and detain the customer, we decided to check all the cashiers in the gift shop for the same activity just in case. It was a good thing we did. The expanded audit of all cashiers on all shifts detected the same activity and more occurring with each cashier who worked in the gift shop. We saw all types of items given away to customers. Most of the cashiers were much bolder than the cashier we first observed. We saw one cashier grab an entire display box of candy bars and hand it out the door to a confederate who ran off the property.

Review of the register reports determined we had massive employee theft occurring in the gift shop. In fact, during the audit we observed the gift shop being restocked with items to replace whatever was missing from the inventory. At the end of each day it was appalling to see how much had been stolen. Unfortunately, as we found by reviewing the gift shop operation reports and financials, the theft had been going on for a long time, probably since the gift shop had opened. We later found out that our company's goods were resold on the streets and at local flea markets.

We had all of the cashiers arrested. They were ultimately convicted and lost their gaming cards. The gift shop manager lost her position and was transferred to another area. The vice president of finance was terminated. If he had paid attention to the daily operational information from the gift shop, he would have detected the thefts in the first week.

3.6.3 Threat Analysis for Surveillance Directors

As a surveillance director or manager it is your duty and responsibility to protect your property from loss and harm. But what exactly should you protect? You, like most surveillance directors, probably suffer from a lack of resources problem: not enough staff, not enough equipment, and certainly not enough time. So, how can you protect the entire casino? The answer is you can't protect everything completely, but you can protect a number of things very well and the rest well enough to detect a problem before it gets out of hand. Using a basic threat analysis approach to identify what to protect is one way to address this issue.

It is important to identify the following:

- Vulnerability: Where are you most vulnerable to loss or harm to your employees or guests? In what area do you expect loss, harm, or injury to occur? Is the threat more often external or internal? Base this on your past loss experience, criminal trends, gaming losses, and other statistical information. What are you required to protect by regulation or by your company?

- Probability of event occurring: Certain events may never happen (an earthquake or flood), some may occur almost every day (employee theft, distract and grab). You should prepare for an earthquake, but you can't look for it to happen every day. You know employee theft can occur every day; are you addressing it as a threat?
- Frequency of event: How many times will the event occur in a day, month, year, or several years? How many times do you get cheated by a major scam in blackjack in a year? What about slots? How often are your players hit with distract and grab teams?
- Impact of event: If (or when) the event occurs, what will it cost and how will it impact your employees, guests, and company? What about the company's reputation?

Once you've identified where you are vulnerable, the probability of the event occurring, how many times it may occur, and what it may cost you in dollars and reputation, you can then lay out your protection plan and strategies to prepare for, deter, or detect the event. It is much better to be ready for an event that is virtually certain to occur rather than being surprised and unable to respond in time.

For example, you must protect table games. Each game can be cheated by various scams. You can't watch each game and wait for the event to occur. It may happen today or never on some games. However, you do know that mini-baccarat gets hit on a fairly regular basis throughout the industry. You also know that when it does get hit, it is usually for a substantial amount. This tells you that preparing for an attack on that game is important and should be done as soon as possible.

3.6.4 Protection Plan and Strategies

Once we've identified where we are vulnerable, the probability of the event occurring, how many times it may occur, and the impact of the event, we must now establish a protection plan. For example, we know that the game of 21 will be attacked by employees, cheaters, and advantage players. It is a known vulnerability. It is probable that theft, cheating, and advantage play will take place, and on a fairly regular basis. Left unprotected, the impact (loss of revenue for the company) can be tremendous, not to mention precarious for the surveillance director!

Knowing that 21 will be attacked provides us an advantage. We can prepare beforehand for the types of attacks expected. The types of attacks we can experience are fairly well known and the majority of their tells are documented. New scams are often variations of older scams and can often be detected using traditional tools.

Developing a protection plan and strategies to combat a known type of attack will be more effective in stopping the attack from occurring or reducing its impact than hoping it doesn't happen at all.

Breaking a gaming property into its various departments helps to isolate, categorize, and identify general threats and protection strategies that we can use to counter them. Make sure you perform a threat analysis for each department on your property.

3.6.5 Apply Countermeasures

The purpose of identifying the vulnerability is to allow you to eliminate it. What can you do, within reason and cost-effectiveness, to protect the asset? Using the examples above, you could protect the baccarat and blackjack tables in several ways, such as monitoring the games for certain activity, types of play or certain players, or for levels of wagers or wins. You could protect POS from illegal employee use of the Void key by requiring that only a supervisor can perform that function. There are many ways and methods to protect your business. You can decide what works for you. The point is to protect it from unnecessary loss.

Countermeasures can and should be applied in each department based on its particular type of internal (and external) threat. As discussed above, once you have identified the specific threats in a specific department, it is essential that you develop and implement the controls, policies and procedures, and trip wires or alarms to detect the threat should it occur.

3.6.6 Monitor and Investigate Exceptions

One of the primary characteristics of employee theft is that the employee will attempt to hide it from you and, unfortunately, can be very good at it. Think about it. Who knows your operations, security, and controls better than anyone? Your employees! Fortunately for us, they can't hide everything. There is always a trail.

What that means is that you must proactively search for clues and exceptions. I am convinced that most employee theft continues much longer than it should because the people in charge or those responsible for the security of the business are not looking at information that already exists.

Again to use the examples discussed above, if someone looks at the daily table game win/loss reports, that person may see unusual losses or trends. Investigating the loss may develop further information and identify existing scams and thefts.

At POS, usually a list of voids is generated daily by accounting. If someone looks at this list daily, he or she may find that one particular cashier has many more voids than anyone else. Knowing this you can then monitor that cashier specifically and find out what's going on.

3.6.7 Obtaining Buy-In from Top Management and Program Partners

In order for your loss prevention program to work effectively, you must have the support of senior management and your fellow loss prevention departments (security, risk management, audit). Without their support you will not have access to the resources you need and your program will not succeed. Take the time to get everyone on board. When presenting the program to executives, focus on the following facts:

- Losses are certain to occur.
- Losses occur in each and every department.
- Losses can be reduced considerably with a loss prevention program.
- A loss prevention program will identify loss areas in each department and will allow the development of countermeasures and detection methods.
- An effective program will reduce losses and increase profits.
- Program can be developed and implemented at minimal cost (usually everything that is needed is already in place (loss prevention departments and personnel, controls, except for employee hotlines).

- Assessing each department for threats and risks will allow development and improvement of internal controls, policies, and procedures.
- Employees prefer to work in a defined and well-controlled environment.

The executives may not even know that loss can be such a huge problem. Most of them will agree that you have to keep an eye on the gaming side but may disagree that other areas warrant such attention. You may have to remind them of the losses that can occur in food and beverages, warehouse/receiving, or even the employee cafeteria.

As far as the cost of the program goes, the loss prevention teams are already in place, and developing/upgrading controls, policies, and procedures usually costs nothing but time. You may have to pay for a third party to operate your employee hotline, but the cost for such a line is usually around $2,500 (and well worth the investment).

It is also critical to your success that you work closely with the other loss prevention departments. Normally, these are security, risk management, investigations, and internal audit, legal, and compliance. Of course, human resources shouldn't be left out either. Each of these departments has a role in the protection of the property and should be included in the program.

I recommend that you meet with department heads for each of these departments and go over their roles and responsibilities. Determine who will do what and when. This should be very clear to prevent overlap and misunderstandings. The property will best be served by effective cooperation between these departments and not constant bickering about whose job it is to do this or that. People get very territorial, so you may have to be the team player to put things together. Once the program is set, the property wins overall.

3.6.8 Determine Program Objectives

Knowing and communicating your loss program objectives to all employees is paramount to a successful program. I think we've all seen such programs fail and fade away. Usually, these programs fail because they lack direction, cooperation between involved departments, employees and management, awareness and consistency. Stay focused, you are trying to accomplish the following objectives:

1. Make employees aware of how losses affect the company and themselves, their role in the protection of the company, and how to report suspicious activity.
2. Train department heads and managers in loss prevention skills for their area of responsibility.
3. Identify potential and existing threats or risks to the property for all departments. This must include internal and external theft, fraud, cheating and advantage play, and the opportunities for collusion that may exist for each area or transaction.
4. Develop and apply effective countermeasures to prevent and detect existing or developing losses for each area or transaction.
5. Properly investigate the incident to identify perpetrators and to allow successful prosecution.
6. Determine how and why every incident occurred and what could or should have prevented it from developing.

7. Develop and implement controls to prevent incidents from reoccurring. This includes working with the department where the loss occurred to improve awareness and detection capabilities.

3.6.9 Case History

As one gaming corporation began implementing a loss prevention program, managers came across substantial conflicts of interest in an area they never thought of before, their gift policy. Most companies have a gift policy that details what an employee can accept from a customer, guest, or vendor. However, these policies are rarely enforced so they often are ignored by employees and management.

In this particular case the new loss prevention policy required that employees of every level report any gift received from a customer, guest valued over $100. Managers and above were prohibited from receiving any gifts whatsoever and were to report offers.

Pandora's box was opened. The company received report after report of employees and managers receiving gifts of well over $100. Gifts such as cases of steaks, show tickets, football tickets, and bottles of wine were the norm. At the extreme level was a retail manager who received a $1,000 gift card. Another manager regularly attended expensive golf outings. Of course, these gifts were usually not from customers or guests; they were almost always from vendors! It is difficult to make an objective decision about a vendor who just paid for your golf trip!

By installing and enforcing a gift policy, the company was able to eliminate a number of conflicts of interest that were clouding the judgment of their managers and executives. Please note that the managers and executives were the major abusers in this case, not the front line employees. Those employees tend not to be involved in this type of issue as they do not make those types of decisions and thus are not bribed to do so.

3.6.10 Train Program Participants to Operate Program

There are key positions that are critical to your program's success: the surveillance director, security chief, risk manager, lead investigator, internal auditor, director of human resources, and legal counsel, to name a few. There are also key personnel who must be involved in the program. Each department head, manager, and supervisor must have a role in proactive loss prevention, as well as each employee. Training all of these people requires time and resources. It would be ideal to have the time, money, and resources to spend training everyone to prevent losses. This isn't going to happen at most properties. It is usually wiser (and easier) to start out smaller.

First, I recommend you begin with new employee orientation. Along with safety and other security information, new employees should hear from the top loss prevention executive on the property about the costs of internal theft, fraud, waste, and abuse how these can affect the company and the employee personally (profits, wages, staffing, benefits, etc.). It is important at this stage that the employees are informed about reporting suspicious activity or persons, including how to report activities through the employee hotline, human resources, or security or surveillance.

Second, I recommend that each director, manager, and supervisor attend a fraud awareness class at hire and annually thereafter. This class should discuss what occupational theft and fraud are; why they occur; their costs, red flags, behaviors, and other indicators; and how to prevent and detect them.

Third, I recommend that each department head, manager, and supervisor be provided specific loss prevention training for their department. For example, food and beverage managers should be taught how losses can occur in kitchens, restaurants, and bars and how such losses are detected. Slots staff should receive training for preventing losses in the slots.

Remember, there are not a lot of "experienced" supervisors, managers, or executives in the gaming business anymore. At most properties a games floor person was a dealer just six months earlier. Same in food and beverages; that beverage manager may have been a bartender and recently was promoted. I'm only saying that as far as knowing what to look for and how to prevent employee theft or collusion, these relatively inexperienced managers and department heads do not as of yet have the ability to do so. You must assist them.

You will find that if you take the time necessary to train your fellow department heads to look for internal theft and fraud, they most often will cooperate. You are helping to protect their department, aiding them in the reduction of loss in their area, thus improving their profitability and making them look good. You establish good rapport and protect the property as you should. A win–win situation!

3.6.11 Perform Daily Analytics

One of the most effective ways to detect and reduce employee theft and fraud (for that matter, almost all theft and fraud) is to review the information and reports you already have available! We've discussed this throughout the book and won't belabor it here. Just a few points:

- Almost all theft and fraud can be detected through paperwork, exceptions reports, statistics, and the electronic trail.
- Most department heads and managers and loss prevention personnel do not review this information at all or if they do, they do so inconsistently. Audit personnel often do review this information but often they are not trained to recognize red flags for each department.

It is absolutely critical that each department management team review daily operational reports, exception reports, and statistics in order to detect suspicious activity and trends. They must question each and every red flag or questionable transaction and determine why it occurred.

It is equally critical for surveillance to review daily the same information for the simple reason that many thefts and frauds are perpetrated by or involve the management of the department, or by those responsible for overseeing the department's activities such as finance, accounting, and audit personnel.

I realize that not all jurisdictions allow surveillance personnel to review financial and department information, but that is a mistake. I don't know how I could do my job without this information. At the very least I could not work proactively and would not catch the criminal activity I should. I would be forced to work reactively, and that is not a good thing. Fight for this information; it is in the company's best interest.

I also know that one person can't review all of this information on a daily basis. My solution was to delegate this to my staff whether they were supervisors or investigators. They loved being involved at that level and tore those numbers apart looking for crime! I could not have done as thorough a job as they did in their various assignments. We caught a lot of developing crime in this manner. Not only did this help in their career development, it also freed me to focus on other issues.

3.6.12 Implement Program

Now it's time to put the program in place. Start the training in orientation. Begin the fraud awareness programs with the managers and executives. Install the employee hotline. Communicate to the employees what you're doing. This program should not go away; it is too important to the continuing success of the property!

By the way, surveillance does not have to take the lead on the loss prevention program. It should be the task of the top loss prevention executive. However, if no one else does or will, then step in. It's that important.

3.6.13 Monitor Program

Ensure that you have a good idea where your property is as far as the type, frequency, and cost of the losses that occurred prior to the implementation of the program. This will provide you with the ability to determine how successful the program is. This is always important at budget time when the company is looking for ways to cut costs. You don't want to lose your hotline to save a few thousand dollars a year. Have your numbers and statistics ready.

3.6.14 Evaluate Program Results

Monitoring your program also allows you to evaluate its results. Where are you having success? Why? Where are you not seeing results? Why? What is working and how can you improve on it? Are there improvements to the bottom line? All these questions should be asked and more. If you're having success, build on it, keep the momentum going. If the program isn't working, find out why and fix it. Use your results to determine what area needs more time, resources, or countermeasures. Some areas will not require as much. Knowing this information will help you apply your resources effectively.

Developing such a program requires extensive research and discussion. It is beyond the scope of this book to discuss all that is required. There are many excellent books on the subject that you can use to develop your program. However, below is a checklist of what a proactive program should include:

- Preemployment screening and background check program
- Threat analysis and risk assessment

- Employee confidential hotline
- Employee orientation program (that includes security awareness information)
- Effective and up-to-date company and departmental internal control
- Code of ethics
- Internal theft and fraud awareness policy and training
- Employee security and safety awareness training
- Exit interview program
- Property access control
- Employee package check
- Computer security and access control

3.7 KEY DEPARTMENTS TO MONITOR FOR INTERNAL THEFT AND FRAUD

All departments and areas within today's casino hotel are vulnerable and exposed to internal theft and fraud. The proactive surveillance team must operate in a fashion that will allow consistent detection of theft and fraud in each of these areas. That said, there are areas that are more critical than others due to the money or value involved. It is up to the surveillance director to perform the threat assessment and determine how and when he or she will apply the necessary resources to them.

You must find a schedule and system that will allow you to provide the most support in your critical areas, yet also be able to routinely look at the others. Tables 3.2–3.6 list critical areas, common scams, and detection techniques for key departments:

3.7.1 Case History: Theft in Players' Clubs

Another example of a key casino area that is extremely vulnerable to internal theft and fraud is the player's club. These clubs in the past decade have become critical to marketing the property and retaining customers and are now the targets of internal and external fraudsters.

A number of gaming properties have been hit by internal scams targeting their player reward programs. These types of scams target the player reward programs for three reasons: (1) there is a lot of value (cash. comps, prizes) available, (2) there are few effective controls in place, and (3) even if controls exist, these programs are seldom monitored until it is too late. Let's look at a typical scam and determine how it was carried out, what allowed it to occur, and how it could have been prevented.

The scam described here actually happened; it went on for about eighteen months and cost the casino where it occurred at least $100,000. A pit clerk found that she could access and edit player accounts. Although her job responsibilities were to enter table game player information from a card provided by floor personnel into a data screen on a computer terminal, this clerk accessed and manipulated both table games and slot player accounts. The clerk accessed player accounts that had a point value, but showed little or no activity in over a year's time, usually if the account owner lived out of state. Once she had this information she accessed the account and removed the account owner's name

Table 3.2 Common Scams in Table Games and Detection/Protection Techniques

Type	Tells	Detection/Protection Techniques
False fills/credits	Personnel fail to verify properly Not enough signatures as required Fill/credit not placed or removed from game or sent to another game Game is a loser without appropriate play Fill/credit paperwork not in drop box	Require notification to surveillance of large fills or credits Audit fills and credits on regular basis Monitor game win/loss daily
Fraudulent markers/buybacks	Poor or nonexistent verification Failure to check identification Dealer fails to present checks for verification Failure to use lammers Table game numbers incorrect Same signatures used on documents, possibly false names or incorrect names	Require notification to surveillance of larger credit transactions Audit credit transactions frequently
Fraudulent player ratings	Incorrect/inaccurate information on rating cards Pit personnel have player accounts or their friends/family do Individual play can't be located or is nonexistent Large wagers can't be verified	Surveillance must compare completed rating cards to video frequently Compare database of players to employee names and addresses
Progressive jackpots (Let it Ride, Caribbean Stud, Bad Beat, etc.)	Same player or groups of players win jackpots Card switching tells observed prior to win Incorrect shuffle by dealer prior to win	Review progressive jackpots thoroughly prior to payment Review all or a good portion of the individual or group play Closely review dealer activity
Dealer/agent	Dealer pushes and pays are sloppy, unclear Card totals can't be seen Dealer favors one or more players Table leaking consistently	IOU patrol to detect same player(s) following a dealer IOU patrol to detect poor dealing procedures IOU to detect consistent loss on game

Table 3.3 Common Scams in Slots and their Detection/Protection Techniques

Type	Tells	Protection/Detection Techniques
Fraudulent/false jackpot	Same player(s) winning Coin-in minimal or nonexistent Same employees pay off jackpots to same player(s) Verification signatures unclear, or always from same individuals Certain machines or banks of slot machines losing consistently	Audit jackpots on a monthly basis Review slot statistics daily for machines that are consistent losers Review daily slot winner list for same names
Fraudulent/ counterfeit TITO ticket	Employees fail to verify TITO Verification number unreadable or written in Same employee(s) consistently redeeming TITO or same players present Same employee(s) making manual or computer adjustments to TITOs	All TITOs must be verified A minimum of two employees (one a supervisor) must be present to redeem manual or returned tickets , or when correcting/adjusting tickets manually or on the computer Surveillance must audit TITO redemption areas frequently
Slot technicians set up machines for jackpots or overpays	Same player(s) winning consistently Same employees consistently involved Coin-in minimal or nonexistent Same machine or bank of machines in play constantly by same player(s) Employees may be toked frequently	Review slot winner list for same name(s) Review slot daily machine win/loss reports Observe players consistently winning for suspicious activity Observe employees who loiter about same players or are toked frequently

and replaced it with her own or that of her boyfriend or their roommate. These accounts were now under her control. Because they were not local accounts and were also old, there was little or no risk that the owners would return to question the whereabouts of their points.

The point value that originally belonged legitimately to real players was now merged into the clerk's and her accomplices' accounts. Their account value was inflated to an extremely high value and they put it right to use.

At this particular property point values could be redeemed a number of different ways: for cash, rooms, or food and beverage. This gang of three took advantage of all the benefits. While they usually redeemed points for cash, they also redeemed their points for room nights, often in the more expensive suites, and comped themselves to the gourmet restaurants and enjoyed the best of food and beverages.

The clerk walked over to the redemption booth every day after work and collected her cash and comps. Although she was in uniform and recognized as an employee, no one asked her about her account or even thought it might be suspicious. In fact, she wasn't even treated or recognized as a top player (her account value put her near the top of the list). As

Table 3.4   Common Scams at the Point of Sale and Detection/Prevention Techniques

Type	Tells	Protection/Detection Techniques
Bartender theft/ fraud	No receipt issued Frequent use of No Sale key Undercharges and pockets difference Comps cash paying customers Uses matches, straws, and so forth to keep track of stolen funds	Patrol and audit bars/bartenders frequently Review void and no sale lists Monitor bartender tokes for excessive amounts
Cashier theft/fraud	No receipt generated or issued to customer Frequent use of Void or No Sale key Frequently counts down bank Has access to or uses manager's swipe card Does not void coupons, sets aside for later use	Patrol and audit each POS on a regular basis Review void and no sale lists Monitor employee, senior citizen, local, and other such discounts for abuse by cashiers
Restaurant cashier theft/fraud	Counts down bank frequently Access to and uses manager's swipe card Frequent use of Void or No Sale key Rings up excessive "walk outs" or customer returns/refunds Frequently "splits" tickets to cover selling for cash comped items	Patrol and audit restaurant POS stations on a regular basis Monitor waitress/cashier activities Review for legitimacy voids, no sales, etc. Investigate excessive "walk outs" and customer refunds Investigate excessive "split" tickets

I mentioned earlier, this went on for about eighteen months. Obviously, no one was paying attention.

So how was the clerk caught? Pure luck, made possible by an alert surveillance agent. The agent was actively monitoring floor personnel for accuracy and legitimacy as they completed player rating cards. While doing so he happened to swing the surveillance camera over to the clerk and observed over her shoulder as she entered information into the computer. As he happened to know the clerk's name he was stunned to see her delete the name on the account and enter her own. The agent called his supervisor over and the rest, as they say, is history. The clerk was so brazen that she, in the middle of the pit, would not even bother to hide her list of targeted accounts. She wasn't even working on pit player accounts. She was working in the slot area of the account program while working as a pit clerk! The investigation ultimately revealed the whole scam and each member of the gang was arrested.

Some of you reading this may be thinking that what happened at this casino can't happen at yours. Maybe you're right. But please withhold judgment and ask yourself two questions first: when was the last time you took a good hard look at any one of your many reward programs? Further, if you did, or if you assigned an agent to do so, what type of

Table 3.5 Common Scams in the Back of the House and Detection/Prevention Techniques

Type	Tells	Protection/Detection Techniques
Warehouse/ receiving theft/ fraud	Failure to inspect or weigh goods or product as required Failure to perform inventory of goods received or issued to departments Deliveries to departments frequently short or damaged, subpar quality	Surveillance audit of warehouse/ receiving on a regular basis Require complete inspection or weighing goods and products Prohibit warehouse/receiving personnel from parking their private vehicles near the warehouse Require all packages removed from the property to be inspected by security
Trash/recycling area (commonly used by employees to hide stolen items for later retrieval)	Restaurant silverware, linens, and other company property spotted in trash/recycling Guest room items such as shoes, articles of clothing, jewelry, electronics, alcohol found in trash	Surveillance audit of trash/recycling areas (if you don't have cameras in this area, put them in as soon as you can) Trash handlers and recyclers are prohibited from parking private vehicles near the area Package inspection by security Investigate any company property or items of value found in trash and recycling
Employee cafeteria	Excessive food costs Packaged goods such as butter, jam/jelly, cereals require frequent replacement Hot line food must be continually replaced Same employees observed in line to eat frequently (even on days off)	Surveillance audit of cafeteria and number of meals eaten by employees Replace packaged goods with bins of product Strictly enforce one meal a day policy Package inspection by security

training do you have or did the agent have to recognize the illicit activity that occurs in this specific area?

Present reward programs are intended to reward players and have too much value and access to information to be ignored by surveillance teams. A loss of $100,000 is extremely difficult to explain to a general manager.

Now let's discuss the controls that were in place at this property and the red flags that went up and should have sounded the alarm.

3.7.1.1 Computer Access Security

Access to the higher levels of a software application, such as the player rating management program discussed, are normally limited to supervisors or management with a need for that function. The "edit" function is one level. In this case the clerk was able to access the edit function in violation of internal controls. How did she do it? She didn't. It was given

Table 3.6 Common Scams in Marketing Programs and Detection/Prevention Techniques

Type	Tells	Protection/Detection Techniques
Players club theft/ fraud	Frequent entry and manipulation of players accounts, points, PINs, comps, slot free play, etc. by same employee(s) Same player(s) frequently redeeming with little or no play Player(s) on win list with little or no play	Surveillance audit of players' club on a regular and frequent basis Review club daily operating reports and exception reports Review player database for employees and friends/family of employees Review daily point adjustments and investigate suspicious activity
Promotional drawing fraud	Same player(s) frequently win or consistently win larger prizes or cash amounts Employee(s) or friends/family of employees win frequently	Always monitor those promotions with large value Ensure drawing storage areas or drums are under continuous coverage (to protect against stuffing barrel) Ensure employees only give customers proper number of tickets Review winner list for suspicious activity and/or relationship with employees
Coupon fraud (two for ones, match play, free drinks, etc.)	More than usual coupon redemption at one area or by same employee(s) Same guests redeeming Cash receipts decrease while coupon redemption increases Employee tokes increase	Surveillance audit of POS and other locations that accept coupons Review daily activity reports from such locations for increased coupon use

to her. Her immediate supervisor, who trusted the clerk, had gone on vacation and gave her a personal logon and password in case she needed it for anything. So much for access control! That's all it took and then the password wasn't changed upon her return or thereafter. The supervisor's login and password also allowed access to the slot accounts where the clerk spent much of her time.

Computer usage reports, when reviewed, showed clearly that the supervisor was logged on to the computer during periods while she was off duty. While she was off, the clerk was on using the supervisor's logon and password. As you can imagine, the supervisor had a lot of explaining to do, and, in fact, was initially considered a suspect.

3.7.1.2 Computer Security Controls: Breached
3.7.1.2.1 Exception Reports
Almost all computer applications and software monitor and report certain conditions or exceptions to normal activity. Just as a cash register will maintain a log and report the number of voided transactions performed by a clerk, player management software

maintains a log and reports activities considered as exceptions and already identified as potential suspect activity.

In this case, every time the clerk changed the name on an account an exception was generated and listed on a "name change exception report." This report was put together daily to allow management to review for illicit activity. Unfortunately, this report wasn't reviewed by anyone and no one in surveillance even knew the report existed.

3.7.1.3 Exception Reports: Ignored
3.7.1.3.1 *Players' Club Redemption*
You would think that employees and management personnel working at the players' club would begin to wonder about this clerk who routinely redeemed high levels of points, especially because the clerk was a uniformed employee. Although employees were allowed to play at this property, most did not, and any employee who was playing at that level should have raised some suspicions. At least someone should have wondered where the money to do all that the gambling was coming from!

A simple and quick check of the clerk's account would have shown that she didn't have any recent play activity. A simple and quick check of her job duties would have raised some eyebrows: an employee with access to player accounts redeeming points almost daily!

A quick call to surveillance or security would have solved the case almost immediately. I don't think the club employees ignored it on purpose. They certainly were not trained to recognize illicit or suspicious activity or how to report it if they did. So the department responsible for the protection of the club ignored or failed to see the red flags and suspicious activity. Further, the director of that area obviously failed to review the exception reports in his own area of responsibility.

3.7.1.4 Players' Club Protection: Failed
Stupid? Yes! Common? Unfortunately, yes. All too often in our industry, we place people in charge of critical areas and transactions, responsible for handling large amounts of money or sensitive information, and we fail to train them, monitor their activities, and hold them accountable.

We can go on and on, but I think you understand what I'm getting at. So what do we do to proactively protect the player reward programs?

3.8 PROTECTION STRATEGIES AND BEST PRACTICES FOR PROMOTIONS

First, we on the protection side—security, surveillance, loss prevention, and certainly senior management—must recognize that our marketing programs, promotions, and player rewards are continually at risk. They are vulnerable to both internal and external threats.

In my career, I have never seen a program or promotion *not* get ripped off in some fashion. It can be someone stuffing a drum with his or her own drawing tickets or players taking advantage of an incorrectly calculated game promotion, but it can happen and usually does. Usually it occurs because of poor planning and preparation and the failure to monitor the program or promotion by the responsible departments.

Listed below are my recommendations for best practices to protect player reward programs.

3.8.1 Best Practice #1: Review Marketing Programs and Promotions

The surveillance or loss prevention departments should review each marketing program or promotion for weaknesses, vulnerabilities, or security concerns. For example, coupons for a free meal or drink without an individual serial number prevent you from tracking where the coupons were issued and by whom. It may not sound like a big deal, but when you're trying to find out why so many employees and their friends are staying in the hotel or drinking at the bar, it will be.

Another example of why reviewing a program or promotion is important is that sometimes marketing people don't always do the math right and they unintentionally put forth a program where the house edge on a table or slot game is reduced or even eliminated by the edge given to the player! We in surveillance can't let this happen. Review marketing programs and promotions. You'll be glad you did.

3.8.2 Best Practice #2: Monitor Marketing Programs and Promotions

After the program or promotion has been reviewed and approved, it is time for it to be launched. While you may think your job is over, it actually is really beginning. It is after the launch that most programs fail. It is at this time that unforeseen problems and vulnerabilities will arise. In other words, this is when it will be attacked.

Expect this to happen and you'll be prepared. No matter how much time you spend reviewing the program beforehand, scams will happen. This is because you can only plan for what you expect or believe will take place. We usually don't know how employees, our guests, or the bad guys will react.

Surveillance and other loss prevention personnel should familiarize themselves with the program or promotion. Information such as who is eligible (and who's not), entry and contest/drawing information, program operation, and department responsibilities is critical in order to protect the program or promotion and should be readily available and understood. Training should be provided if necessary.

Once the program or promotion is launched, take the time to monitor it to ensure the rules, policies, and procedures are in place and followed. It's important at this point to monitor what type of response and which players or guests you are getting to the promotion. Are you getting the responses and players or guests the program or promotion was designed to attract?

For example, an overwhelming response to the program or promotion may indicate you came up with the right program or promotion at the right time, or it could mean that it was poorly designed and players or guests are aware of the "hole" and are taking advantage of it.

I remember a promotion designed to increase slot play. The slot players would receive a ticket or tickets from a slot floor person whenever they hit various levels of winning combinations on their machine. Each ticket was worth so much in point value and the player could redeem his or her points for cash or prizes. The promotion was an immediate success. Players were on almost every machine, people were winning, everyone was happy! Then the results came in. The property was spending so much money on cash and prizes that it didn't make any money on the increased slot play. In fact, it had lost money! Why? It was too easy for the players to win. The levels of winning combinations on the slot machines were set too low. It seemed like every time players had a three of a kind or even lower they won prize tickets. The slot staff was overly busy (and on overtime to handle the load). Everyone was winning. In this case, the promotion was stopped but only after an unnecessary loss occurred. Always monitor your programs and promotions.

3.8.3 Best Practice #3: Review Exception Reports

Exception reports list exceptions or violations to internal controls. Every critical transaction has or should have controls that must be adhered to in order to protect the organization. When these controls or procedures are broken, an exception report is generated. Normally these reports are automatically generated by the computer application or put together by the audit department. These reports should ultimately be directed to and reviewed by the director or senior management of the department where the exception occurred.

Remember the pit clerk we discussed earlier. Every time she changed a name on an account an exception report was generated. No one ever reviewed it. The crime went on for eighteen months and cost the company a considerable amount. If someone had looked at the exception report the theft could have been stopped the first day with only minimal loss.

Consistent review of exception reports and information will deter and detect potential and existing problems, issues, vulnerabilities, and internal/external theft. It is extremely important to remember that during most incidents of internal theft and fraud a control was bypassed, ignored, or broken. Proactively searching for these exceptions and determining why they occurred are the most effective steps to protect an area or property.

I highly recommend that the surveillance department review exception reports and information from key areas and critical transactions. If you don't, you're trusting that someone else will tell you if anything is wrong. What if they don't review the reports or, even worse, they are involved or are the actual perpetrators? The fate of your department and your property rests with you. Review your exception reports!

3.8.4 Best Practice #4: Train Your Personnel to Recognize and Report Suspicious Activity

Most surveillance and loss prevention teams are not trained to look for or recognize theft or fraud occurring within marketing programs and promotions. Furthermore, most supervisors, managers, and directors who work within the department running the promotion are not trained to recognize theft or fraud.

If you accept the premise that theft and fraud will occur (and you should) in this critical area, you must be prepared. Train yourself and your agents to recognize the scams and methods used to beat these programs and promotions. Study exception reports until you understand them. Work with the auditing staff to learn what reports should be reviewed and help one another spot trends and anomalies.

I recommend you train key departments such as auditing and the departments responsible for operating and monitoring the program/promotion to spot and report unusual activities and transactions. These employees are in the front lines and see these things. They are a wealth of information. They just don't know what you want to know or even how to report it to you. Use them, they are a great resource. Train your personnel!

3.8.5 Conclusion

Player reward programs and promotions are important to every gaming property's marketing plan. From drawing a ticket from a barrel to downloadable credits issued by a clerk in the rewards center, a considerable amount of a company's money is exposed and vulnerable to new and old scams, theft, and embezzlement, not to mention advantage players. Traditionally, these areas have been overlooked for too long by surveillance and the loss prevention team. Yet, due to the growth and implementation of new technology, we lose more money and value here than we do normally in other areas.

Fortunately, you can succeed in the protection of these key areas through the application of tried and true surveillance techniques. You just need to step in and make it happen.

3.9 LOSS PREVENTION AT THE POINT OF SALE

In today's world thieves are using technology to steal more and at a faster rate than ever before. Fortunately, loss prevention professionals obtain benefits from technology too; we can protect more points and detect crime at a much faster rate. Technology also provides businesses the ability to install cameras and exception reporting systems cost-effectively. In this section we will discuss how digital surveillance systems can be used to protect the POS to reduce theft and fraud.

The Association of Certified Fraud Examiner's 2008 Report to the Nation states that employee theft and fraud is on the rise. The University of Florida's "2008 National Retail Security Survey" by Richard C Hollinger states that businesses lose about 1.54 percent of their total annual sales to shrinkage, a significant portion of that due again to internal theft and fraud.

Employee theft and fraud often occur at the POS because that is where the assets—cash, credit, and the ability to manipulate them—are located. The improved ability to deter and detect theft at the POS reduces the majority of our losses.

3.9.1 Important First Steps

- *Install surveillance cameras at each POS location.* Cameras are relatively inexpensive and provide both deterrence and the ability to detect theft and who is perpetrating it.

- *Record all activity using a digital recording system.* Again, technology has reduced the costs of the equipment and most businesses can afford them. The security they provide and the impact they can have on the bottom line are well worth the expense.
- *Combine an exception reporting system with your surveillance system.* Exception reporting will let you know any time an employee performs or doesn't perform a critical transaction. For example, a transaction that is voided by an employee is recorded and reported to you for your review. If it's legitimate, great! If the transaction is not legitimate or appears suspicious, you can investigate further.
- *Use remote monitoring.* You can't always be at your business, yet your business must operate while you're away. More than likely, it is while you're away that the majority of theft will occur. Today's technology allows you to monitor your business wherever you are. All you need is access to a computer and the Internet. Again, this is a relatively inexpensive solution that will impact your bottom line positively.

3.9.2 Deterring and Detecting Employee Theft and Fraud

- *Operate your system regularly.* Most people don't until they need it and then they realize they have forgotten how to operate it. If you operate the system daily you will become familiar with it and become better at using it. You will also see things within the system such as employees fooling around instead of working, breaking your procedures, or even stealing.
- *Respond to observed activity.* In most cases it is a great deterrent to make your employees aware that you observed them doing something they weren't supposed to. Usually you can correct these minor issues before they turn into major issues. It may even just be an issue that can be corrected through additional training. The point is they know you're watching and checking and that is a good thing. There are some observations you will make that will require further investigation before you respond. If you suspect someone may be stealing, be patient and gather your facts or get outside assistance before you confront the individual. It may turn out the person is not stealing or there are others who may be involved that you need to identify.
- *Identify and alarm critical transactions.* Identify the transactions that increase your exposure to theft. For example, an employee voiding a transaction may be legitimate, but it also may be a way that an employee is covering his or her illicit activity. Use your system to notify you of such transactions for easy review. A well-designed system can locate such transactions and any other transaction you desire in seconds.

3.10 SUMMARY

Employee theft and fraud exist. There are steps a business can take to deter and detect theft activity. These steps aren't difficult, but the efforts must be consistent. A loss prevention program is well worth the investment and will return profit back to the bottom line.

4

Security Surveillance

4.1 THE EVOLUTION OF SECURITY SURVEILLANCE

A number of gaming properties separate their surveillance duties between gaming and security operations. Gaming surveillance is usually assigned the games and the casino floor in general. Security surveillance is usually assigned retail operations, back of the house, and parking lots.

I prefer when surveillance duties are kept to one department in order to centralize skills, training, and response; a security surveillance department can work provided it is treated like a surveillance department. Most security surveillance departments fail because they are treated like stepchildren of the security department. Usually, officers are assigned to these areas with minimal (if any) training in the use of the equipment or what their duties actually are. In fact, the officers assigned to the security station are normally rotated and do not get the time they need to operate successfully.

Usually the reason a security surveillance function is established is to allow gaming surveillance to focus specifically on gaming and for security to focus on the other areas in the hope that both areas will perform more effectively. This usually doesn't happen. What does happen is security isn't trained well enough to operate the equipment and must call on gaming surveillance to assist. In fact, I had a standing order that whenever something critical happened on the property (murder, suicide, stabbing, fight, etc.) our surveillance supervisor was to immediately assign an investigator to go to the security surveillance room and provide any assistance necessary. Normally, the investigator was used to locate necessary camera coverage, help review video to locate suspects and witnesses, and prepare video evidence. Our investigator was always needed!

While I don't agree that having a separate surveillance room is a good idea, I have seen some that do work, and I would suggest some things to help your security surveillance station be a success. In fact, there are reasons why you may want to have security surveillance stations in nightclubs, European pools, and retail malls.

4.2 TIPS FOR SUCCESSFUL SECURITY SURVEILLANCE OPERATION

Assign a permanent staff: As mentioned previously, most operations rotate through the station, allowing no continuity. If you're going to operate a security station, do it the right way: find officers who want to work behind the cameras and keep them there.

Identify areas of responsibility for the security surveillance function: Perform threat analysis/risk assessments for those areas within the function. Establish specific objectives for the station to attain. For example, let's look at what a typical threat list for security might be:

- Threat of terrorism
- Employee/guest safety
- Building/property perimeter
- Parking lots/valet
- Hotel floors and guest areas
- Retail malls, gift shops
- Nightclubs
- Pools
- Employee areas
- Warehouse/receiving
- Trash/recycling areas
- Attractions

This list is not meant to be exhaustive or in order of priority. What the list indicates is that there are a number of security threats to be dealt with that are not prepared for (and most gaming surveillance rooms are not prepared to handle incidents in those areas!). Let's look at one of these threats and determine some appropriate measures that should be taken by a proactive security surveillance room.

Nightclubs are in the news a lot lately for drugs, prostitution, fights, gang activity, underage drinking, too much drinking, theft, tip hustling, and so forth. For almost any nightclub there are increased calls for service by casino security, local law enforcement, and medical response units. Nightclubs represent a high threat/risk level to the property and can cost the property profits, loss of licensing, and fines by regulatory bodies, as well as loss of reputation and bad press, to mention just a few consequences that may be due to just one incident!

Nightclubs are such risks for a hotel casino that I would ensure my officers were trained to recognize and respond to any incident that may occur in that area. I would establish a schedule requiring security station officers to patrol with their cameras throughout the club. In fact, it may be a good idea to assign an officer to monitor the club whenever it's open!

By the way, a lot of nightclubs are operated by outside companies. They often provide their own security. I don't agree with this. Unless the security is provided by a reputable provider, I would rather use casino security staff who are usually better trained, accountable, and don't have any interest in the tip pool. Nightclub security can be part of the problem because they are part of the tip pool and tend to allow activities they shouldn't.

I would also audit the club regularly. A lot of internal theft occurs in these areas at the bars, the cashier station (door charge), and through the sale of booths and bottle service.

Ask yourself this: Do you really think that the employees working in the club don't know what's going on? They are very aware and probably profiting from it. You must let them know you will catch them.

You must also audit the bouncer (or security) at the door to ensure identification is checked and minors are turned away. Individuals not dressed appropriately or in gang colors or attire should be turned away.

How problems and incidents are handled by nightclub staff, security, and management should be monitored closely. A lot of fights begin in the club and often spill out onto the casino floor. Often club security calls casino security too late (or not at all) and the casino security team has to try to quickly identify the nature of the problem and those involved. This usually doesn't work well.

In essence, the nightclub should be patrolled by the security surveillance team on a regular basis. Just observing for potential problems and developing issues and reporting those observations to the casino security team will help identify and reduce the threats and risks to the property and their actual incidence.

I hope you can see how performing a threat/risk assessment of an area within the security surveillance assigned area of responsibility provides the information to develop a security plan and objectives to protect the casino. Evaluating each area in such a fashion allows proactive surveillance operations.

Train security surveillance in surveillance tradecraft: As mentioned previously, most security surveillance stations are manned by officers who receive little, if any, training. This is why they are not successful! If you have responsibility for a security surveillance station, you must train your officers to be security surveillance officers, not security officers. I recommend you train your personnel in surveillance tradecraft and operations and everything else necessary (aside from gaming) that you are responsible for. Key areas I would recommend are:

- Surveillance camera techniques
- Patrols, IOUs (identify, observe, understand), and tri-shots
- Audit and close watch techniques
- Threat assessment
- Standard operating procedures for security surveillance
- Standard operating procedures (for all areas/departments of responsibility)
- Loss prevention techniques for food/beverage/retail operations
- Loss prevention techniques for employee areas/warehouse/hotel
- Nightclub and pool security and risk management

Develop security surveillance standard operations manual: Once you understand your responsibilities and assignments and have started your training program, start your standard operating procedures (SOP) manual. You could put it together in the beginning, but it is best to wait to see what you actually will be doing.

I find that the better the SOP manual is the better the department will run. It should detail the department mission, its objectives, and how it operates to attain them. Your personnel need to know what is expected of them and how to go about doing their jobs. A critical area is response to incidents. If you want your officers to respond properly to an incident, tell them what responding properly is. If you want them to use common sense or if they have flexibility in a type of decision, let them know what those situations are.

Security incidents are often emergency situations. Make sure your people are trained and ready to go.

4.2.1 Case History

Cooperation between security surveillance and gaming surveillance is important, as this case shows. A man was found dead in the hotel of a casino resort property. The maid found him lying on the floor as she entered to clean the room. Police were called and quickly determined it was a homicide (the victim had been beaten to death). The police immediately requested a tape review to identify the murderer.

Security surveillance began a review of the hotel elevators and the cameras on the hotel floor where the incident occurred. A gaming surveillance agent was sent to the security monitor room to assist.

Gaming surveillance quickly determined that the victim was a player and had a player's card. This allowed his play on the table games to be located. Due to proper IOU patrol techniques used by the surveillance agent at the time of the play, an identification shot of the player was obtained. A photo of the player was released to security surveillance for their use.

Once both surveillance teams knew what the victim looked like, a tape review of his movements and activities was initiated. Gaming surveillance was able to track the victim to the bar where he was recorded talking to a young woman (the woman appeared to be a prostitute; this was later confirmed by the police investigation). Gaming surveillance, through additional tape review, tracked the victim as he left the bar accompanied by the prostitute and entered the elevator to the hotel floors.

Security surveillance was advised of the entry time and they picked up the review as the couple entered and then exited the elevator on the victim's floor. The hall cameras were reviewed and located the couple entering the victim's room.

Twenty minutes later into the tape review a black male adult was observed knocking on the door of the victim, and when the door was opened he quickly entered the room.

About thirty minutes later review of the tape located both the prostitute and the black male exiting the room. The victim was not observed at that time and was not seen on video again. No other persons entered the room until the maid arrived the next morning and found the victim.

The black male hid his face from the cameras in the hotel hallways and elevators to prevent his identification. However, he could not avoid the cameras placed on the casino floor and at the doors. An excellent face shot of the suspect was obtained and shown to the police who immediately identified him as a known pimp and criminal.

Both the pimp and the prostitute were quickly located, arrested, and held for the murder. The crime was solved within two hours after the victim's body was found. This case is a great example of how both surveillance teams can and should work together.

5

Standard Operating Procedures

5.1 SURVEILLANCE DEPARTMENT OPERATIONAL POLICIES AND PROCEDURES

Policies and procedures are the fundamental backbones of any business operation. Without them, a business will not operate as effectively and efficiently as it should. This is especially true for gaming companies. In our world we must operate successfully; protect our games, employees, and guests; abide by state and federal statutes, and do it in a manner that won't expose us to risk or liability.

One of the most critical factors for the successful operation of a gaming property is the surveillance department. It *must* operate effectively. Failure to do so has resulted in losses of significant amounts of money and jobs.

Most surveillance departments do not protect the property or its profit-making ability very well. Surveillance personnel, in reality, are not trained well and are usually focused on the wrong things and in the wrong areas. If you think about it, we spend most of our time protecting the game of 21 from card counters and not on what is really going on in the casino and the back of the house.

While the road to a successful and proactive surveillance operation is a long one, the first step is developing and implementing standard surveillance operating policies and procedures.

5.1.1 Standard Operating Procedures

A number of surveillance departments don't have standard operating procedures (SOPs). If they have them, they usually consist of policies regarding employee absenteeism and tardiness. Procedures such as calling in are usually stressed and perhaps some guidelines on detaining someone may be included. Obviously this will not suffice in today's environment of ever growing risk and exposure to liability. Human resources would have a field day with most surveillance SOP manuals. However, that really isn't the biggest problem. A surveillance department that does not have a well-written and up-to-date SOP manual that contains specific policies and procedures on how surveillance personnel are to perform their duties will not be effective over the long term. In fact, proactive surveillance departments almost always have good SOP manuals.

Take time to develop your SOP manual. It will take effort to put it together correctly and will always be a work in progress requiring constant revision. Once developed and implemented, your SOPs serve as your entry into the proactive surveillance world

5.2 KEY SURVEILLANCE POLICIES AND PROCEDURES

Of course, you should begin your SOP manual with those policies and procedures required by your particular company or corporation. These are, as mentioned previously, policies and procedures regarding absenteeism, punctuality, company organizational chart, requesting days off, and so forth.

Once these are in place you must develop the key surveillance policies and procedures your department will operate by. These SOPs will be the foundation you will build your department upon. It makes sense to ensure that you develop SOPs that will inherently cause your team to operate in a proactive and successful manner. Some key SOPs you should include are:

- Camera assignments and positioning, including "at rest" positions, for all cameras in system
- Required set-up and display of cameras and monitors based on property needs, regulatory requirements, crime trends, and gaming statistics
- Patrol techniques and requirements
- Recording techniques and requirements
- Audit and close watch technique and requirements
- Department notification requirements
- Required trip wires
- Player evaluation standards
- Surveillance detection and response techniques
- Evidence gathering
- Training requirements for surveillance personnel

These SOPs serve as the core operating procedures. Using these allows each surveillance officer to operate successfully in a framework of established and proven technique and protocol.

Implementing these SOPS establishes how the department will detect or be informed of key events, transactions, or activities that may require observation or response from surveillance and how surveillance will do this. For example, a table games player wagering $100 per hand (based on type of casino property) must be evaluated by surveillance for indications or tells of cheating or advantage play. If the player is cheating or is using advantage play, he or she can be stopped in a timely manner. If he is just a normal player, the pit and surveillance can move on to the next player.

Another example of a key SOP is the trip wire. Let's say that the player is wagering $50 per hand and is below the required notification limit for the property. Thus the player will not be reported or reviewed by surveillance. The problem with this is that this player can still win a lot of money or can work in collusion with the dealer to dump the game. For this situation, a trip wire requiring the pit to report to surveillance any player win of $2,500 or more (based on type of casino property and maximum allowed wagers) again results in a surveillance evaluation of the player.

The point is to get your people to where they need to be and to perform the necessary activities to protect the property. Without SOPs in place you can only hope that things are done the way you want them done or even done at all. Again, as mentioned earlier, this is how a lot of surveillance rooms operate. They are depending on the individual surveillance officer rather than a solid and structured system.

While you may have some good personnel, you will also have some poor performers. A good SOP manual will help even the poor performers operate at a higher level or will assist you in identifying where the weaknesses are.

5.3 KEY SURVEILLANCE FUNCTIONS

5.3.1 Audits

Surveillance departments must perform regular and routine audits of all departments to protect the property successfully. It is the single most powerful weapon the surveillance department has at its disposal and it should be wielded.

In order for a surveillance audit program to be successful it must be included in the SOP manual. The SOP should include:

- Audit description and requirements
- Normal audit parameters
- Departments requiring audit
- Transactions and activities requiring audit
- Tools used in audits for specific departments, transactions, and activities
- Audit scheduling and assignments
- Audit reporting

A strong audit program *will* detect unusual and suspicious activity. It *will* often detect theft and fraud. It is highly recommended that surveillance managers and directors incorporate an audit program into their operations!

5.3.2 Officer Training

Another key function that should be detailed in the SOP manual is the training of surveillance personnel. Most surveillance rooms do not spend enough time on this and consequently fail to detect new scams and even old scams.

Another problem is most employees usually will not take responsibility for their training unless forced to do so. Your top performing personnel, of course, will do so. But how many top performers do you have?

The SOP manual should include training parameters and guidelines for each job title/level (trainee to supervisor/manager) within the surveillance department. Standard components included are:

- Knowledge of property policies and procedures
- Knowledge of each department's policies and procedures
- Game protection techniques for all games presented for play at the property
- Basic strategy and card counting
- Internal theft and fraud detection/prevention
- Laws, statutes, and regulations
- Risks and liability
- Investigation, interviewing, evidence gathering and securing, and report writing

Surveillance personnel must be the most knowledgeable employees on the property. In order to protect a department they must know how it operates and how it looks on a normal day-to-day basis. This is true from the back of the house to the front of the house.

Remember, the people you must go up against will conceal how they are stealing from you, whether they are employees or outside agents, or both in collusion. You must prepare yourself and your people through training.

The SOP manual should detail for each level the specific knowledge and job skills that are required for that position. How that training (self-guided, instructor provided, off property seminars, etc.) is to be accomplished or provided should be included. The manual should also include how an officer will be compensated or rewarded (promotion, increase in pay, etc.) or held accountable (fail to complete probation, progressive discipline, etc.) (see Chapter 7).

5.3.3 Summary

A well-written SOP manual is the foundation for a successful surveillance operation. Including the key procedures and functions described above will improve your surveillance operation. The manual is a living document that must be constantly revised and updated to address current trends and changes. It should be reviewed at least four times a year. In fact, since it is so critical to the success of the department, it is suggested that a senior supervisor or manager be permanently assigned to oversee and update the SOP manual on a monthly basis.

The standard operating procedures listed in the appendix to this chapter are representative of what we've been discussing. Hopefully, you can see the detail necessary for each policy and procedure. Please feel free to adopt these as your own.

I recommend that each member of your surveillance team be issued his or her own SOP manual for ready reference. One of the most effective ways to train your personnel is to select an SOP weekly and go over that SOP at a preshift briefing. This method also allows SOPs to be checked for need to be updated or revised.

5.4 APPENDIX

5.4.1 Mission Statement

The surveillance department proactively protects the assets and profit-making ability for the company. We provide maximum deterrence, rapid detection, and response to internal and external theft and fraud, cheating of our games, harm to our employees and guests, and losses due to inefficiencies of operation.

5.4.2 Key Objectives

- Protect and serve the company, the property, and the departments under our protection to the utmost of abilities and skills.
- Ensure surveillance personnel are highly and consistently trained in all aspects of surveillance operations, gaming, and loss prevention knowledge and skill.
- Provide and maintain top quality equipment to utilize in the performance of our duties.
- Rapidly detect and respond to any threat or incident of cheating of our games, internal and external theft or fraud, or harm to our employees or guests.
- Maintain the integrity of the company, the property, and our gaming product through the enforcement of our rules, policies, and procedures.
- Investigate reports or indications of cheating, theft, fraud, and loss of revenue or property, emphasizing the identification of involved individuals and the methods used to perpetrate the crime, their apprehension and prosecution, and the prevention of the crime from reoccurring.

5.4.3 Investigator Code of Ethics

1. Investigators shall, at all times, demonstrate a commitment to professionalism and diligence in the performance of their duties.
2. Investigators shall not engage in any illegal or unethical conduct or any activity that would constitute a conflict of interest.
3. Investigators shall, at all times, exhibit the highest level of integrity in the performance of their duties and assignments.
4. Investigators will comply with lawful orders of the courts and will testify to matters truthfully and without bias or prejudice.
5. Investigators, when conducting investigations, will obtain evidence or other documentation to establish facts and a reasonable basis for any opinion rendered.
6. Investigators shall not reveal any confidential information obtained during an assignment or investigation without proper authorization.
7. Investigators shall reveal all material matters discovered during the course of an investigation, which if omitted, could cause distortion of the facts.
8. Investigators shall focus on the evidence, not the position or status of the parties to the investigation.
9. Investigators shall continually strive to increase his or her professional knowledge, expertise, competence, and effectiveness in all duties performed or assigned.

5.4.4 Function of Surveillance Department

The function of the surveillance department is to operate and maintain a closed-circuit television surveillance system within the guidelines and regulations set forth by the Gaming Commission, and via this system, operated by a staff of trained personnel, strive to:

- Provide protection for our employees and guests
- Proactively protect company assets
- Ensure adherence to systems of internal control, policy, and procedure
- Detect internal and external theft and fraud, advantage play, and cheating at gambling, in full cooperation with the Gaming Commission and other law enforcement agencies, to maintain the integrity of the company, augmenting the development of public confidence and trust

5.4.5 Authority Specific to Surveillance

1. The surveillance department has no specific authority over other departments. The surveillance department has a direct responsibility to actively protect other departments from criminal activity, loss or damage to company assets, and loss of revenue or profit-making ability.
2. Gaming Commission regulations govern equipment and some operational procedures. Those concerning contact or interaction with Commission members or their agents and surveillance personnel are listed below:
   a. Members of the Commission, and their agents, with proper identification, shall at all times be provided immediate access to all surveillance areas and records.
   b. Surveillance personnel shall record and provide documentation, video, videotape, or photos of any views, activity, or location as the Commission or its agents require.
3. The Gaming Commission shall be notified regarding activity that is considered irregular, suspicious, or criminal. The established surveillance chain of command will be used to make such notifications.

5.4.6 Surveillance Chain of Command

1. The chain of command is important for effective operation of the department and shall be followed except under extreme or emergency conditions or as per the company's "open door" policy.
2. Special requests, complaints, concerns, or questions should first be directed to the employee's immediate supervisor. In the event the supervisor is unable to resolve the issue, the supervisor shall pass the issue on to his or her supervisor to resolve.

5.4.7 Surveillance Monitor Room Access

The surveillance monitor room is a restricted access area.

1. Authorized access
   - Surveillance personnel
   - Gaming Commission regulators and agents
2. All others must have the approval of director of surveillance.
3. Visitors for the purpose of reviewing tape shall be directed to the designated review area.
4. All visitors must sign the visitor's log.
5. Immediately upon request and presentation of proper identification, agents of the Gaming Control Board are provided access to the surveillance monitor room.

5.4.8 Surveillance Daily Operations

1. Surveillance personnel must arrive on time for their assigned shift.
   a. The off-going shift of investigators shall be relieved at this time.
2. The off-going shift supervisor or senior investigator shall brief the oncoming shift concerning:
   a. Operations and incidents of the previous sixteen hours
   b. Ongoing investigations, assignments, audits, and close watches
   c. Current information concerning active players, advantage play, cheating, or theft activity
   d. Any other information pertinent to shift operation
   e. Investigators must familiarize themselves with operations and incidents that may have occurred during their days off
3. Cameras and system equipment shall be checked for proper positioning and operation.
   a. Playbacks and time date checks shall be performed on a monthly basis
   b. Malfunctioning or failed equipment shall be reported immediately and listed in the repair log
4. Shift supervisor or senior investigator shall assign on-duty investigators as needed to:
   a. Area/department of patrol
   b. Audit/close watch
   c. Special assignments
5. Investigators assigned to routine patrol of an area or department shall use the IOU method of patrol:
   a. IDENTIFY: Employees and guests in area or on game. Identify specific location/ID of area or within department, and status of any company assets (gaming devices and equipment, table checks, cash, etc.).
   b. OBSERVE: Monitor activity for indications of violation of policy or procedure and indication of advantage play or criminal activity.
   c. UNDERSTAND: The investigator must understand that the activity observed is normal and is not unusual or suspicious in any way prior to moving on

in the patrol. Unusual or suspicious activity must be monitored continuously until proven that it does not represent a threat or it is determined a threat and appropriate responses made.

6. The use of, at the minimum, a triangulated camera set-up (tri-shot) is required when monitoring:
   a. Unusual or suspicious play
   b. Criminal activity or any activity that affects the assets or profit-making ability of the property
   c. High action play
   d. Audits and close watches
7. The tri-shot will be maintained until the activity is resolved. Player evaluations will be continued until the play is determined not to be a threat.
8. Player evaluations are required for a player wagering $100 or more, buy-in of $2,000 or more, or winning $2,500 or more.
9. When the investigator determines the play or activity does not pose a threat to the property, tri-shot coverage may be dropped to routine coverage. The investigator will continue to check the play or activity to ensure it remains normal or has not exceeded wager/win parameters.
10. Incident and evaluations must be completed prior to end of the shift.

5.4.9 Surveillance Tri-Shot Coverage

1. Tri-shot camera coverage is the basic technique used by the surveillance department to establish camera coverage of an area, event or incident, or suspicious activity.
2. Tri-shot coverage is used to obtain and provide detailed video records of an event or incident for review, investigation, and for use as evidence.
3. Tri-shot coverage is placed in any situation considered critical for the protection of the company's assets or of its employees, guests, and customers.
4. The three components of the tri-shot are:
   a. Overview of the game or activity (table layout, face of slot machine, area, etc.)
   b. Identification shot of the player(s) and employee(s) on the game or in the area
   c. Specific or detail shot of the suspected activity or critical information such as player wagers, player's hands, currency/ticket acceptor, cash register, etc.
5. Tri-shot coverage shall be placed immediately under the following circumstances:
   a. $100 action or more
      i. Upon determining the play or activity is not a threat to the property, tri-shot coverage may be reduced to routine coverage.
      ii. The play or activity should be rechecked on a regular basis to ensure it remains a nonthreat or has exceeded win or wager parameters.
   b. Detection of criminal or suspected criminal activity
   c. Security incidents
   d. Routine walk-outs, ejections, eighty-sixes, etc. do not require tri-shot coverage but coverage should be placed if at all possible.

e. Tri-shot coverage should be placed during an incident that may result in litigation such as guest injury, medical response, security approaches and handling of hostile, volatile or inebriated individuals or situations.

6. Tri-shot coverage shall be displayed on the agent's working monitors until the activity has ended or the agent has determined the activity is not a threat, with the following exceptions:
   a. Games with wagers of $500 or more or on a game where a player has won $2,500 or more shall be moved to other monitors with continued tri-shot coverage.

7. During peak business periods or emergencies it may be required that routine monitor displays be dropped and replaced with tri-shots or other monitor/camera adjustments. This is authorized during these conditions.

5.4.10 Evaluation and Coverage of High Action Games

Games with wagers of $100 or more shall be considered high action games and require surveillance coverage and response.

1. Players wagering $100 or more shall be assigned to an investigator who will perform the following:
   a. Establish tri-shot coverage of the game
   b. Obtain identification shots of each player in the game
   c. Check any unknown players through player and criminal databases
2. Evaluate play for tells of cheating, theft, or advantage play.
   a. Report any indication of the above to the on-duty supervisor immediately.
3. Evaluate player to determine wagering method, level of skill, and strategy.
   a. When the investigator "understands" that the play does not represent a threat to the property, the coverage may be reduced to minimum coverage (one monitor).
   b. Such minimum coverage must remain until the player has ended the session.
   c. Routinely check player to ensure that the player continues to play as previously observed and has not exceeded establish wager/win parameters.
   d. Log information as required.
4. Players wagering $500 or more or who have won $2,500 or more require tri-shot coverage until the play is ended.
   a. Upon determining that the player is not a threat to the property the tri-shot coverage may be moved from the investigator's working monitors to other monitors in the display.
   b. A final player win/loss summation is required.
   c. Log information as required.
5. Further analysis and evaluation is required if the player wins $10,000 or more in one session or several within a twenty-four-hour period, or if the play is suspicious in any aspect. The investigator shall enter the play into *BJ Survey* or other appropriate evaluation software, if available.
   a. An incident report detailing the play is required for all player wins of $10,000 or more.

6. Table games personnel shall notify surveillance of the following types or levels of action:
   a. Players who buy in for $1,000 or more
   b. Players wagering $100 or more
   c. Players who have won $2,500 or more
   d. Credit transactions of $1,000 or more
   e. Refused name players
7. Surveillance personnel must not depend on table games personnel to notify the surveillance department of action or players. Keep in mind that pit personnel may be involved in a scam or working in collusion with others to cheat or steal from the property. Ideally, surveillance will locate play that should be evaluated prior to a notification from the pit. The above notifications are to be used as final alarms should the action or play not be detected by surveillance patrol.
8. Upon being notified of action that meets or exceeds the above parameters the investigator shall:
   a. Check the game for presence of a known cheat or advantage player.
   b. Check game and players for indicators or tells of cheating.
      i. Alert supervisor immediately of any such tell or suspicious activity.
   c. Evaluate player for threat to the property.
9. When the investigator has determined the play is normal, coverage may be reduced to minimum coverage as required by established player evaluation parameters.
   a. Play should be covered until the end of the session.
   b. The investigator shall check such games frequently to ensure cheating or advantage play has not developed after the initial evaluation and to update the player's win/loss.
   c. Log play as required.

5.4.11 Advantage Play

1. Suspected advantage play shall be responded to immediately by the surveillance department.
2. Shift supervisors shall assign an investigator to initiate tri-shot coverage and evaluate the player(s) suspected of advantage play.
3. An evaluation shall be performed in order to determine the threat level, if any, of the player(s) and shall determine the response, if any, made by the surveillance department.
4. The investigator shall evaluate for:
   a. Amounts of bets
   b. Bet variation to count
   c. Basic strategy deviations
   d. Tells of team play, back counting, shuffle tracking, hole card play
5. The investigator shall attempt to identify the player(s) through appropriate player and criminal databases.

6. Players who are evaluated shall be checked through both positive and negative shoes to ensure an accurate representation of the play. The on-duty supervisor will determine the number of hands that must be analyzed for the final disposition.
   a. *BJ Survey* can and should be used to provide an accurate and expert evaluation of all players on the involved game.
7. Upon detecting advantage play the investigator shall advise the on-duty shift supervisor immediately.
8. The shift supervisor shall advise the casino shift manager (CSM) of the detection of the advantage player(s). The CSM will make the decision as to how the advantage play will be handled.
9. The authorized response to advantage play are as follows:
   a. No response due to low level of bets or amount of win/loss (minimal threat)
   b. Shuffle upon increase of bet
   c. Player(s) restricted to flat bet
   d. Prevent mid-shoe/deck entry
   e. Wash the cards
   f. Change the dealer
   g. Back off from further 21 play
10. Verified and known advantage players and their team members once identified may be responded to without an evaluation at the shift supervisor's discretion.
11. A complete log entry and an incident report are required.
12. Photos of verified advantage players and team members should be broadcast on the Surveillance Information Network (SIN).
13. Photos of verified advantage players shall be enrolled into Biometrica and other appropriate databases.

5.4.12 Response to Criminal Activity

1. Upon the detection of criminal activity or suspected criminal activity, immediately contact the on-duty shift supervisor.
2. Initiate coverage of the activity using, at a minimum, tri-shot coverage.
3. Determine if a crime has occurred or is in the process of occurring. If time allows, notify security and any other appropriate personnel for review of incident and coordination of response.
   a. If unable to verify that a crime has occurred or is occurring, or a crime did occur but there is not enough reasonable cause to believe that a specific suspect perpetrated the crime, an investigation into the event or activity must be conducted. No one will be detained at the request of the surveillance department unless these facts are established.
   b. The investigator should make every attempt to identify the suspect prior to the suspect leaving the property.
4. Notify all individuals, departments, or agencies necessary to facilitate the investigation of the crime and to detain the suspects.

    a. Upon notifying a state agency or local police, follow their instructions as to procedures for handling the case and detaining any suspects.
5. Notify the director of surveillance (DOS) of the incident and the status of the investigation or response.
6. Gather and secure all evidence related to the case and ensure proper handling requirements are followed.
7. Prepare video, evidence, obtain witness statements, and write an incident report.

5.4.13 Reporting Violations of Policy or Procedure

In the event the investigator observes a company or department policy or procedure violation the investigator shall perform the following:

1. Determine if the violation is indicative of criminal activity. If criminal activity is detected, advise the on-duty shift supervisor immediately.
    a. Do not call down to report the violation until the crime has been stopped or it is determined there is no criminal activity.
2. If the event is indicative of criminal activity the investigator shall:
    a. Report the violation to the on-duty shift supervisor.
    b. Review video with supervisor to verify validity of the observation.
    c. Report violation to appropriate department head, manager, or supervisor.
    d. Review video with department head, manager, or supervisor, if necessary.
    e. Attempt to ascertain what type of corrective action will be made, if any.
    f. Enter observation into a log or file an incident report as directed by supervisor.
    g. Place video into evidence, if necessary
3. Not every violation of policy or procedure will require a response by surveillance or at any given time. The on-duty shift supervisor will determine, based on the seriousness of the violation or the pace of business, if and when a surveillance response is made or necessary.
4. The DOS may have to be contacted in the event a violation of a control, policy, or procedure is allowed to continue by the involved department and the company is believed to be at risk for any reason.

5.4.14 Close Watch and Audit Operations

1. Close watch operations are defined as a surveillance observation of an individual, area, or department that is maintained for an established period of time to determine the existence of cheating, theft, or violation of control, policy, or procedure. Close watches are usually initiated as a result of information obtained from an audit or statistics or a tip from an employee or guest.
2. Audit operations are defined as a surveillance observation of an individual, area, or department that is maintained for an established period of time to monitor and verify certain and specific monetary and procedural transactions to determine the existence of cheating, theft, or fraud or violation of controls, policies, or procedures.
3. Investigators assigned to a close watch or audit must maintain observation of the subject assigned throughout the assigned period of the audit. This will require

the investigator's complete attention and he or she shall be excused from routine duties whenever possible. Close watches and audits may only be terminated by the shift supervisor.

4. Close watches and audit assignments shall be passed on to another investigator or to the shift supervisor during break periods.
5. The investigator shall maintain the close watch/audit on the assigned monitors and use the assigned cameras to observe and monitor the subject.
6. Exceptions and suspicious activities observed during the close watch/audit and any pertinent investigator comments shall be listed in the case file provided.
7. Close watches and audit operations that continue for extended periods shall be updated on a regular basis by the case manager. The status of the operation should be part of the shift briefing to ensure all are aware of the necessary information.
8. The case manager or shift supervisor will ensure that the proper numbers of personnel are assigned to the close watch/audit at all times.
9. A thorough and detailed report of the observations, activity, and exceptions noted during the operation shall be compiled and written by the case manager and submitted to the DOS.
10. Close watches and audits may only be terminated by the shift supervisor in the event of emergency conditions such as incidence of cheating or theft, fire, or evacuation.

5.4.15 Required Incident Reports

Incident reports are required for the following incidents, events, or occurrences:

1. Criminal activity.
   a. Surveillance is reasonably certain a crime has occurred
2. Significant regulatory, control, policy, or procedure violation has occurred.
   a. The on-duty shift supervisor will determine if the violation requires an incident report
3. Detected advantage player or known cheat.
4. Variances of $200 or more.
   a. Shift supervisor will assign an investigator to the case if the variance is not located in twenty-four hours.
5. Security activity or responses where the incident or the suspects are located on video, when video is held for potential evidence, or if the incident has the potential to reoccur.
6. Employee or guest injury where video exists.
7. Surveillance investigations, audits, and close watches.
8. Any information deemed important enough to record that will further our basic surveillance requirements.

5.4.16 Writing Incident Reports

A report narrative is the essence of an incident report. It provides the reader with the details of an incident. Generally, a report narrative should contain the following basic elements:

an introductory paragraph, an investigative paragraph, an action paragraph, an optional notifications paragraph, and a disposition paragraph. These are explained below.

1. The introductory paragraph serves as the introduction to a report narrative. It should briefly state when and where an incident was observed or first reported and briefly give an overview of what the reader will be reading about.
   a. If the report is a request for service from an outside department (i.e., video review, request for coverage, etc.), list the reporting party by name and title and state what the requested surveillance needs to do to assist.
   b. In some situations, it may be necessary to provide the reader with a background or other relevant information prior to continuing with the report. This can usually be done following the introductory paragraph.

2. The investigative paragraph states the details of the incident and what the investigator observed during the course of the reported incident. The investigative paragraph should contain a chronological and accurate account of the incident. This paragraph should be very detailed and leave no question in the reader's mind as to what happened or what was observed. In many cases, more than one paragraph may be required.

3. The action paragraph states what actions were taken immediately following the investigation or observation. It is a follow-up to the investigative paragraph. For example, it would state if a player was backed off for being an advantage player; or if security was notified and detained suspects for a gaming control board or law enforcement agency.

4. The notifications paragraph states who was contacted regarding the reported incident. This would include persons not directly involved in the incident, but where policy mandates they be advised (i.e., surveillance director or manager).

5. The disposition paragraph closes the report. It should include disposition of the incident video and items attached with the report (i.e., witness statements, etc.), if the case is to be forwarded to another department or agency for further investigative response or review.

6. The following are requirements and guidelines for writing an effective report narrative.
   a. When writing a report narrative, report only the facts as they are known and as they are on video. Investigators will never lend opinion, report hearsay information, or speculate in a report. A report should sound factual and unbiased to the reader. The reporting investigator should be mindful that the reader was not witness to the incident and is relying on the investigator to paint a factual, concise, complete, and accurate picture of the events reported.
   b. Gather as much information as possible about the incident. More information is always better than not enough. An investigator can always omit nonpertinent information, but cannot always go back and get information needed for the report.
   c. Always introduce (the first time an individual is mentioned in the report narrative) persons by first and last name, along with their title or position. When referring to this person later in the body of the report, refer to him or her by

last name only. Putting a person's last name in all capitals throughout the body of the report helps it to stand out in the reader's mind and makes it easier to find at a glance.

  i. When reporting an unknown or unidentified person(s), describe them by race, gender, approximate age, clothing description, and any other notable characteristics. Thereafter, refer to the individual as "Subject #1," "Subject #2," and so forth. Do not continually refer to the individual as the "WFA," "HMJ," or "BMA" as the reader may misinterpret this as prejudicial.

  ii. After introducing two or more persons with the same last name in a report, refer to them by first initial and last name thereon.

  d. Writing in first person (investigator referring to self as "I") or third person (investigator referring to self as "this investigator" or "this writer") is acceptable when writing a report; however, the reporting investigator must be consistent throughout the report.

  e. A report should be factual, complete, chronological, detailed, clear, and accurate. The questions of who, what, where, when, and how must be answered in a report.

  f. Use paragraphs when writing reports. Not only does this look neat on paper, but it also shows organized thought. Paragraphs also eliminate confusing "run-on" sentences. Always use proper punctuation and capitalization.

  g. When using abbreviations that will be used later, first fully spell them out followed by the abbreviation in parentheses: for example, director of surveillance (DOS). This will eliminate any confusion as to what the abbreviation means.

  h. The writer will proofread each report and utilize spell-check.

  i. Reports will be given to the on-duty shift supervisor or lead investigator. The supervisor or lead will proofread the report, direct changes as needed, and initial or print his or her initials in the lower right-hand corner of the final report. The report will then be held for pass-on purposes and distribution as needed.

  j. When writing a report, investigators should remember that incident reports are official documents that are often viewed by outside departments or agencies. In some cases, incident reports may be subpoenaed for criminal or civil litigation.

REFERENCES

Hill, Robert A. 2005. Writing Incident Reports.

Hannum, Robert C. and Anthony N. Cabot. 2005. *Practical Casino Math*, 2nd ed. Institute for the Study of Gambling and Commercial Gaming, University of Nevada, Reno.

6

Investigations

Although each case is different, investigating a crime or incident always comes down to who, what, where, when, and how. The investigator must answer each of these questions to solve the crime properly and successfully and to prepare for its prosecution, whether it is through the judicial system or within the company.

The investigator working with the gaming environment should prepare his or her case as if it will go to trial. Often our cases do go to trial, as criminal matters, or, even more frequently, as employment or civil matters. Working the case with that perspective compels the investigator to be thorough and accurate in the investigation.

6.1 FUNDAMENTAL INVESTIGATIVE TECHNIQUES

The fundamental investigative techniques that will help the investigator conduct a successful investigation are listed in the paragraphs that follow. It is recommended that each surveillance agent receive, at a minimum, training in the basic investigative techniques described below. Advanced training should include professional interviewing skills and specialized training for the gaming environment, such as in statistical analysis, department financial and accounting information, and exception reports, to name just a few. The better trained and more knowledgeable your investigator, the more successful he or she will be.

Investigate: A lot of investigations fail because they were never started. Frequently it is assumed that there will not be enough video or evidence, or that the suspect is too powerful or related to someone too powerful to allow investigation. Do not let this occur. An incident must be investigated. Many major cases are developed from one small lead or minor issue. I was involved in a gift shop case at one property that started from what appeared to be a minor shoplifting issue that ended with the arrests of everyone who worked in the shop for embezzlement and larceny.

It shouldn't matter who committed the crime regardless of how powerful they are or whom they are related to. I know that's easy to say and harder to do. All I can tell you is that I have never regretted going after anyone, regardless of their rank. I have regretted it when I did not. It always comes back and it is always bigger than when it was first

97

detected. You will also always be questioned about why you didn't report it the first time. It is better, in the long run, to handle every case consistently.

Identify the objective of the investigation: Know what your objective is! Is it a criminal incident that will be submitted to law enforcement? Is it an employee issue that must be handled through human resources? Knowing where the case will or how it should end successfully helps you plan the investigation.

Identify which elements of the crime or incident must be proven: Which specific elements must you be able to show or prove to prosecute your case? For example, if you are investigating a case of a player accused of marking the cards, how will you prove that the player did not just accidently mark the cards? How will you prove the player used the markings on the cards to gain information and then put the information to use? Prepare your investigative strategy to address this critical issue.

Define its scope: Who are the people that are involved? Who do you suspect is involved? Who should have known but didn't report it? Why? Are other employees involved and would they know something helpful to the investigation? What departments may be involved or have information you can use?

Scope is often defined by why and how an incident happened. In gaming, we ask where the floor person was while the dealer dumped the game. We ask or should ask why the table games manager didn't notice that blackjack table seven lost daily for thirty days straight! Of course, we ask these questions because they must be asked to hopefully prevent the incident from reoccurring and also often because there are others involved. The dealer or other employee doesn't always work alone. Always consider that there are others involved. If they are not involved, there is a strong possibility that some or all failed to perform their duty.

This is all the more reason to position your cameras properly. Proper camera positioning will allow you to review the video and determine what the floor person or others in the area were doing while the crime was in progress.

Determine the resources you will require: How many investigators should you assign to the case and for how long? Is overtime authorized? Who can the investigator contact for assistance and information (and who should not receive information; work on a "need to know" basis)? Is there any special equipment needed? These questions will arise. It's best to address them as soon as possible.

Assign a specific individual to investigate: It is highly recommended that you assign one person to be the lead investigator. If it will not be yourself, ensure that you assign the best person possible. The lead investigator will manage day-to-day investigations and direct the activities of other investigators. Too many investigations are assigned to the entire surveillance room and can be hindered or even fail due to disorganization.

Again, if not yourself, assign one investigator who will report directly to you and update you regularly. This individual should carry out your instructions and maintain all information involving the case. Additionally this individual should be available to you to assist or to make presentations regarding the case to executives and law enforcement.

Interview witnesses and suspects: It is very important to identify potential witnesses and suspects. Too often we depend only on the video and do not attempt to develop further information or leads. Witnesses to the incident, bystanders, employees in the area, and co-workers should be interviewed for potential information. That means professionally interviewed! Invest in the proper training for yourself or your investigators. You will develop further information and will often obtain confessions, including who else was involved.

Call in the experts: If you don't know what you are looking for (or at), if you know something is going on but can't determine what it is, get some help. Bringing in a department head, manager, or supervisor who may be able to help you interpret what exactly occurred or how the crime is being perpetrated as well as save you man hours and possibly ensure the success of the investigation.

For example, I had a case in which we knew a food waitress was stealing but couldn't figure out how. We reviewed the video and her transaction records to no avail. Finally, we called in the manager of the department and asked him to look at the video. Within five minutes he determined that the waitress was splitting cash tickets and comping off items that were paid for and pocketing the cash.

Finding the right expert can be key to your investigation. Words of caution, if you are going to use someone from outside the department, make sure that person can be trusted. If you have any doubts whatsoever, don't involve such persons. They will destroy your investigation. Too many people can't help talking about what they know. Either find someone else or find another way. By the way, fellow surveillance directors can be very helpful in this area and don't mind helping.

Save the evidence: All of it: video, cards, receipts, everything that pertains to the case. If the case is significant or appears that it might be, I recommend immediately saving all video in and around the area, and any areas that may become involved. Cases and investigations have a way of developing quickly, and if you don't pull everything at once, you will regret it later. It's better to have it than not.

Of course, you must also store your evidence securely and maintain a chain of custody. Find out what the requirements are in your jurisdiction and follow them accordingly.

Maintain a case file: A case file should contain everything to do with the case in an easy-to-read and logical format. You will find the investigation much easier to manage and perform when you keep all records together.

Prepare for questions: Your investigation (successful or not) will generate questions and concerns: from "Why didn't you catch this earlier?" to "Great job, when do we get our money back?" Or, and really most important, "How can this be prevented from ever happening again?"

To me, surveillance personnel are not operators or agents; they are investigators. We investigate through our cameras as we go through our patrols. As we discussed previously, when we observe a tell or indicator of cheating or advantage play, or a violation of a control, policy, or procedure, or just something that doesn't look right, we must investigate the observation until we "understand" if its "normal/legitimate" or "unusual/suspicious." To get to that point almost always requires investigation.

I highly recommend that you ensure your surveillance personnel are trained in investigative techniques. There are many great books, seminars, and courses on the subject. They are usually available at a relatively low cost. This is an investment in your personnel that will pay off immediately and often.

I close this section by saying that surveillance audits often turn into investigations. As we know, during most audits we will observe activity that warrants further investigation. This is where most audits fail. Most surveillance personnel are not trained in what to do at the point of investigation and usually just write it up in the log and continue on. This is a missed opportunity.

For example, when performing an audit on a bartender, an investigator may observe that the bartender is not issuing receipts and properly writes a report. But the scenario begs the question: Why is the bartender not issuing receipts? We are at the point where an audit becomes an investigation requiring further observation and review of sales as compared to the register tape. As I said, some surveillance people would miss this opportunity and report a violation of procedure.

6.1.1 Case History

It is extremely important that surveillance directors understand that certain investigations must be conducted by the surveillance department. Even when security normally investigates or assists surveillance, there will be times when you must run the investigation. Taking the time to learn how to investigate an incident or report properly is critical. The following case history illustrates this point.

The surveillance director received an anonymous tip that the security manager and some of his supervisors were taking cash and other items from the lost and found. Because the tip concerned security, it wouldn't have been wise to turn the investigation over to the investigator who was in the security department himself (in fact, it was later determined that the tip had initially been given to the investigator who ignored it).

The surveillance director decided to investigate it. A close watch was initiated. First, a covert camera was installed in the lost and found room to confirm the tip's veracity. Only the CEO and legal counsel of the company were advised of the camera installation to protect the confidentiality of the investigation. The hidden camera quickly confirmed that security supervisors and managers were frequently entering the lost and found area and leaving with items. Now that the suspicious activity had been observed, additional hidden cameras were installed and other cameras were adjusted to cover the entire room and the outside area of lost and found.

The surveillance department then had an undercover investigator turn in a camera to the lost and found desk that had been marked for later identification. This was done in order to track what happened to the camera as it went through the lost and found system. The investigator was able to observe that the camera was properly logged into the system by the security officer on duty.

As the close watch continued it became apparent that security supervisors routinely entered the lost and found to check items that had not been claimed and were due to be given to the person who had found the item. If the security supervisors wanted the item, they would simply take it and put into the record that the item had been claimed by its owner! Items taken ranged from clothing to watches to electronics.

The security managers really shocked the surveillance department with their thefts. Both of the individuals had worked at the property from day one and were highly trusted and respected. Both had worked directly with the surveillance department on a number of cases. They were really the last people you would expect to be involved in theft. Yet, here they were.

The managers were observed counting all the cash that had been turned in to lost and found the previous week. The surveillance director was astonished at the amount that was turned in; during the investigation the cash averaged about $1,000.

The cash was supposed to be counted and verified by the security managers (I guess they figured that they wouldn't collude) and then submitted to the cage with accompanying paperwork. What was observed on camera was an entirely different story. The managers actually skimmed most the cash off the top, split it up among themselves, and turned in what was left to the cage. Usually the managers would split up $600–800 and turn in about $200. These guys were so dishonest that they were observed even splitting up the change!

Again, anyone inquiring about the money was told that it had been claimed by the owner. If the owner of the property or cash called in to check whether the lost property or cash had been found and turned in, their question would be directed to, you guessed it, the security managers.

When the investigation was completed, the results were presented to the CEO who wanted everyone involved fired. The investigation provided enough evidence to do so, but as so often happens, the company didn't want the knowledge of the thefts to get out and damage its reputation. Both security managers were fired and two of the security supervisors received severe suspensions.

The fact that information had been received earlier and had not been investigated did not go over well with senior management and negatively affected the careers of a number of individuals.

6.2 INTERVIEWING SUSPECTS AND WITNESSES

During my career I've learned the importance of interviewing witnesses, potential witnesses, suspects, and perpetrators. Not only can they fill in pertinent details of the case or point to those involved, they often are the only way to solve the case!

Over the years my surveillance teams have been very successful in detecting all types of criminal activity. We were so good that we were often asked to investigate crimes outside our realm of responsibility. This was great for the ego, but really didn't work very well. The reason was because we didn't have any video to look at and didn't know what else to do. We were not professional investigators nor were we trained as such.

Consequently, even though we tried to solve such cases, we often failed. Yes, we should have turned such cases over to someone else or some other department. However, sometimes you can't do this because you know that other person can't or won't do the work or that other department is also undertrained or doesn't care.

I hated to walk away if I knew the case would be swept aside. So I learned a few methods to help us in these cases. The art of interviewing was one methods and it helped us immediately.

Keep in mind that a lot of crimes are solved without videotape. In fact, most are. They are solved through good old-fashioned police work involving reviewing the facts and circumstances of the crime, gathering of evidence, and interviewing likely witnesses and suspects. Of course this doesn't always work, but it works quite often!

So in those cases where we had a crime and we could not locate it on video, or if we had video but not enough to specifically identify the suspect or the method used, we used traditional methods.

A case in point. One day we received a hotline call that said that our pit manager was selling dealer jobs to newly arrived immigrants from Asia and Eastern Europe. The going rate was apparently $1,500, and you allegedly did not have to know how to deal.

Now obviously we would not have any video of such activity. I guess we could have installed hidden cameras and possibly some audio recording in the manager's office. However, there are some major legal issues in doing so. We also could have asked security to lead the investigation, but some of the senior management was allied with the manager in question and the information may have leaked. We also could have reported it to local law enforcement, but it would not have received the attention it deserved, and it would have taken too long.

So we took the case. After discussing how we would handle the investigation with our team, we determined that it could only be done through interviewing dealers who likely paid for a job they weren't qualified for and see what we could develop.

Working with human resources we identified several dealers who matched the parameters: recently hired, recent prior work or educational history in Asia or Europe, and hired by the suspected manager.

Fortunately and unfortunately, we identified several dealers almost immediately. We also found that the dealing schools they each listed on their applications as having attended either had not been heard of or were nonexistent! (A case for pre-screening!)

We actually solved the case pretty quickly after that. At the first interview we conducted, the dealer required an interpreter to answer our questions! She had functioned at bare minimum in the pit. Anytime a customer asked her a question, she had to call a floor person over. Sad, but true. The manager covered this by explaining that no other people were applying for dealer jobs so she had to hire them. Eventually the dealers told us what happened and we broke the case. The manager was terminated and eventually left the industry. Obviously a lot of things went wrong in that situation. The point is that it was solved through investigation and interviews.

It is very important that you train at least some of your personnel in professional interviewing techniques. I trained my key people and allowed any level-two investigator or above who was in good standing and had a genuine interest to attend the course provided by the Reid School of Interviewing. This is a great course and relatively inexpensive. I highly recommend it or another comparable course. This training provided us with the ability to develop further information, solve cases, and obtain written confessions, which aided us tremendously in the prosecution of the case.

Additionally, even when you have access to security personnel who have interviewing training, it is likely that they will not have the casino knowledge or expertise that a surveillance investigator develops. The learning curve for some things may take too long for a specific case, so sometimes a trained surveillance investigator is the way to go.

6.3 EVIDENCE GATHERING AND HANDLING

Surveillance personnel do gather evidence in the course of their investigations. Usually, it is through the lens of our cameras. Hence, the need for the IOU (identify, observe, understand) patrol and tri-shot coverage we discussed previously.

When a surveillance investigator detects something suspicious or that for any reason doesn't look right, he or she must set up the tri-shot immediately to allow for the gathering of evidence. Although, you may not know what you are dealing with at this time, do not waste this opportunity to obtain as much data as you can. Remember, you can't go back and pull the shots you need if you didn't record them or place the shot on the right area.

A minimum of three cameras is necessary for the tri-shot; however, don't be shy. If you need more to solve the crime, use them (use common sense). What you record is what you will present as evidence to the department head, your general manager, gaming agents or law enforcement, and possibly in front of a jury. It must be gathered with this in mind. You are a professional and should perform your duties as such.

It is important when you place your camera shots that you seriously consider what you suspect is occurring and what you will need to prove the activity. Camera shots and angles should be based on the need for proof.

For instance, if you believe a player is counting cards, a typical tri-shot showing the game layout, an identification (ID) shot of the players in the game, and a bet shot to monitor and read the wager amounts are appropriate and necessary. You would set up cameras differently if you suspected card switching. In this case, a game layout, an ID shot, and a cards/hand shot should be placed on one player. In this scenario, you must consider who is receiving the switched cards and attempt to record the pass of the cards from one player to another. Another element you may wish to add is what cards were originally dealt to the suspects. This coverage requires at least an additional three cameras, possibly more. Obtaining these views will assist you tremendously in proving your case at any level. Remember, too many cameras are better than not enough!

You will hold video for evidence and at times you will obtain other items that will be held as evidence. Items such as cheating devices, marked cards, counterfeit tokens, photos, paperwork, and receipts used in the commission of a crime may be held in the surveillance room. Every surveillance room should have a secure evidence storage area. This can be a locked drawer or cabinet large enough to contain videotapes, CD/DVDs, cards, dice, and any other items of evidence.

Assign one person as the evidence custodian and maintain a log showing whenever the area is opened, an inventory of the evidence (including associated reports/case numbers placed into storage), and when it was removed by anyone. The list should detail the date and time entered, printed name and signature of person entering, reason for entering, item entered or removed from evidence, and who evidence was transferred to. All this is extremely important to maintain the chain of custody.

The above is a reasonable setup that works in most jurisdictions. I recommend that you check with legal counsel to ensure you are within the requirements in your state or area. As an aside, you may want to assign an alternate evidence custodian in the event the primary person is unavailable for any reason.

To complete your set-up make sure the process is documented, well laid out, and described in your standard operating procedures manual and follow it strictly. You may be asked about your evidence control process by a defense attorney one day; so be prepared.

7

Surveillance Training and Education

7.1 SURVEILLANCE TRAINING AND EDUCATION PROGRAM

As mentioned throughout this book, training is critical to your operation and the key to your success. If you don't think training is that important consider this: the bad guys practice their moves all the time, for years. Advantage players are experts in basic strategy and card counting. They train all the time. Why don't we?

In our field new scams and methods to steal or cheat arise almost daily, and there are also those scams that are just variations on the same old theme. In other words, cheats and thieves adapt to new technology and controls. So must we.

One of our major problems today is that technology allows the criminal to steal more, faster. Look, for example, at coinless slots. Thieves used to have to steal buckets of tokens, coins, or cash. Nowadays, a ticket in, ticket out (TITO) voucher can list any amount of money. How about the players' club? Through those terminals flow points, prizes, comps, cash back, and free slot play. When fraudsters find a way to commit theft in this sensitive area, the losses can be staggering. You cannot afford to allow your property to suffer these types of losses unnecessarily. You must train your personnel to protect these areas.

How do you train without resources? I know most of you would like to train, but your training budget is minimal or maybe even nonexistent. I also know that most surveillance investigators say they want training but fail to motivate themselves to even memorize basic strategy. Additionally, you must provide training on a regular basis for it to be effective. How can you do it?

How we handled training over the years after trying many different methods was to develop the Surveillance Training and Education Program (STEP). This program allowed us to train our personnel from the trainee position all the way through to lead investigator, a first step position for those personnel interested in supervision and management.

The program is a combination of managed and self-guided instruction that allows those who are self-motivated to move quickly up the ladder. For those who are not so motivated, a minimum amount of progression is required. In the end, basic training criteria are established that allow the department to field highly trained personnel. This program, I believe, will work for any surveillance department. Here is how it works.

7.2 PROGRAM SETUP

The STEP program consists of three levels:

- Investigator I
- Investigator II
- Investigator III

Each level requires that certain training criteria be met prior to the taking of an exam for that level. Successfully passing the exam allows the investigator to move up to the next level and begin the training program for that level.

Each investigator level has established training guidelines, subjects, and skills that must be learned and demonstrated to management. These are listed in the sections that follow (you may adopt these or make up your own for your property's particular needs).

7.2.1 Trainee to Level I/Investigator I

A thorough knowledge and understanding of:

- Each games rules, policies, and procedures (all games offered at the property including table games, slots, bingo, poker, etc.)
- Minimum internal control standards (MICS)/internal controls
- Surveillance department standard operating procedures (SOPs)
- Surveillance patrol and camera techniques
- Each department SOPs
- Basic strategy of 21
- Card counting techniques
- Tells of cheating and advantage play

7.2.2 Level II/Investigator II

- External cheating and internal theft tells
- Detection and initiation of response to fraud, cheating at gaming, and advantage play
- Methods, schemes, and scams used by internal and external individuals to commit fraud, cheat at gaming, or otherwise pose a threat to the assets
- Criminal and civil laws and applicable to gaming statutes as they apply to a gaming operation
- Key gaming regulations and MICS
- Case file management
- Surveillance department databases
- CDS, Biometrica, Surveillance Information Network (SIN), scams, Casino Management System (CMS), Griffin Gold, International Casino Surveillance Network (ICSN)

- Required training/reading manuals and reference materials will consist of surveillance department standard operating manual, Title 31 of United States Code, and Certified Fraud Examiners Report to the Nation

7.2.3 Level III/Investigator III

In order to participate in the Level III Investigator program, an application must be completed and submitted to the surveillance management team through the property manager. The following will be part of the application process:

- Explanation as to why you are qualified to be a Level III Investigator
- What you hope to accomplish through participation
- What your future goals and objectives are within the surveillance department

The surveillance management team will review all applications received and determine if the applicant is qualified to participate. The following criteria will be taken into consideration:

- Investigator performance
- Training seminars attended
- Leadership practices
- Minimum two years' surveillance experience
- Annual reviews

Applicants denied will receive an explanation as to the reasons for denial and actions needed to reapply along with a time line (no less than three months). Applicants granted participation will be monitored on their progress by the training manager. Assistance will be provided by the property manager or designee, when requested. After the applicant has successfully completed all required material, an oral board review will be conducted by the surveillance management team to decide whether or not the applicant will advance to Investigator Level III. The Investigator III requirements are:

- Application to participate
- Board review
- Minimum of two years' surveillance experience
- Required knowledge will consist of:
  - Key gaming regulations
  - Understanding of Sarbanes/Oxley Act of 2002
  - Case file management
  - Homeland Security
  - Statistical analysis
  - Slots
  - Net win, drop variance, extended handle, type report, location report
  - Table games
  - CMS, flash report
  - Food/beverage cost of sales

- Required training /reading manuals and reference materials will consist of gaming regulations, and Sarbanes/Oxley Act of 2002

Required participation:

- The investigator will develop a training presentation to be presented to the surveillance department based on a topic chosen by the participating investigator.
- The topic will be approved by the surveillance management team.
- The training presentation will be presented and approved by the surveillance management team before being presented to the surveillance department.
- The investigator will be required to attend all corporate management training courses as provided by the company. The investigator will keep records on classes attended.
- Case management will require the investigator to initiate, follow through, and close an investigation based on the statistical analysis information reviewed. The investigation must determine an explanation or change in policy/procedure and review results with the department head or department management staff from which the investigation was conducted.
- The investigator will review each required report of statistical analysis of each area listed for their respective property. This will assist the investigator in learning how to read company reports.
- A monthly performance summary is to be completed and submitted to the property manager that details the investigator's progress and accomplishments.

7.2.3.1 Compensation and Rewards

One of the reasons our program was successful is that we (with human resources) developed a compensation program for the investigators that rewarded them for attaining each level. Overall, it didn't cost much, but it meant a lot to the individual investigators.

For the promotion from trainee to Investigator I the individual received a twenty-five cent per hour raise and a certificate awarding the new title. For the promotion from Investigator I to Investigator II, the individual received a fifty cent per hour raise, a badge and wallet to carry it in, and a certificate awarding the new title. Investigator III is the biggest and most difficult step requiring the most work and personal motivation. It also resulted in the biggest reward, an additional dollar per hour. We also had a department party (paid for by the company) during which the certificate was awarded. We made it a big deal because it was a big deal. Individuals who attained this level were always our best. They were the ones promoted to supervisory positions.

Please note that these raises were not part of their annual raise programs that they were eligible for. This was additional compensation they earned through the program. If they worked hard they could increase their earnings quickly. On the other hand, if an individual did not bother to participate in the program, he or she was quickly left behind by the others. Their inactivity was also reflected in their annual evaluation. Needless to say, individuals who failed to participate in the training program usually ended up leaving for another casino surveillance room, which was strongly encouraged.

7.2.3.2 Program Benefits

We reaped many benefits from our STEP training. Some are as follows:

- Investigators were self-motivated to participate and complete the program. If they didn't go through the steps, they did not obtain the raises their fellow investigators did.
- The STEP training was easy to manage. As the program established the criteria, guidelines, and resources for each level, investigators worked independently and at their own pace. Each investigator was assigned a mentor (usually an investigator one step higher) to assist and answer questions where necessary. This turned out to be great succession training.
- As we trained constantly at all levels we put together a very good training program that attracted the right individuals to work in our department. Although we didn't have a high starting wage, we did provide excellent training. If you wanted a career in surveillance, our company was a good place to start. By the way, we didn't lose as many people as you might think. We were always able to keep a solid core of highly trained and motivated investigators.
- As we trained our investigators to detect crime in all areas of the hotel casino, we caught a lot of crime and bad guys. We consistently detected illicit activity. I know that our executive staff was amazed at what we were able to do. Our department was well recognized and rewarded for our results.
- We had a solid chain of command. Each level essentially followed the instructions of the level above when necessary. For example, if there was an Investigator II and Investigator III on duty and an event occurred requiring someone to take command, it would be Investigator III's duty to do so. This eliminated wasted time arguing about what to do and who was going to do it.
- We always had trained individuals ready to be promoted into supervision and management.

I highly recommend you design and install your own training program. The above program worked very well for us. Please feel free to take it and adapt it for your own needs.

8
Statistical Information and Analysis

One of the most effective methods you can utilize to detect loss is to review each department's "numbers." As mentioned previously, each department, particularly in gaming, compiles daily statistical information detailing handle, drop, and win, usually overall, and for each game type and individual game. You can use this information to help locate where losses are occurring.

Areas where numbers are especially helpful are:

- Table games
- Slots
- Keno
- Bingo
- Race and sports book
- Food and beverage

I highly recommend that you review the numbers from these key areas daily. Doing so will lead you directly to losses that may otherwise remain hidden. If you can't review the numbers on a regular basis, then delegate someone to do so. It is that important.

8.1 TABLE GAMES

Some basic formulas for determining win percentage, hold percentage, and house advantage are:

$$\text{Win percentage (actual)} = \text{win/handle}$$

$$\text{Hold percentage} = \text{win/drop}$$

Tables 8.1–8.3 list some of the house advantage percentages for common games and bets. You should be aware of these percentages. This information will assist you in determining if a game is set up incorrectly (as an example: a poorly calculated marketing program) and to determine if a specific game or game type win percentage is below industry standards.

Table 8.1 House Advantages for Casino Games

Game	Percentage
Roulette (double-zero)	5.3
Craps (pass/come)	1.4
Craps (pass/come with double odds)	0.6
Blackjack (average player)	2.0
Blackjack (six decks, basic strategy)	0.5
Blackjack (single deck, basic strategy)	0.0
Baccarat (no tie bets)	1.2
Caribbean stud	5.2
Let It Ride	3.5
Three card poker	3.4
Pai Gow poker (ante/play)	2.5
Slots	5–10
Video poker	0.5–3
Keno (average)	27

In table games there are a number of reports you should review. These are:

- *Soft count report or "stiff sheet"*: This usually lists the details of each individual game: opening amount, closing amount, fills/credits, credit transactions, drop, handle, and win. This report often lists the numbers by game type also. This report is used to check game losses to known play (or to locate unreported losses) and activity (fills/credits, etc.) and to verify soft count accuracy.
- *Table game flash report*: Lists player wins/losses over a certain amount for each shift, where the win or loss occurred, and the shift manager's estimate of the overall win/loss for the shift. Used by surveillance to check that they aware of the play of each of the listed player's win or loss amount and that there were no significant losses that were not reported or observed. This report also lists the shift manager's estimate of what the shift won or lost, including the win percentage. It can be used as an early indicator of unexplained loss and an estimation of how you are doing against the grind (all other play minus your high action play). For example, you should normally win more percentagewise against grind play. The players are usually novices or tourists or lower action players with less money and less skill (higher action players tend to be better players). If you back out high action play from the numbers, you'll get a rough estimate of the grind. If the grind is consistently lower than expected that may indicate significant theft. At one casino, the surveillance director suspected theft once he backed out the high action play and found the grind was consistently low. Ultimately he identified theft in the soft count. Soft count personnel were stealing at such a level that it affected the numbers.
- *Casino games report*: The daily report lists how the casino performed overall by game type. It is used to quickly check if the games won what was expected. Discrepancies should be investigated.

Table 8.2 House Advantages for Common Casino Wagers

Game	Bet	House Advantage (%)
Baccarat	Banker (5% commission)	1.06
Baccarat	Player	1.24
Big Six	Average	19.84
Blackjack	Card counting	−1.00
Blackjack	Basic strategy	0.50
Blackjack	Average player	2.00
Blackjack	Poor player	4.00
Caribbean Stud	Ante	5.22
Casino War	Basic bet	2.88
Craps	Any craps	11.11
Craps	Any Seven	16.67
Craps	Big 6, Big 8	9.09
Craps	Buy (any)	4.76
Craps	C&E	11.11
Craps	Don't pass/don't come	1.36
Craps	Don't pass/don't come w/1× odds	0.68
Craps	Don't pass/don't come w/2× odds	0.45
Craps	Don't pass/don't pass w/3× odds	0.34
Craps	Don't pass/don't pass w/5× odds	0.23
Craps	Don't pass/don't come w/10× odds	0.12
Craps	Don't place 4 or 10	3.03
Craps	Don't place 5 or 9	2.50
Craps	Don't place 6 or 8	1.82
Craps	Field (2 and 12 pay double)	5.86
Craps	Field (2 and 12 pay triple)	2.78
Craps	Hard 4, hard 10	11.11
Craps	Hard 6, hard 8	9.09
Craps	Hop bet—easy (14–1)	16.67
Craps	Hop bet—easy (15–1)	11.11
Craps	Hop bet—hard (29–1)	16.67
Craps	Hop bet—hard (30–1)	13.89
Craps	Horn bet (30–1 and 15–1)	12.50
Craps	Horn high—any (29–1 and 14–1)	16.67
Craps	Horn high 2, horn high 12 (30–1 and 15–1)	12.78
Craps	Horn high 3, horn high 11 (30–1 and 15–1)	12.22
Craps	Lay 4 or 10	2.44
Craps	Lay 5 or 9	3.23
Craps	Lay 6 or 8	4.00

Continued

113

Table 8.2 (*Continued*)   House Advantages for Common Casino Wagers

Game	Bet	House Advantage (%)
Craps	Pass/come	1.41
Craps	Pass/come w/1× odds	0.85
Craps	Pass/come w/2× odds	0.61
Craps	Pass/come w/3× odds	0.47
Craps	Pass/come w/5× odds	0.33
Craps	Pass/come w/10× odds	0.18
Craps	Place 4 or 10	6.67
Craps	Place 5 or 9	4.00
Craps	Place 6 or 8	1.52
Craps	Three, eleven (14–1)	16.67
Craps	Three, eleven (15–1)	11.11
Craps	Two, twelve (29–1)	16.67
Craps	Two, twelve (30–1)	13.89
Keno	Typical	27.00
Let It Ride	Base bet	3.51
Pai Gow poker	Skilled player (nonbanker)	2.54
Pai Gow poker	Average player (nonbanker)	2.84
Red Dog	Basic bet (six decks)	2.80
Roulette	Single-zero	2.70
Roulette	Double-zero (except five-number)	5.26
Roulette	Double-zero, five number bet	7.89
Sic Bo	Big/small	2.78
Sic Bo	One of a kind	7.87
Sic Bo	Seven, fourteen	9.72
Sic Bo	Eight, thirteen	12.50
Sic Bo	Ten, eleven	12.50
Sic Bo	Any three of a kind	13.89
Sic Bo	Five, sixteeen	13.89
Sic Bo	Four, seventeen	15.28
Sic Bo	Three of a kind	16.20
Sic Bo	Two-dice combination	16.67
Sic Bo	Six, fifteen	16.67
Sic Bo	Two of a kind	18.52
Sic Bo	Nine, twelve	18.98
Slots	Dollar slots (good)	4.00
Slots	Quarter slots (good)	5.00
Slots	Dollar slots (average)	6.00
Slots	Quarter slots (average)	8.00
Sports betting	Bet $11 to win $10	4.55

Table 8.2 (*Continued*) House Advantages for Common Casino Wagers

Game	Bet	House Advantage (%)
Three card poker	Pair plus	2.32
Three card poker	Ante	3.37
Video poker	Selected machines	−0.50

Table 8.3 Typical Table Games Win Percentages

Game	Type	Low Percentage	High Percentage
Blackjack		12	15
	Single deck	12	14
	Double deck	12	14
	Six/eight deck	14	16
Craps		15	18
Crapless		20	25
Roulette	Double 0	20	24
	Single 0	11	12
Mini-Bac		12	14
Pai Gow poker		20	24
Caribbean stud poker		25	30
Let It Ride		22	27
Three card poker		25	30
Slots	Local	Up to 6	
	Strip	Up to 8.2	
Keno		26	28
Bingo		1	2
Race book		18	22
Sports book		2	4
Overall table games		16	18

- *Table games analysis report*: As mentioned previously, this report breaks down the games by type and by individual game, as well as overall. Information is usually broken down by day, month to date, and year to date. This report will help you quickly locate games or game types that are consistently not holding what is to be expected.

The above are the basics. There are many other reports. Nowadays a lot of these reports are located on the company computer network. Use them to help you protect the property.

8.1.1 Case History

At one property the surveillance director noted during his daily reviews of table games reports that the single zero roulette wheel was not holding well, in fact it was well below what was expected. He continued to monitor the game, but the numbers did not improve

115

over time. The director ordered the surveillance team to monitor the wheel for irregularities and suspicious activity. Nothing was located. Nobody in the pit had any ideas about what was wrong (nor were they concerned, which is often the case). They began monitoring the count team and the "stiff" sheet. That's where they found the problem!

A couple days a week a few of the count team members who didn't understand that there were two different types of roulette games on the floor misapplied the funds from single zero to double zero wheels. Once that misconception was corrected, the numbers returned to normal.

8.2 SLOTS

The slot department also has its own numbers and reports that should be reviewed daily. As with table games, these numbers are broken up by individual games, game types, sections or banks of machines, totals and time periods. Some of the reports that are available are:

- *Net win report*: This report lists slot machines by denomination and individual machine and details jackpots and fills, the par percentage (what the machine is set up to hold with optimal play and strategy), and the actual win/hold. It is used by surveillance to locate slot machines not performing to par.
- *Location*: Statistical report by machine location.
- *Numeric*: Statistical report by machine number.
- *Type*: Statistical report by machine game type.
- *Extended handle report*: This report shows the dollar amounts of coins circulated through any given machine. For example, if you put $1 into a machine and hit max bet to play $1, it will register as $1 coin in on the handle report. From that $1 play, you win and your credits now reflect $5. Any coins played from the credits of $5 will register as coin handle through the machine.
- *Bill drop variance report*: This report lists any variance from the electronic count validator and the manual drop/count. For example, the electronic count is $1,500, the manual count is $1,000. The validator is missing $500 and should be investigated.
- *Daily override report*: Lists manual overrides that were performed by the staff: amount of override, the machine it occurred on, the reason for the override, and who performed the override. Used to verify the override was legitimate.
- *Jackpot/fill ticket void report*: Details jackpots or fills (fills on coin machines only). Amount of void, time, location, who initiated the void, and the reason for doing so are usually listed. Used to verify the void was legitimate.
- *Jackpot ledger*: Lists all jackpot hits for the previous day. Amount of jackpot, location, and time are listed. Used to ensure surveillance is aware of all significant jackpots and has reviewed them for legitimacy.

8.2.1 Case History

A surveillance director reviewing a report found that several machines registered millions in coin in for the handle for one day. Machines were all one penny denomination. The director recognized this as a red flag. The director checked other available information such as the jackpot ledger, which did not show enough jackpots to justify this type of handle. The director requested the slot's technical manager to have the machines physically checked on the floor.

When the check was conducted, the machines were found to be set up incorrectly as a nickel denomination instead of the correct denomination of one penny. This resulted in five times the actual amount played. This, of course, increased the handle reading of the machine, and for each person who played the machine, it also registered a much higher amount played for their accounts through the players' club. Basically if you were playing twenty-five credits per spin, this should have registered a quarters played, instead it was registering as $1.25 played, along with the undeserved win amounts of five times what they should have received. (I'm sure the players would have reported this problem on their own if we had given them the time to do so!)

As a result of this, the property had to identify the players on the machine and their accounts had to be adjusted. Auditing had to adjust and correct all slots' reports. This was the result just from one error. It is important to note that the error was detected by a proactive surveillance director. If he had not caught the error, who knows how long it would have gone on.

8.3 KEY DAILY REPORTS

Both table games and slots reports should be reviewed daily, along with reports from the players' club. You will also find reports from points of sale, such as void reports, no sale reports, and variance reports, very helpful in the detection of losses and negative trends. I recommend the following reports be reviewed on a daily basis or at least on a regular basis:

- Table game flash report
- Casino games report
- Slot net win report
- Slot daily override report
- Slot daily fill/jackpot void report
- Player club exception reports
- Point of sale void report
- Point of sale/no sale report
- Variance reports

On a weekly basis you should review:

- Table games analysis report
- Slot extended handle report
- Bill drop variance report
- Bingo
- Keno
- Race and sports book (especially during football season)

The above are the basics. As mentioned previously, if you can't review this information personally, delegate the responsibility to your supervisors and leads. Reviewing reports is excellent training and you can cover a lot more ground (detect more) by delegating this.

I would say that most surveillance departments work in a vacuum. They don't use the information that is available to them and thus don't see the red flags or negative trends developing. Reviewing your numbers is key to your success.

8.4 KEY BUSINESS INDICATORS (KBIS)

Surveillance too has or should have its own statistics. When I was a director for an individual property I always noted key statistics that I tracked daily so I always had a good idea of what was happening on the property. These statistics were the daily handle amounts and win percentages for 21, craps, baccarat, and roulette.

As time went on I added other information specific to surveillance. I tracked a number of detections the surveillance department made, whether they were proactive (detected purely by surveillance) or by report from another department. I also broke down detections by shift. Such information was valuable because I could immediately see if the department or a shift was operating well (consistent detections) or not (everything was always okay—always a danger signal).

As I was given more responsibility and more surveillance departments to run, KBIs became even more important. I required the surveillance manager at each property to send me a KBI form every day. This allowed me to quickly check what was going on at each property and respond as needed to developing trends or problems.

Table 8.4 is an example of a KBI sheet. Such information gives you an excellent feel for what is going on at your property, especially if you are running more than one property.

Table 8.4   Key Business Indicators Form

PROPERTY NAME:				
Date:				
Table games:	Handle	Win% (Daily)	Win% (MTD)	Win% YTD
21				
Craps				
Wheel				
Baccarat				
Significant Wins/Losses:				
Slots	Handle	Win% (Daily)	Win% (MTD)	Win% YTD
Jackpots:				
Issues/Problems				
Significant Variances				
Audits:				
Department				
Results				
Significant Incidents/Reports/Detections				

9

Surveillance in the Future

When I started in surveillance in the late 1980s closed-circuit television technology was in its infancy. We had very few cameras. The ones we used were either black-and-white fixed cameras or black-and-white pan-tilt-zoom (PTZ) cameras. The PTZs were extremely large units.

Additionally, when PTZs were not in use, we had to drop their view to the carpet. If we left the PTZ on a bank of slot machines or area with any lighting, the lens had a tendency to burn that image into itself, destroying its clarity. Thus, we could not place the PTZs in appropriate at-rest monitoring positions.

We also could not record everything we can today. Then you were normally limited to what you had displayed on your monitors and what was recording through quad units. Because recording was done with VCRs, which could accept only certain and limited amounts of video input without great expense, our systems were small and simple.

Because we could only record certain areas, what we looked at, how we placed our cameras, and what we recorded were extremely important. This situation (for me) forced the development of the IOU (identify, observe, understand) technique, the tri-shot, proper camera positioning, and effective monitor display.

Today, we are in an entirely different world. We record 100 percent of our camera inputs 24/7. Cameras are much cheaper and now record in color. PTZ units are much smaller and see farther. We cover much more of the property besides the gaming areas: hotel, parking lots, points of sale, back of the house. There are few places that someone can commit a crime on any casino property without being recorded on a camera somewhere.

Of course, we also now have digital technology. VCRs are essentially gone and most properties are moving to digital systems. Our tape changing days are over (or fast disappearing). Digital recording brings us a whole new world of technology. Megapixel cameras allow us to use two cameras instead of three or four, and also include a zoom function. DVRs and NVRs allow immediate recall and review of specific cameras and times. It is an exciting time to work in surveillance.

When I think about the future of surveillance, most often I think about technology, not just for surveillance but about where it's going in the gaming world, how it will affect our operations, and most importantly, how the bad guys will use it against us.

Casinos are using increasing amounts of technology in every area of the property. Look at table games: they now utilize radio-frequency identification (RFID) checks, "smart tables" that monitor wagering activity, dealer payouts, and can monitor player counting!

How about slots? We already have free slot play that we use for marketing promotions. Server-based slots are coming online. Slot machines have already switched to ticket in, ticket out (TITO) and you can play any denomination on any machine. We are also talking about online gaming and even wireless gaming. Imagine a guest using a device to play blackjack while at the pool!

My point is that technology will always outpace loss prevention capabilities. Providing necessary security for new technology is usually not high on the priority list. Nor are the loss prevention and surveillance personnel charged with protecting the technology trained to do so. In fact, we often have to fight to attain access to the technology and information we need to protect the property from using the technology against us.

We in surveillance must realize that technology is changing how we should operate. The days of looking around and catching someone grabbing cash or tokens and running out the door are over. They are over because the bad guys don't have to use this method to steal from us.

The theft and fraud that occur nowadays are based on the technology we use. Employees and outside agents are attacking us with and through the systems, networks, computers, applications, and programs we use in gaming operations and for customer service.

One of the best things about computer-based operations (the ability to process transactions and information extremely fast) is also its weakest point (from a loss prevention perspective). In essence, it allows more to be stolen faster! This is one of the primary reasons you see gaming losses to theft and fraud climbing so drastically. Bad guys can steal more and faster using technology so what used to be a $100 loss can now be $10,000, and what used to be a $10,000 loss can now be hundreds of thousands. We are also now seeing $1 million losses in slot and players club frauds!

We must use technology to detect and defeat the bad guys who are using technology to beat us. Ultimately, this means that surveillance must change how we operate to protect our properties. As I said, you probably won't see someone steal some money and run out the door. What you'll probably see is a clerk hunched over a computer entering information and data. This, of course, is routine and appears normal. Yet those clerks and other employees are some of your biggest threats and they could be stealing right in front of your camera and you wouldn't know it! We aren't using the right method to detect today's theft and cheating.

Surveillance departments and personnel, in addition to their cameras and systems, must use computer-based information, operating reports and statistics, exception reports and events to detect today's crime. That means that on a daily basis we must review operational reports and results and exception reports in order to detect illicit activity. This is where we will find the red flags and indicators of technology-based crime. Once we find the indicators, we can then place our cameras on that clerk hunched over the computer and understand that what is entered might be used to steal from the company.

I stress again the importance of reviewing daily those critical areas and transactions for illicit activity. If you do not do this, you will be routinely victimized by those individuals who will use your technology against you.

Future scams will revolve around new systems and technology. Of course there will be ample opportunity for old scams, but the most damaging to gaming properties will be technology-based.

Consider one recent case at a casino in Las Vegas. Three slot technicians devised a way to connect a slot machine used for tests in their shop to live machines on the floor. Doing so allowed them to set up false jackpots on the live machines. The technicians managed to steal over $1 million from the casino in a time period of about a year before they were detected! As I mentioned previously, this type of theft will not be caught through random patrol (although a curious surveillance investigator might, we just can't depend on that happening), but rather through review of reports or a live audit. In this case, reviewing jackpot paid reports and the list of winners would have picked up suspicious trends. A live audit of, of course, will quickly detect the same players winning on the same machines.

Currently, players clubs and marketing programs and promotions are hit on a regular basis. Again, for the most part, you will not catch this type of internal theft, fraud, and collusion with outside agents through random observation. You must combine a review of department transactional activity with an audit of club personnel to detect this type of activity.

For example, a recent scam with marketing promotions concerned "hot seat" promotions. A hot seat promotion involves using a computer program to select at random a slot player who is currently playing a slot machine and has his or her players' club card placed in the machine. The winner (in the hot seat) receives cash or other prizes.

At one property it was noticed that the same people were winning frequently. The prizes ranged from cash to high-definition televisions to Broadway show tickets. Upon investigation it was determined that the manager of the promotion was able to continue "selecting" the hot seat winner until her agent was selected. The manager received kickbacks from the winners (her friends and family). Cost of the loss: over $100,000!

Scams such as these usually require a review of reports, such as the list of winners, to identify trends and patterns and a review of computer access and activity records. Obviously such promotions should not be controlled by just one person. Someone must look over the shoulder of those who operate promotions.

Another concern is the possibility of bad guys hacking into our networks to disrupt operations for blackmail or extortion purposes (denial of service attacks) or to cheat gaming devices. My thought is if they can hack into the Pentagon, they can certainly hack into a casino system.

I've heard of a case where a few undisclosed large casino race and sports books were hit with a denial of service attack right before the Super Bowl and were then extorted by the criminals. The criminals threatened to flood the sports book wagering systems and prevent customers from wagering during this peak season. Apparently the casinos in question bowed to the threat and paid a "fee" to prevent this from occurring.

A case recently in the news was an online poker scam. Employees working for the online company figured out a way to "see" the hole cards (pocket cards) of the players. This information was communicated to their inside man playing in the same game who, of course, won consistently. At the time of this writing losses to the players are estimated at $20 million.

121

Another famous case involved the Dennis Nikrasch gang that hit Las Vegas casinos for over $10 million. This gang was able to access the inner computer system of slot machines and set up jackpots of $10,000 and up. These gangs were able to access these machines right on the casino floor and were never detected by casino surveillance (or anyone else). They were finally caught when one of their own turned them in over a money dispute.

Of course it isn't all bad news. What technology does for the bad guys it can also do for us. While criminals can steal more, faster, we can catch more of them faster. We just haven't completely realized it yet.

Technology allows us to continuously monitor selected activities such as access control, points of sale, table games, slots, and people just to name a few. Let's discuss a few of these applications.

Access to the property and to sensitive areas within it can be controlled through access control technology. Today's systems allow access to be defined by an individual, job title or classification, and work schedule, to name a few. Most surveillance rooms now have access control terminals that can display photos of the employees as they access areas of the property and alarm conditions such as an individual attempting to enter an area that he or she is not authorized for or a door left unsecured. Such systems are a tremendous benefit to surveillance when attempting to track an employee's or a vendor's movements through the property for investigative purposes. Additionally, the system can be used to determine who accessed an area at a particular time or date. Since access control systems can be interfaced with the property's camera system, we usually can identify who accessed an area in the event another individual has used an authorized person's card or access code.

Points of sale can now be used continuously to monitor those conditions that may indicate a potential theft situation, such as voids, no sales, incorrect price for a specific item, or the cash drawer left open for too long. Such conditions can be alarmed to immediately be displayed on a monitor or reviewed on command. Having such a system run in the background allows the surveillance team to focus on areas that require live observation, such as table games or slots, and also keep tabs on all points of sale on the property. For example, a bartender at any one of the bars on the property who enters a void into the register triggers an alarm that displays on a monitor in the surveillance room the register and the transaction for surveillance review or investigation.

Table games technology is improving by leaps and bounds. Smart tables, radio-frequency identification (RFID) checks, along with cameras placed on the game allow tracking of players' wagers for rating purposes. Automatic game protection is also available to check card totals for appropriate and accurate payouts as well as monitoring for card counting activities. In other words, the table can report to surveillance that a dealer is dumping the game or that an advantage player is on the game.

Slots seem to be a never-ending source of new technology. Already, slots can provide us with alarms indicating doors or drops opened illegally or improperly, coin in and out, jackpots hot, and so forth. If a player uses our players' club card in the machine, we now can obtain everything we need to know: name, address, daily win/loss, career win/loss, as well as all kinds of other information that we may or may not use (favorite sports team, favorite drink, etc.).

Certainly, slots technology can report malfunctions and attempts by internal or external agents to manipulate the machine or its operating system. Again, this equipment continuously runs in the background during routine surveillance operation.

One of the advantages of digital technology is tracking of people. We discussed the tracking of employees through the use of access control. Technology also allows us to track and count customers as they visit our various venues and attractions within the facility. For example, the marketing department may want to know how many are coming to the casino as a result of a new promotion, or a restaurant manager may want a count of customers for breakfast. This type of information is available from a digital surveillance system. All you need is a camera focused on these areas and the appropriate computer application and that information is almost automatic. Again, this information is gathered in the background and requires little, if any, surveillance intervention.

Successful surveillance operations in the present day and for the near future will combine the surveillance system and surveillance operations with technology. You must patrol and audit with your camera, and you must investigate and audit the information provided by technology.

Section II

Physical Security in Gaming Operations

10

The Gaming Security Officer's Role

10.1 OPERATIONAL SEPARATION FROM SURVEILLANCE AND REASONS

In today's gaming environment, the majority of operations make a distinct and often dramatic separation between the surveillance function and that of physical security. In many jurisdictions the regulators mandate this separation, and in some instances control of even basic communication between these departments. From a legal and public perception point of view, they are one and the same. They are transparent in many civil and criminal legal cases and are combined.

The concept of surveillance in gaming was born within the physical security function. Prior to closed-circuit television (CCTV) systems, there was merely visual observation through a series of one-way mirrors with catwalks above the gaming area or in the walls next to a cashier in the back of the house. A more experienced security officer or manager would walk into these areas and make observations discreetly to make sure that employees and customers were not taking the house money. In the early stages of gaming history, even the pit bosses and managers would walk these areas and be sure that employees observed them as they entered that secret door into the surveillance world.

Prior to the catwalk era, there were only the watchful eyes of the pit boss or casino manager who would make an observation directly or sometimes use what most customers thought were decorative mirrors. If the pit boss thought a customer was cheating, the ramifications were sometimes brutal, ending in the customer lying in an alley bleeding from unknown causes. Thankfully, the industry has changed a lot since legalized gambling was born in Nevada in 1931 (Figure 10.1).

The functions are very distinct and yet they are quite similar in basic applications. Security and surveillance directors have differing strategies on how to protect the people and assets of the operation and are often at odds with each other in the methods to accomplish this daunting task. Surveillance has an inherent tendency to want to observe and report on security personnel behavior (sometimes on marginal minor infractions) to the executive manager. The security management will sometimes complain to the very same executive that surveillance never gets the important incident or arrest on video.

Figure 10.1 Modern gaming operation.

Security and surveillance certainly need to work together and communicate absent any direct regulatory environment that prohibits it. Even in those restricted situations, executives of each department should have a method in which to accomplish good two-way communication for effective management of the protection of people and assets. One-way communication will not work and the operation will suffer as a result.

A simple and direct method of improving communication between these two important security functions is to meet weekly, even if only for a few minutes, with the senior executive discussing issues and possible solutions between the enforcement arms of the gaming operation. These meetings will often start out intense and will progress to the point that they will become the driving force for proactive and effective security management by increasing communication and problem solving in the early stages of a potential conflict.

Surveillance is charged to "follow the money" and to make observations and report them to ensure compliance with regulators and applicable laws. This includes the important function of observing the security officer as he or she escorts cash or chips across the gaming floor or in areas not visible to the naked eye. The gaming security officer needs to be very aware that surveillance is watching and keep the assets where they belong. Security personnel are the same as other employees who handle cash or negotiable instruments, and they need to accept the fact that they are being watched.

Surveillance needs to understand that it is easier to sit in a room and criticize or play Monday morning quarterback during an arrest or other dynamic situation as it occurs on the screen in front of them than to actually apply a set of handcuffs on a resisting offender. The supervisors, managers, and directors of both departments should work at communication and understanding of each function and work as a team to accomplish the mutual task. The daily reinforcement of this effort, along with the weekly meetings with the senior executive, is sure to change the attitudes of the employees positively in the protective function.

10.2 PROACTIVE PRESENCE

Being reactive as a security professional is certainly part of the job when protecting the people and assets of a gaming operation. The security officer must be able to respond to an emergency or situation in a calm and professional manner. This is accomplished through experience and training. The important presence is a proactive one that will deter, detect, and hopefully prevent the criminals from preying on the customers and employees of the casino or targeting the assets. Between the open and obvious CCTV cameras and mirrored domes and the presence of obvious security personnel, a first line of proactive presence should be in place in most casinos. Although cameras cannot fully deter criminal activity, they certainly enhance the concept of being caught to the potential perpetrator of a crime. It should also be kept in mind that a highly motivated offender will not typically be deterred by traditional security measures.

By the late 1960s Nevada casinos were finding that by placing a security officer in a raised podium in the casino would not only afford high visibility, but it would also function as a positive public relations tool for the customers who needed directions or who had lost a personal item somewhere between the slot machines. This concept was well received and security began to establish this early standard for security in casinos. These podiums were typically placed next to the cashier's cage, which would also be the logical place for a security officer as a deterrent.

This podium officer position developed so well that in many operations the officer eventually had the new CCTV monitors and key controls, as well as checked the hard count employees, answered the telephone, and dispatched the security officers on the radio. In many operations this became the focal point for security and the podium officer became the dispatcher. This certainly worked as an organizational position and, as a consequence, it made this position almost impossible to function as an effective deterrent due to the lack of time the officer had to make actual observations. The mere presence of a uniformed security officer, however, even if he was obviously busy, is still a deterrent to some offenders.

The proactive presence should be a concept that is frequently revisited and evaluated by the supervisors and managers of security. Fixed positions, podiums, and uniformed security officers will all play a part in the proactive presence of security in a casino. The security officer who appears alert and attentive to the surroundings will certainly be a deterrence versus one who is slouched over appearing bored and uninterested in anything but the next scheduled break.

The job of the shift supervisor should be one that will frequently observe the actions and presence of the various security officers and apply typical human resource management in discipline and positive reinforcement to make the entire shift proactive in their approach to managing the protective functions.

Even in the parking lots and garages there should be a proactive presence to deter criminal activity and protect the guests and employees. I once asked a security director I know in Las Vegas why I routinely saw two security officers on bicycles stopped and talking to each other when I drove into his property. He smiled at me and told me that it was intentional that when most people entered his parking lots or garage facility he wanted high visibility of security officers.

He designed the patrol patterns of his bike officers and mandated that if and when they needed to speak to each other while on patrol, or needed to rest, they were to do it in specific places. These locations were designed to be highly visible to the public and the criminals. He would still manage the patrol functions, and with this feature he was able to increase the proactive perception of security without adding additional officers.

When I first started working as a security officer at a casino in Lake Tahoe in 1978 it had two security patrol vans. Each van had a yellow flashing light on it that was hard-wired to be on as long as the engine was running. When working the parking lot we were instructed to patrol in opposite areas and offer customers rides to the casino, jump start vehicles with dead batteries, and approach anyone wandering in the parking lot and inquire if they needed assistance even if they were acting suspicious.

I quickly learned that this application of proactive security worked very well and created the safest parking lot in the region. The highly visible flashing lights constantly moving, interaction with people in the parking lots, and the public relations all fostered a very positive security environment. Many security officers preferred not to work outside and thought that a plain marked vehicle lurking in the back of the parking lot was a much better way to catch criminals. Those officers were rarely placed outside under my watch. Personally, when I was in uniform, I liked the parking lot patrol and volunteered whenever possible.

The concept of obvious security presence is not a new one and can be found in even medieval times when the king's castle was protected by numerous armed guards ready to thwart off any potential threat to their charge. If a guard fell asleep at the post, he would be severely disciplined or even killed. Today's security functions are much the same in application, although beheadings have softened to more modern methods of discipline. The obvious presence of the guards was typically enough to deter threats to the crowned leader.

If there are several businesses around a casino, or other casinos, and there is an obvious security presence around the exterior of your casino, the criminals who are deterrable will most likely go to a property with less security presence. Another important factor to consider is that there are people who are not deterrable by contemporary security measures, and must be dealt with in a more direct method. Those hardened criminals are not threatened by the ramifications of incarceration and are willing to take higher risks when committing crimes.

As I moved up the ranks to chief of security, the local sheriff told me that I had the safest lot and proved it to me with a report comparing crimes at my facility as compared to crimes at other properties, which was dramatic. These early versions of police calls for service were invaluable in future security planning. He explained to me that the combination of security components created an image that made the perpetrators of crimes move to the casino next door, which had the highest crime rate in the area. This phenomenon is known as *displacement* in the criminology world. For example, if a criminal observes two casinos side by side and the objective is present at both, he or she will evaluate the perceived security and chances of being caught and decide which environment he or she wants to work in. Proactive presence works in these situations.

The concept of security deterrence is different when compared to law enforcement and community policing. In the police environments officers are charged with overall reduction of criminal behavior, which involves many different approaches. They instead want to attempt to reduce the entire crime picture, as opposed to the security approach, which is to deflect the criminal away from your property to somewhere else.

Another routine task that is seen but rarely discussed is the concept of slots stool arrangement and security proactive presence. Moveable slots stools are placed throughout the facility and many marketing professionals suggest that these stools always be placed uniformly in front of slot machines to appear inviting and organized to the serious and casual gambler. I always recommend that security officers assist in this process to increase presence and interaction with the guests. It is important, however, to make sure everyone knows that this is a courtesy and not the primary job of the security officer.

The officers can make casual observations between machines, suggest to female patrons not to leave purses on the floor or between machines, and communicate positive greetings to customers as they straighten up the casino floor. Again, approaching persons who are just walking through or with no obvious purpose will go far in deterrence of criminal activity. Some retail giants across the country have a policy to greet every customer as he or she enters and to make full eye contact. This is a proven method of deterring undesirable behavior by making that perpetrator think someone will recognize him or her. In those operations, the shrinkage, or level of pilferage and theft, is significantly lower as a result.

Another simple method to increase the patrol presence whenever possible would be to make simple changes in routines. As an example, the security officer who is charged with patrolling the north end of a casino floor can be instructed to walk out the doors onto the sidewalk and check the trash cans and exterior areas around the building walls that surround the designated patrol area. The officer can exit one door and enter another, which will take only a few minutes. Calling in the exterior check to the dispatcher will document the number of times the officer makes this simple patrol that will be high profile to the casual observer. The outside patrol officers still patrol the same area, and you accomplish double the patrol without adding an additional security officer.

Creative methods for higher visibility should always be explored and exploited to give the appearance of a formidable force of obvious security around a gaming property. Simple routines can significantly increase the visibility of security personnel. Combining the increased presence with positive observation and patrol techniques will reduce exposure to gaming-related crime.

Recording the proactive actions that are routine and repetitive will become invaluable in the event of a claim or litigation over a serious crime where someone is injured or killed. Because the actions are routine and repetitive, the security personnel can become complacent in performing proactive security functions. They must be supervised, trained, and motivated to protect the people and assets of the gaming operation.

10.3 PUBLIC RELATIONS AND SECURITY

Both management and the customers demand positive public relations from all employees and especially security officers. No matter how many times a security officer is asked the most obvious question in a casino—Where is the bathroom?—the officer must answer it as if it were the very first time and assist the customer. In today's competitive gaming environment, many companies encourage the concept of the security officer to respond to the customers' questions by actually showing him or her where the bathroom is, time and circumstances permitting.

The way that security should give directions to a customer is equally important. The message should be short but informative and accomplish the request. Long and complicated directions for an impatient customer who has an overly filled bladder will not fare well in the eventual outcome. The customer will only go as far as the first part of the directions they remember and then ask another employee for the next set of directions. Sarcastic and unprofessional answers to basic questions of revenue-generating customers will surely create a letter of complaint to the general manager or more importantly the loss of that valuable customer and all of his or her friends and family members.

The customer also has basic expectations of security officers in a casino. Those expectations are basically to respond to disruptions, to act professional, and to minimize obnoxious behavior. Watching four security officers dog pile on top of a suspected shoplifter from the gift shop is not a desirable event to the average customer.

The customers are used to watching television programs that depict unrealistic casino security and many believe that is how it should be done. They dramatize and exaggerate the conditions to serve their purpose, which is entertainment. The professional security officer appears neat, clean, and professional when observed. He or she responds professionally, with firmness when necessary, exerts compassion when warranted, and has a smile when in public.

When approaching customers it is desirable to make them feel more secure and comfortable. Even a simple head nod acknowledging them is a signal that the officer is aware they are there and that they are important. Customers will normally welcome these gestures and appreciate them. Those customers who do not will generally let you know through very strong nonverbal communications such as a scowl or frown.

As an example, checking identification (ID) is something that all security officers will do on a daily basis in virtually any position. There is a significant public relations component to ID checks. When checking the ID of a customer, care should be exerted not to offend him or her. The approach is huge in the public relations aspect and one security officer with poor people skills can create a sizable group of irritated customers over a relatively short period of time. I always found that a simple "Hello" goes a long way as the opening line followed by "Can I ask how old you are?" This establishes the greeting and purpose of your contact quickly and will also circumvent many follow-up questions.

If the initial approach by the officer is "Let me see some ID," you are sure to receive negative feedback and the question requires more inquiries. By asking how old a visitor is, the ID may not even be required if the person is under the legal age. Most minors would rather just admit their age and leave rather than go through a prolonged ID check.

Then the manner in which you request a person to leave the gaming area will determine how the rest of your shift will go. An officer with an attitude will turn this very simple function into a disturbing the peace arrest and hours of paperwork for the security officers and the supervisor. If the ID is produced and a person is of legal age, a compliment should be given and a brief explanation of the applicable law should be ready for those who seem irritated at the request. Keep in mind that the thousands of underage people security officers request identification from are future customers.

In the early 1980s drink tokes were the normal perk of all employees, including security officers. I found that if I offered to buy that underage customer a drink on his or her twenty-first birthday (the legal age in Nevada), he or she would remember that gesture. In reality that one gesture made many people come back years later and approach me to tell me about it and how the casino became their favorite place over competing ones in the immediate area. What was more amazing is that there were less than a dozen out of the thousands of kids who actually came back and took me up on the offer. My goal was to accomplish the regulatory requirement and still keep them as future customers. It worked!

The professional security officer should be able to withstand minor insults when performing routine tasks such as ID checks. These comments are a reinforcement why laws are enacted that require a certain age or maturity to patronize a casino. Provocative comments will be made to any security officer in the gaming industry during his or her career, and how the officer responds will determine his or her professionalism. It is also important to understand that customers will be observing the exchange and will make their own evaluations of your professionalism and actions.

It is still amazing to me that every day there are people even well into their eighties who have never been inside a casino before. All security personnel need to be aware that many are not familiar with how casinos operate and need to be politely informed rather than in gruff or uncaring tones. They are ignorant of the concepts of a casino that you are intimately aware of. It should always be remembered that the customer is truly the one who pays your wages and is the driving force of why the casino is in the business of gaming.

Another thing that should be considered is that people from around the world come to the United States and other democratic nations from places where security and police are not always trusted and abuse their power and authority. When dealing with people from other countries and cultures, you may find these customers to be quiet, aloof, or sometimes actually scared to even speak with you.

Having a list of employees who speak various languages will always be appreciated when dealing with foreigners. In many operations, the human resources department will log employees as they are hired who speak languages other than English. The list is then periodically sent to the security department where it is maintained until a person they are dealing with speaks only a certain language. The security supervisor will consult the list and look for someone on staff who can assist in interpreting to help the customer, which should always be the goal.

The public relations aspect of the gaming security officer's daily duties is constant. With the inventive and creative television and movies produced today, the public's perception of what security is in a casino is quite different from reality. The public has very distinct expectations and demands of gaming operations. The high level of competition in various markets makes public relations crucial to an operation's ultimate long-term survival.

133

If you recall an incident in your personal history where you were treated badly by an employee, you will most likely also remember that you never went back to that business and it lost you as a customer. You will also probably recall telling numerous friends and relatives about the unfortunate experience who were most likely influenced by your story and also did not patronize the business.

10.4 UNIFORMS AND APPEARANCE

Throughout the history of casinos and gaming operations, the uniforms have undergone various stages of changes and cycles based on many different factors. The incoming chief has distinct ideas of what he or she likes in a uniform, the general manager has a very different idea, and the marketing department has other ideas that sometimes create security morale issues.

The traditional approach is the uniforms with epaulets on the shoulders, patches on the sleeves, and a shiny star on the chest of the uniform, enhanced with proper leather and accessories. In today's casino security world, the radios are attached to an ear bud device, which allows for private communication, as opposed to the days when I first started and the radio was hung on the belt with the volume cranked up so the officer and the world could hear what was happening. These hard uniforms seem to have withstood time and are the predominant uniforms for gaming security officers inside most casino buildings.

The soft uniform, however, is fast approaching as the common uniform in many major casinos. This uniform consists of slacks, a blazer, and suitable tie, which gives a softer and more pleasant appearance of the security officer. As an example, I am always impressed when I enter the lobby of a certain large casino resort in Las Vegas and see the security officer standing at parade rest in the middle of it wearing a coat and tie, name badge clearly visible, radio ear bud in place, and gesturing welcomes to customers.

These soft uniforms are clearly visible and most customers will recognize who the security personnel are. Old school security directors, and even some experts, believe that customers cannot tell who security is without a traditional uniform with badges and patches. They have obviously never worked in the environment with soft uniforms and enjoyed the benefits from employee morale to positive customer comments on the appearance and professionalism of the security personnel.

Both styles of uniforms are acceptable and used widely in the industry. The concept should be that the security uniform should be easily recognized by the customer and more importantly by the local or visiting criminals. There are other employees with radios and ear buds and in coats and ties, which could make this difficult if colors and designs are not coordinated. There is of course the concept that if hundreds of people look like security then that is a good thing. Many security professionals will argue on these points.

The exterior security officers are quickly becoming uniformed outside the traditional uniforms. Law enforcement bike officers started the trend of wearing bright yellow or lime green shirts and black pants or shorts for comfort and visibility. Very large letters on the back and smaller ones on the front identify them as security (Figure 10.2). With parking lots and outside areas having higher exposures to third-party assaults, robberies, and other person-on-person crimes, this proves to be effective in many different ways.

Figure 10.2 Security uniform with large lettering.

The high visibility of exterior security is obvious in larger metropolitan cities where there are many casinos in a relatively small area. These security officers are well recognized and observed constantly by customers and criminals alike. Local police departments will also deploy bike officers in these locations with similarly colored uniforms. Bike officers can navigate parking lots and sidewalks much faster than the traditional patrol vehicle, absent dramatic weather conditions.

Limiting the security uniform to official pins and insignia is also desirable. Numerous personal pins and marketing buttons can clutter the uniform and even create issues rather than solve them. I would recommend a very clear and definitive uniform policy be incorporated into the security operations manual and in the rules of conduct for employment. The written policy will ensure that there are no public interpretations of the company arising from security uniforms.

The marketing gurus also like to further increase the security uniform presence to the customer by attempting to create a themed concept and outfit the personnel in very nontraditional uniforms. This can be very demeaning for security officers who have to take the brunt of ridicule by obnoxious customers or other employees. There are successful operations that use themed uniforms, although very few have withstood a measurable amount of time. Very careful consideration should be given before allowing this to occur in any operation.

In 1983 the casino in Lake Tahoe where I was director of security underwent a major name change and theme change due to market conditions. The property was converted into a western theme from the aesthetic appearance all the way to the uniforms. I was mandated to outfit my officers into cavalry uniforms to incorporate the marketing concept. As the rumor quickly spread through my staff, I was furiously fighting this change from the existing traditional uniform. I was finally told to come up with an alternative after threatening to quit before being dressed up in a casino like a cavalry soldier. My uniform for the grand opening was that of a cavalry captain with sword, yellow pant stripes, shoulder cords, and so forth.

I quickly assembled my key staff and we went to work and came up with an acceptable presentation that was black slacks, gray cowboy-type shirt, bolo tie, and a badge that

135

looked like the old Texas Rangers from a century earlier. I presented one of my supervisors clad in this quickly designed uniform to the decision makers and they actually liked the idea. As I breathed a sigh of relief and was exiting the executive conference room, my boss asked me what color and type of cowboy hat I wanted my officers to wear. I should have known that was coming. Although I fought long and hard, I lost the battle of the hats. My security officers ended up wearing a light gray Stetson for several years. If they were going to have to wear the hats, they were going to look good in them, and they actually did.

Getting the personnel to buy into the uniforms was not easy. The officers resisted the concept and it was a difficult sell. The hats were the biggest issue for them, as I suspected it would be. The officers were to be responsible for the hats, yet they were concerned about what to do with them if they got into physical altercations. I made the rule that they had my permission to throw the hat if that was about to occur. For years I would occasionally see a hat fly in the distance and then hear the call for backup. Ironically the staff came to like the hats and took pride in them. They found that the opposite sex thought they were cute or sexy, and that worked. The hats and the western uniform faded as the themed operation did not result in major market stimulation and increased revenues. There are themed resorts that are still in operation and the nontraditional uniforms they utilize have passed the test of time.

In time, the western theme and the look of security personnel as marshals faded and the uniforms were once again changed back to the traditional security uniforms with epaulets, patches, and ties. I personally proudly display the badge shaped like an old Texas Ranger badge in my office today as a reminder of that time in my career.

Grooming and appearance standards are always a concern for any security operation. The officer who shows up in combat-style pants and boots and many additional unauthorized attachments to the duty belt should be discouraged. Neat grooming of head and facial hair is important as well as enforcement of accepted hygiene requirements, as these will present a professional staff. Generally the company's grooming policy is sufficient for security personnel.

Creative security managers and supervisors will observe and test public relations from simple customer requests and responses to interviewing incident victims and making sure that the security personnel exerted proper and desired results. Testing how your staff appears and interacts with the public when you are not watching them is crucial to a successful operation. Having a "spotter" approach the security podium and complain about losing a purse or wallet will invoke various responses and will test the customer courtesy of the security staff.

11

Security Patrols and Assignments in the Gaming Environment

11.1 THE FUNCTION OF PATROLS AND ASSIGNMENTS

The majority of what the typical security officer will do during a shift is patrol or be stationed at a particular position or assignment and perform visual patrols of some type. Little is written about the function of gaming patrol or positional assignments other than in various organizational procedural manuals for various casinos. Security personnel should be oriented and trained on company or tribal procedures for each assignment, stationary position, and patrol area. This chapter will examine the basic assignments and duties of the security officer in a typical gaming environment.

Every operation has unique characteristics, customer demographics, and facility designs, and no two facilities are exactly the same. There is no magic formula that all gaming operations use to design security coverage and protective measures. There are, however, very basic positions that have also withstood the test of time.

In the contract security world, the particular personnel assignments will come with what are called post orders that describe each position, the duties required of the officer assigned, the reporting relationship, and instructions on specific duties related to the position. In gaming operations, these are typically incorporated into the operations manual as job descriptions. In either case, it is important to design basic instructions for each position within a security operation for consistency in operations and clarity to the staff.

Stationary security positions will change as a security department evolves and conditions change at a particular location. Directors will have different preferences when dealing with assigning personnel to stationary positions. The traditional approach over the past decade has been to rotate these positions every one to four hours to keep the personnel alert and fresh. Some directors feel that they want personnel assigned who are very proficient at a position and will assign them permanently to that position whenever they are on the shift. Regardless of the time an officer is assigned to a stationary post, there should be a clear and consistent understanding of the duties and responsibilities.

Creative scheduling is required to rotate personnel within a shift, and it can create confusion during an incident when staff members are busy. Many directors merely suspend the rotations until the situation is under control and then switch at the next interval. Rotation of staff will ensure that all personnel can work all positions, which will be of value to the operation. Operations that assign a new position each workday or rotate personnel within the shift will find that it will help morale and efficiency of the department.

Conceptually, the patrol is designed to cover a large area by making rounds through it and watching for any undesirable activity, criminal behavior, and whatever appears unusual or suspicious. As mentioned earlier, a key concept for proactive security is to always make contact with anyone who catches your eye while on patrol. This does not mean that you should ask for identification of every person, but it does mean that even a simple "Hello" and the question "Is there anything I can help you with today?" can deter a potential threat to people or property. Even the obvious recording of a license plate in a parking lot can be helpful in overall guest protection.

Regardless of the patrol area, the security personnel should stay in their assigned areas unless they are specifically called out by a supervisor or dispatcher. This provides for an evenly distributed manpower staff and will ensure that all areas are covered as desired. The process of multiple patrols will in itself be a deterrent. Security personnel are just like other employees and they tend to gather and have social interactions during the work shift. Supervisors must always be watchful when security personnel collect in one spot and neglect the patrol function.

The supervisor can utilize the dispatcher to ensure even patrol coverage of all areas of the property. Designing a system to ensure coverage will ultimately reduce incidents and provide opportunities for early intervention in altercations and undesirable behavior by customers and employees.

11.2 IDENTIFICATION CHECKS AS A CONSTANT

One of the most common functions of the casino/hotel security officer is to check the identification of persons on the property for a variety of reasons. The primary reason is for regulatory compliance of the limitations on the age of persons allowed to gamble or drink alcohol within the establishment. In all areas of patrol this important function is required and failure to patrol can incur a severe penalty to the operation up to and including the loss of a gaming license if not done regularly.

Various age restrictions are in place around the world, with the ages between eighteen and twenty-one as most common to allow legal alcohol consumption and gambling. Regulatory agencies from tribal gaming commissions to state gaming agencies are charged with monitoring compliance with the process of restricting under-aged persons. In some jurisdictions, serious fines have been imposed on licensees for allowing minors into an establishment even when proven unintentional. Diligence in enforcing this important aspect of gaming is vital to the survivability of a casino.

Because gaming is a hospitality-driven environment, people come from different states and countries to U.S.-based casinos on vacation and for various other reasons. They are often ignorant of the rules, laws, and regulations that are in place within a given juris-diction. First and foremost the security officer should understand that not all people are aware of the laws and the requirements of identification. Due care in the approach and request must be managed for positive results in compliance and for positive public rela-tions. As an example, most casino security officers will not be familiar with what a pass-port from Libya looks like or know if it is a genuine document.

The most misunderstood concept in identification checks is the basic fact that in most places it is not a crime to refuse to produce identification for a security officer. There are typically no laws that require a citizen to produce identification when requested inside a gaming establishment. Security officers need to know that the only thing that typically can be done is to ask the person to leave the premises under the local trespass statutes should a person refuse to show identification. The gaming establishment has a duty as a licensee to check identifications of all persons who could be under the legal age for that particular jurisdiction. In other parts of the world it is a crime not to produce ID, and severe penalties could be imposed, sometimes immediately.

From a public relations standpoint, the person who is not quite twenty-one is a future customer and the manner in which the security officer approaches, requests, and executes an identification (ID) check could cause that person to refuse to patronage that establish-ment after he or she becomes of age. Using practice scenarios during the training process is a positive way to accomplish good public relations during identification checks. The security officer who approaches a suspected minor and asks "Excuse me, I am sorry to bother you, but could I please see some identification to verify you are old enough to be in the casino?" would get a more positive response than "Let me see some ID." After a short period of time each security officer will have his or her own approach method and specific language in asking for ID using as few words as possible and still getting the correct message across.

The actual checking of the ID should be careful and deliberate to determine if it matches the person, is valid, and is not altered or counterfeited. Personnel should not be afraid to check the identification for accuracy if it is from a state that the officer does not recognize. The ID should be checked for date of birth, face picture comparison, height, weight, eye color, and so forth. The security officer will have a tendency to get into a rou-tine and become lazy in the process after several hundred ID checks. The ID should be checked for at least three components to make sure they are the person identified. At a minimum, the date of birth, picture, and expiration date should be checked.

Another process is for the security officer to examine the look and feel of the ID as it is checked. A common method of altering an ID is to insert a picture into an existing ID by separating the plastic laminate, making the changes, and the relaminating the docu-ment. Careful examination will reveal the raised edges of the picture or cut lines in the ID. By merely feeling the ID, this can be detected, much like a cashier who can tell when a counterfeit bill is handed to him or her. Cashiers have handled so many bills that the paper difference will stand out.

Features that typically do not change on an official ID can also be checked. Height, eye color, and sex normally stay constant. I found that a close look at a person's mouth and nose will also be a good comparative. Extremes in identity changes can be made to include cross-dressing, color contact lenses, and even platform elevator shoes. The officer should always continue checking an ID until he or she is satisfied that the ID is a valid one.

Typical fraudulent ID issues will involve relatives switching IDs (brothers, sister, and cousins), alteration of the date of birth and other portions of the ID, and the basic fake ID purchased from a magazine or creative college student with access to quality printing equipment. Your local police department and regional secret service office can be helpful with information on the most common form of ID fraud in your area.

In classes that I give regarding ID checks, I always ask how many people in the room had at one time either a false ID, a relative's ID, or an altered ID that they used, and I always get numerous hands raised. If security personnel used counterfeit IDs when they were young, it is probable that today's minors also will attempt it. It is the obligation of the security officer to ensure that all persons gambling and drinking in the casino are of age and have proper ID.

Be careful in confiscating an ID. If you are wrong, it certainly would be problematic. It should be remembered that a false identification is still the property of the person presenting it and if you take it you are in effect taking that person's property. Some gaming properties take possession and advise the presenter that the local police can be called to verify that it is valid and will issue a citation if it is a false ID or return it if it is legitimate. Remember that there is typically no law that says a visitor must present the ID to you as a security officer.

The jurisdiction you are in gives the authority to check the ID for age verification. For those instances where a vagrant or person exhibiting undesirable behavior is asked for ID and refuses, he or she should be advised of trespass regulations and requested to immediately leave the premise. Trespass is a good tool to use when people do not have an ID or their ID has expired.

Most jurisdictions have a local ordinance that identifies presenting a false identification as a misdemeanor. They typically do not give the authority to security personnel to confiscate it. The regulators will, however, come into a casino where identification checks are not adequately enforced and issue a citation, fine, or in some instances close a casino operation for not checking IDs as required.

As a result of some of the larger fines that have been imposed on gaming operations, a common practice has emerged where security personnel call dispatch and the ID checks are logged into the system with the time, location, and number of underage persons checked. At the end of each shift these are tallied and a total is entered. These numbers can be later collectively tallied and can become invaluable when the casino is audited or questioned by the regulators of compliance enforcement.

It also demonstrates which officers are on the floor checking IDs and enforcing this important task. The manager or supervisor can look at the dispatch logs and determine which officers are not calling in ID checks and take appropriate action. Conversely, the officer who seems to do nothing but checking IDs can be tempered to do more desired overall security functions.

Every security position or assignment will involve the checking of IDs in some form. Each officer has personal habits that surface during the routine process, and these should be monitored and corrected before they become problematic or other security personnel pick up the same bad habits through example.

11.3 STATIONARY ASSIGNMENTS

Casino security is basically divided into two categories. First is the patrol assignments, then there are those positions where an officer is placed in one location for a period of time. Stationary assignments usually involve dispatchers, loading docks, employee entrances, and ingress/egress points. Additionally special assignments can be assigned that relate to functions or special events where temporary positions are implemented.

The concept of a stationary position requires a calculation that 4.5 officers will be required to man one stationary position to allow for all shifts in a given week to be covered. This includes vacations, sick time, and breaks. Obviously this is manpower intensive and therefore costly when a casino determines that a stationary position is necessary. Careful consideration of fixed, stationary positions should be made based in part on the fact that these positions cannot be dropped from a shift roster because someone calls in sick or for other reasons.

New Year's eve in cities will require stationary positions specifically for maintaining order where large crowds gather and celebrate in the street next to a casino. Las Vegas, South Lake Tahoe, Reno, and Atlantic City experience this annually. Placing security personnel at each exit, on elevator banks at the ground level, and at various other locations is common.

11.4 DISPATCHERS

As the raised podium form of security, explained earlier developed in the industry and the duties of these early dispatchers became more intense, larger operations began to remove these positions away from the public's eye and into control rooms or command centers. In larger operations, entire surveillance rooms with thousands of closed-circuit television (CCTV) cameras piped into dozens of monitors, several dispatchers, alarm system enunciators, and radio systems have emerged and become the critical command centers for the operation. Many small to midsized casinos, however, still work on basic podium systems and handwritten logs, which are still quite adequate for the basic security function.

In many operations, surveillance plays an important role in dispatching security personnel and functions as the command and control for the security department. In those operations the interaction between security and surveillance is constant. In most operations the security department will have its own set of cameras and monitors and will watch the back of the house, hotel areas, and parking lots and garages.

Surveillance will normally monitor security by listening to radio traffic to determine what is occurring on the facility. The routine calls such as illegally parked cars in the parking lot or area checks can cause them to turn down the radio or scanner that monitors security and turn it back up when there is chatter on an incident. Surveillance has many tasks and is also making observations, so it cannot devote 100 percent of its time monitoring security radio traffic.

Handwritten logs are quickly being replaced with the automated computer-operated programs that increase efficiency, staff management, and analysis of data with the click of a computer mouse. Integrated systems include electronic patrols, alarms, access controls, and many other components that were unheard of only twenty years ago. In my travels, I still encounter numerous midsized and small operations that still rely on the handwritten log for security dispatchers. The cost of the software and hardware prohibits many operations from converting to them.

The dispatcher position is critical to the minute-by-minute operations of security. This assigned officer needs to be patient, efficient, fair, observant, and able to follow commands under pressure. The dispatcher also needs to be able to report to the appropriate executives and outside agencies as an incident or emergency develops, evolves, and concludes. He or she must be literate, have computer skills, and display positive public relations. The shift of security officers will often mirror the attitude and demeanor of the shift dispatcher; therefore, this position becomes one of the most important for any shift of officers.

The dispatcher is the focal point of the security operation from the officer's perspective. He or she is the person who typically controls rest and lunch breaks, patrol assignments, and incident call assignments and is the lifeline to the security personnel in the field with radio contact. The dispatcher is the one who needs to set an example to the rest of the shift in radio procedure and protocol, use of codes, and the orderly flow of communication.

Selection and assignment of the dispatcher are typically the responsibilities of the security shift manager or supervisor. This process needs to be reviewed and managed by the director of security to ensure that the shift attitude mirrors company policy and the department's mission statement. If an officer who has a negative attitude yet possesses good technical skills is placed in this important position, he can cause more harm than good for the overall operation of the shift and department.

The primary function of the dispatcher is to receive requests, or calls for service, and assign an officer to perform each requested task. In addition, he or she is charged with knowing where all officers on the shift are located, if they have received their assigned breaks, and that they are performing the tasks assigned by the supervisor. The dispatcher must have good communication skills and be easily understood on the radio by all who are listening.

The importance of the radio procedures comes into play and must be enforced procedurally through the security dispatcher. Use of proper codes and protocols will maintain an orderly process especially during an emergency situation. If the department uses a phonetic code list (e.g., A = alpha), it should be consistent and used by all the officers. If each officer uses his or her own code, confusion will occur. The dispatcher also controls how each call is received and transmitted for overall consistency. Because many directors have different opinions on proper radio procedures, the details must be clearly defined in the operations manual with the particular procedures and codes. The end result is a professional dispatching system that provides clear and concise communication between security personnel.

The dispatcher is also typically charged with watching a certain number of CCTV monitors while performing communication functions. The monitors are typically limited to nongaming areas and areas that the gaming surveillance department does not actively monitor in real time. Cameras in parking areas, exterior walkways, and at exit locations are usually found piped into the security dispatch center and observed by the dispatcher while performing other duties. This allows the video filming of incidents or locations being coordinated by the dispatcher and records the events whenever possible.

11.5 LOST AND FOUND

Several directors I have encountered have told me that dealing with lost and found property is by far the most difficult task to keep running smoothly and without complaints. In many operations, the lost and found is handled by security and typically by an officer in a podium or stationary position and sometimes the dispatcher in smaller operations.

When people misplace or lose their personal belongings, the central repository for those items is security. The items will range from cash to baby strollers, and organization and control of these lost items can be problematic and require patience. The security officer charged with taking in and recording each lost and found item must have positive public relations skills.

When an item is found by an employee or guest, he or she will naturally gravitate to security to turn the item in unless the person decides to just keep whatever he or she has found. When these items are brought to security, there is usually a log in and written procedure that is to be followed to describe the item, if applicable, and if it should be placed in a lockup area based on value. Every property has its own written procedure on how to handle lost and found items. Many complaints are received in letters or verbally from guests regarding the handling of their property, which can also include accusations that security took an item or removed something of value from a purse, wallet, or bag.

If a wallet (or purse) with cash and credit cards inside is turned in, certain procedures are typically followed. In many operations, security is required to have another officer present as a witness when the wallet is opened to determine the owner's name. This is done by probing through the wallet's contents, which are personal and often considered very private by the owner. Once an identity has been obtained, the owner is paged in the casino in an attempt to locate the rightful owner. Ideally the owner is located and verifies the contents, signs acceptance, and goes on his or her way. If the owner of the wallet is not located, the item is placed in the box or bin with other lost items. The decision is made to donate less valuable items to a local charity at some point in time. In larger casinos, this occurs in a rather short period of time (fifteen to thirty days) and in others the property is held for a longer period.

In the case of the wallet or purse, the most productive, professional, and safest way to dispose of the items is to turn them over to law enforcement as lost property. They can then make attempts to locate the rightful owner of the property if they choose to. If the casino attempts to locate the owner, problems can be created with customers who may not have told their spouses they were at the casino or in other uncomfortable circumstances.

Another area of lost and found that must be handled is when a customer calls and is told his or her item was found. The customer will want the item shipped and sometimes will demand immediate overnight delivery of it. This can create public relations issues yet it can also be expensive to ship thousands of items in a given year. Each property will have its own procedure for shipping and the costs associated with it.

Care should be given to premium customers regarding lost property. A simple check with the players' incentive club representatives will tell you if an individual is a premium customer and may dictate if the casino will send the item back via overnight delivery. The same holds true for hotel guests. As technology is integrated into security command centers, access to hotel and player tracking systems by security will become more common. Getting the lost items back to the owners in a professional manner is the objective.

11.6 INGRESS AND EGRESS POSITIONS

In many casinos, there are stationary positions located at main points of ingress/egress to the gaming area. This assignment can be mandated by regulators, necessitated by dram shop laws (liquor liability legislation), or can be manned as a voluntary position by the casino. These positions require a defined set of post instructions that contain specific requirements of the position. In these positions the primary functions are to watch for intoxicated patrons and to check identification to ensure no underage person enters. Additionally, these positions become critical during emergency operations or when attempting to locate a particular person.

The important function of monitoring for intoxicated individuals is defined by the local or state laws regarding liquor liability, which will be discussed later in this book. The basic premise is to prevent intoxicated persons from entering or exiting on their own. From an egress point of view, the security officer evaluates the level of intoxication, based on his or her training, and prevents the intoxicated patron from exiting, driving a vehicle, and possibly getting into an accident that could hurt or kill others or him- or herself.

Precise options should be available for this officer to be able to prevent this from occurring. For valet parking, it is a relatively simple process in that you merely would not give the keys back. In self-parking lots it becomes more of a challenge to obtain the keys or do what is reasonable to stop the person. The most effective way to solve this problem is to notify the local police of a possible drunk driver, and they will respond and handle the situation. Making it clear to the person who is intoxicated that the police will be called may thwart his or her attempt to drive while intoxicated. Other methods will be discussed later in the book.

Identification checks, as discussed earlier, are more difficult to manage and enforce in ingress/egress locations based on the repetitive function and human nature. Stationary security personnel should have a commercially produced identification guide at each post and use it to verify valid IDs. As indicated earlier, an officer can fall into the bad habit of only looking at the date of birth and nothing else. If underage persons or criminals with false identification can be confident the security officer is not looking at the other information on an ID, it is easy to breach the security position. Common distractions are used to get past these positions and the officers assigned should also be aware of this.

These stationary positions are also important for public relations. This is one of the first employees a customer will encounter and the approach and mannerisms that the stationary officer projects will more likely than not affect the attitude of the customer entering. If the officer has a positive, professional, and expeditious demeanor, the customer will not object to being asked for ID or momentarily stopped for screening. If the encounter is abrupt and mechanical, the customer will not appreciate it and enter the casino with the perception that this establishment does not care about the customer.

As in any public assignments, the officer should be pleasant and smile when greeting the customer, be neat and clean, and present an image that welcomes customers and makes them confident that security is there to protect them and not hassle them.

Stationary positions at all public ingress and egress locations can communicate quickly when an event occurs inside or outside the casino and can be very effective in deterring incidents as well as catching perpetrators. A simple radio transmission to all points at once can literally save a life in these environments.

11.7 EMPLOYEE ENTRANCES AND LOADING DOCKS

Theft or shrinkage in any operation that sells goods and services is always a security concern. Employees and vendors are typically the major culprits of theft, embezzlement, and fraud. The back door or loading dock becomes a focal point for control based on design and activity (Figure 11.1). In order to control inventory theft, there must be some form of security for basic inventory. From a vendor standpoint, all goods go in and out of this location and should be verified by someone. It is common for some vendors to take product that is not associated with their services and put it on a truck. An extreme example would be an electronics vendor who hides a case of lobsters that cost thousands of dollars on a cart with boxes of electronics.

Some operations maintain key controls at these locations and require all access keys to be signed in and out or locate automated key control systems in that location. In addition these positions could also maintain CCTV functions of the back of house areas and

Figure 11.1 Security loading docks are commonly used as employee and vendor exits and entrances—they can also be opportunities for theft.

exterior doors that require monitoring and control. In many other operations, parking lot cameras are piped into this position and the officer is charged with monitoring the activity. This is separate from the dispatch location, although the cameras can also be piped into the dispatch for mirrored surveillance if needed.

Critical gaming supplies such as playing cards, dice, chips, gaming devices, and other valuable items susceptible to access by outside criminals typically come through the back door where the internal controls need to be initiated in acceptance and delivery of these items. Careful inspection is required by regulation in most jurisdictions because of the importance of these consumables. Specially locked areas are designed to prohibit any access unless by preapproved managers. A chain of custody is typically strictly enforced regarding these gaming consumable items.

Employees typically will enter and exit through this dock location area also based on design. In newer casinos the time and attendance system allows for clocking in and out at various locations and dilutes the ultimate control of all employees entering and exiting past a security employee and the ideal ingress/egress control.

Spot checks of bags and packages are also completed without warning as a managing tool against theft. Well-defined policy and procedures for bag and package checks should also be in place and signed by all employees. Security personnel can accomplish these surprise inspections in a positive, friendly, and consistent manner. I have personally conducted or ordered many bag checks unannounced to my staff and the employee population and never had an inspection period where contraband or company property was not found on an employee.

The employee entrance areas are typically called the back door, loading dock, or employee entrance and are designed to keep out persons who are not authorized from entering nonpublic areas such as kitchens, housekeeping, engineering, and other service departments. Presentation of company-issued ID is done in person or in the form of access control systems by swipe or proximity reader, which records the time when any employee enters or exits these areas.

Visitors and vendors are usually screened, must be issued a visitor's badge before entering, and are required to sign out when they leave the building. The experienced security officer who has logged many hours at this position will be able to recognize furtive behavior or cues that will signal nonverbal communication of possible theft from the company and be able to act on them within the law and with professionalism.

In recent years, with economic challenges, many gaming operations have gone to ingress and egress management of these areas by card or other access means to include increased CCTV coverage. They have pulled the security officer from this function to save payroll. This creates additional opportunities for unauthorized personnel to enter the building, including piggybacking, which is the method of following quickly behind a person entering a building and therefore not using an access card to allow the electronic and mechanical access. The same holds true of gate access areas where a vehicle merely follows a vehicle inside and sensors allow the access.

Without a security officer posted at the location where all employees enter and exit the facility, the risk of unauthorized access is greatly increased. The multiple access points into employee areas also dilute the security function of this position if dishonest employees can simply use an exit that is not manned.

11.8 PATROL OF HOTEL AND GUEST ROOMS

If you have sleeping rooms in your facility, there are certain security concerns that come with the transient lodging business. First, you should consider that if your hotel has 500 rooms and is full, you have 500 individual family or group environments in one building. People will generally bring their quirks, habits, and personalities with them, which need to be respected while still attempting to keep a safe environment for your guests.

Until the economic downturn of 2008–2009, it was common for some casinos with hotels to post an officer at the elevator banks to verify that every guest had a keycard and was registered before entering the elevator. This system is a good deterrent for the casual petty criminal who would observe this process and immediately leave. For the professional criminal this is merely a minor obstacle to overcome. Locating any keycard dropped or discarded is relatively simple, and unless there is a verification machine and it is used, it is a simple process to wave the keycard at the officer and enter the hotel. Piggybacking and distractions are also easy to accomplish; when the officer is talking to a guest, the undesirable will merely walk with a guest and act as if he belongs by engaging in conversation as they get on the elevator.

Many operations have gone to the keycard access system in elevators. It requires the guest to use a room keycard to operate the elevator. This security feature can be easily defeated if a person quickly also presses a button or even steals the purse of a patron when the doors are closing. By the time the shocked guest gets to a telephone to report it, the criminal is long gone. These systems are helpful to the security system but should not be relied on as a sole measure of security for a hotel environment.

Patrols of the guest rooms, hallways, hotel lobby, arcade, spas, and meeting rooms should be accomplished as a full-time function, not assigned occasionally when the rest of the facility is not busy. There should be some specific training associated with hotel patrol functions. Security officers need to have consistent post instructions that define what functions are to be completed to provide guest safety to transient guests.

There is no known magic standard ratio of hotel rooms to number of officers patrolling the towers or buildings. The security director needs to evaluate the square footage of patrol areas, tasks required, electronic patrol requirements (if any), and historical data to design the frequency of patrols and staffing. The frequency of patrols in a hotel area will vary depending on the facility and can vary from twice per shift to every thirty minutes depending on the property. Interruptions in patrol can occur for reports and incidents, noise complaints, and other unpredictable events and should be considered in planning.

Patrol of hotel areas should always be documented for reference and investigative purposes. The easiest method to document would be to utilize an electronic patrol system that documents the locations of the security officer using bar codes or buttons and a wand. This system has evolved since the days of the round clock and punched keys of decades past and is quite easy to use. The officer touches the bar code as he passes each location and then, at the end of each shift, downloads it into a reader and computer that then produces a report for management or for use by investigators.

The electronic patrol systems are only as good as the patrolling officer and should not be relied on as a "cure all" for hotel patrols. Proper supervision is still required and the printouts should be analyzed regularly to include time between entries and ensuring that all areas are registered for the required number of times per shift.

These systems can and are easily integrated into dispatch log programs that will give the manager an easy method of checking on, analyzing, and managing security operations in the hotel areas as well as the entire property. Managers should be consistent in making sure that the system is used regularly and that there is an alternative recordkeeping system in place in the event the system in nonfunctional.

As an alternative the hotel officer can merely call the dispatcher on the radio and indicate the floor or area has been checked and is secure. For example, the patrol officer would call on the radio "eighth floor, code four" or something similar that is coded and simple. The dispatcher should have a sheet of paper that has a log of the locations and times of those calls for the record and for supervisors to manage and ensure the areas are patrolled at desired frequency.

Patrol of the guest floors should be accomplished in a random manner, leaving which floor or area to be patrolled up to each officer (Figure 11.2). Care should be given in random patrol functions to make sure every area is covered regularly. Security officers may not be able to recall which floors have been checked and might miss a floor after an incident call or event. Dispatchers and supervisors can check this regularly to ensure best patrol

FIGURE 11.2   Patrol of guest floors and hallways.

coverage. Patrol officers can keep track by notebook or patrol log if they are required to document each shift.

Functions of the hotel patrol officer should include making sure all guest doors are closed and locked, ensuring no loud parties or juvenile gatherings are occurring, managing noise complaints, checking fire suppression equipment, checking maid's closets and maintenance rooms, and stopping all nonregistered guests from wandering the hotel. Typically, if there is a hotel-related report to be completed, the hotel officer will complete the paperwork unless the property has a report writer, a person who completes all reports for the officers. These positions are usually found in larger gaming facilities.

Security officers are also charged with escorting and assisting guests who are having difficulty with keycards that won't work or lock problems in accessing their rooms. The security officer will verify the ID of the registered guest and not let anyone in who is not registered to be in the room. In addition, the security officer can ask a simple question like what is the brand name of a personal toiletry in the bathroom. Once inside the room, verification of ID will ensure the person is the registered guest and not a scam artist.

Challenging unregistered guests is a constant proactive function of any hotel security officer. All persons should be asked for a room keycard and thanked after they produce one. Any person wandering a hotel floor who is not a registered guest should be identified and the information logged with date of birth and description in the event a problem is discovered at a subsequent time. This process will often also deter the person from committing a crime knowing that security has his or her name and details. A recurring theme in this book is to approach, speak to, or identify anyone who appears to be loitering anywhere.

If the officer is suspicious that the person is not a registered guest yet has a keycard, the officer can escort the person to the room and call to verify the guest name against an ID. If the person does not belong, he or she should be clearly identified and a field interrogation card, or contact card, should be filled out from the identification presented. This process not only identifies who has been wandering the hotel and might have committed a crime, it also sends a clear signal that there is security patrolling the floors and has information on any wanderers.

Employees entering a hotel room that has been rented by a guest should be an exception and specific procedures should be followed. Each state has its own innkeeper laws that govern the rights of hotel guests regarding access and property. The guest has rented the room for a specific period of time and the basic rules of landlord and tenant should be followed. Employees cannot enter the room without permission unless for an established industry protocol such as maid service. Then the maid is not permitted to search the customer's luggage. The same holds true for security personnel.

Noise complaints are common where a group of people have a party or engage in arguments that are loud enough to disturb other patrons. Calls are typically made to the hotel operator who either takes the information or transfers the call to security. The first thing that can be done before making any contact is to verify the person who is complaining and the offending room number with a check to the hotel front desk. Hotel folios or registration card printouts will assist in this process. The front desk can also research prior history of noise or chronic complaints from the same rooms and provide this to the responding security officer. The only exception to this field investigation would be responding to a fight or potential life-threatening event where time is of the essence.

Once security personnel have the guest information, they can then stand outside the offending room for a brief period and verify the noise complaint before knocking on the door and asking them to quiet down. In many circumstances, incorrect room numbers or floor locations are given and the staff will have to answer the complaint letter of the guest who was awakened mistakenly by security. This verification process can be helpful in confirming the noise.

For the guests who will not comply with the request to quiet down, the legal eviction process can be started when all other attempts to resolve the issue have been tried. If the situation involves the removal of a guest from the hotel, the simplest method is to refund the night's hotel charge. Hotel management will resist this and will not understand that it will only exacerbate the situation if you throw someone out and not refund the money paid to stay in the room. In any event, an eviction should be a last resort and be done lawfully.

Hotel officers should also be pillars of public relations while patrolling in the hotel areas. They should be seen frequently and not heard (loud radios without ear buds or lapel microphones). Hotel patrol officers need to have compassion and understanding in dealing with upset customers, whether they were stuck in an elevator or victimized by a criminal.

People tend to get comfortable in a hotel and act as though they are in their own homes. It is not uncommon to observe a guest go to the ice machine clad only in his underwear or leave the entry door blocked open. Managing guest behavior in the hallways and hotel areas is important but should not be dictated by security personnel.

As with any assigned patrol area, a good management practice is to have a supervisor actually complete one full round of an area to familiarize him- or herself with the process and to evaluate the work load of the officer patrolling. The supervisor should be quite familiar with how long it takes to patrol a hotel tower or other area.

11.9 PATROLLING THE CASINO FLOOR

As in all gaming environments, the main function of security will be to patrol the casino floor and venues within the general gaming area. The first task is to divide the gaming area into patrol or beat areas that will identify locations for security functions and design areas of responsibility for each patrolling officer. The primary design of these areas should be made based on an absolute minimal staff to ensure coverage.

There are two basic types of casino patrol used in the industry: specifically assigned areas and roamers, where all officers are left to roam the area in random fashion. Careful consideration should be made when using a roaming casino patrol to include coverage, training, and supervision of the officers. I recommend the assigned area approach under normal casino conditions and environments. Absent intensive training and supervision, roaming systems traditionally are not effective in even coverage of a facility.

In the assigned area approach a blueprint is used, and the best document for this would be the property exit plan used by the fire department. This document is a footprint of the facility and is a good representation of the occupancy loads and fire and emergency exits and will accurately depict the property. The next document that is useful would be the slot plot map, which all casinos use to identify locations and denominations of slot and table games and generally shows basic locations. The slot plot maps depict slots, table games, and other features but will be limited to the casino floor.

Casino patrol areas can be designed in such a manner as to accomplish minimum mandated staff levels and maximum staff levels. As an example, a 30,000-square-foot casino can be split in half and assigned patrol zones one and two as the minimum level of patrol. Each zone can then be split in half again for maximum staffing of four officers during heavier customer volumes.

Supervisors and managers of security should also walk each patrol area to ensure the officer can patrol it at desired intervals. If any cash dispensing machines or bill validators are to be checked during the patrol, ensure that there is sufficient time to complete these also. Any ancillary change booths or banks, kiosks, vending machines, liquor storerooms, bars, restaurants, exit doors, and any other place that falls within the patrol area should be included in this zone of patrol.

For a new casino, I recommend that the casino patrol areas should start at approximately 10,000 square feet per patrolling officer. The director can adjust up or down in coverage area from that level of patrol based on other venues and factors as the business changes. These patrol areas should be marked and on display in the security office areas where all officers can clearly see the general boundaries of patrol. This is a recommended starting point and cannot be used as a standard by any operation, and many other factors should be considered when staffing a new operation.

At the beginning of the work shift, the supervisor will make the schedule assignments and assign an officer to each zone as his or her primary job assignment for the shift or for a specific time if positions are rotated. Rotation schedules are used in some environments to stimulate officers by changing the mundane assignments at specific intervals. Some directors feel that this is a positive way to keep staff alert and a fair method of assigning those jobs that are considered boring by the security officers.

When the shift starts, the officers are deployed with all of their equipment and begin work. The officers should also have a basic written description of what this patrol area consists of and what they are supposed to check and how they are supposed to patrol, as discussed earlier. These job positions, or post orders, will guide the staff through the basic functions that are unique to that area of patrol. If there are no unique functions or areas, the officer can follow the base policy and procedures established for the department. Some jurisdictions will mandate certain functions or positions in patrol areas and the regulations and the minimum internal controls need to be reviewed to ensure compliance.

The security officer should patrol the assigned area as the primary area of responsibility for the shift or hours assigned. The officer may be called out of the area to assist or back up another officer but should always return as the primary assigned officer of the original area. The officer will become familiar with the customers and surroundings and will be the best person to identify any unusual behavior or circumstances. Some properties require a daily activity report for each officer, including the casino patrol officers; however, the majority of gaming operations will merely have the dispatcher log activity as it occurs through radio communications. After a complete and full patrol of any gaming area is completed, the officer can call information to the dispatcher who logs it as completed. The dispatch then becomes a record of the patrols for any area of the property.

The casino patrol officer should first and foremost attempt to protect the people within his or her assigned area. This would include customers and employees as well as any vendors or outside agency employees. Patrol officers do this by watching out for safety hazards and third parties who might harm others for personal gain or other motives. Part of this process is to again stop, talk with, and identify any person who acts outside the normal patterns of a customer or employee.

This becomes more challenging in the gaming areas, and the officers need to approach and engage people regularly. By saying "Hello," straightening slot stools, and checking IDs of suspected minors and persons not gambling, officers will send clear and convincing signals that the area is patrolled. Other things that can be done are making sure customers do not leave purses, luggage, bags, coats, or other personal belongings in places that can be easily removed by others. An example would be placing belongings between machines where someone could reach through from an opposite direction and steal them.

As strange as it may sound to the outsider, the trash should be checked regularly by security personnel while on patrol of the casino. People will dispose of wallets and purses after they have removed the cash and other things that may be unwanted by a perpetrator. Empty alcohol bottles found regularly in a trash receptacle could be an indicator of employee alcohol abuse or a regular customer not following the established rules. I always recommend that casino patrol officers also do spot checks of trash removed by cleaning personnel from gaming areas. This can turn up some interesting items and is a good source of intelligence for activity in any area. People will typically discard all items in the trash with the assumption no one will check it.

When a person is merely walking around a casino, not gambling but rubbernecking (looking right and left), he or she should be watched to determine what the person is doing and where he or she is going. Security should always make its presence known to these individuals. In addition, surveillance should be notified to enable them to watch the person when possible. Care should be exerted to make sure the person is not legitimately merely waiting for a spouse or there for an innocent reason. There are customers who will spend a long period of time looking for the perfect slot machine that will give them large jackpots and they should not be confused with undesirables.

The undesirables are people who are up to no good and have been nicknamed many things over the years. In past years these people who prey on gamblers and casinos have been called slot walkers, seagulls, and scammers because of their typical behavior. They will walk through areas of slots or stand behind players on a table game looking for an opportunity to palm a chip, take a slot TITO (ticket in, ticket out) slip, an unattended purse, or any item that presents an opportunity for them. They are not always homeless or offensive in appearance.

The first method of deterring these unwanted persons is to identify and engage them in conversation and either determine their intentions or at least make them nervous. They typically will not have ID when requested, so they may be immediately escorted to the door and advised that they are on private property and they must be identified to remain there or are just unwanted there, if the circumstances warrant. Surveillance photographs can be taken from video for documentation and future briefings in the event the person becomes a repeat offender, which is usually the case. It is very important to watch for and legally remove these predators from the casino floor regularly to keep the people safe from minor petty crimes as well as those that may develop out of desperation like robbery or assault.

As previously discussed, any ingress or egress point in the assigned area should be thoroughly checked. The officer can walk outside and patrol the designated area of the exterior near the doors, inspect any trash receptacles, look for any vagrants or undesirables, and enter back in to the facility. This will create an overlap in the patrol function with the exterior patrol officer in this important area.

Restrooms are often overlooked within any environment, including casinos. If there are restrooms within the area of responsibility, the officers need to patrol them regularly. For those smaller operations where a female officer is not available, another department female supervisor can assist in this function. Because restrooms are not covered by CCTV systems, they are vulnerable for crime, scams, and safety hazards.

When I was a security director we had a very popular nightclub that was frequented by university students on the weekends. The security officers assigned to the nightclub were not patrolling the restrooms just outside of the main doors as I had instructed. I required the supervisor, as part of his duties one day, to sit inside a stall in that restroom at peak times and make observations of what he heard and saw. In just a thirty-minute time period he discovered the world of bathroom crime and activity, which solved my patrol issue. I had learned this technique from a manager when I was assigned bathroom stall duty during training.

Many crimes can occur inside a restroom. Very highly publicized homicides and violent crimes have occurred over the years as casinos pop up in all jurisdictions. The case of the molestation of seven-year-old girl in a southern Nevada casino near an arcade ended tragically as a homicide. Although this was a highly unusual incident, it illustrates what can occur inside a restroom.

In another casino, and at a local security chiefs' association meeting, I learned of a team of criminals who were preying on victims inside restrooms. In the Reno, Nevada, area, a group of two men and one woman targeted restrooms for people to rob of their cash. After marking them (identifying them as good victims), they would wait for victims to enter the restroom and follow them in. The woman would enter the adjacent stall, wait, and then remove the purse of the woman sitting on the toilet by merely reaching over the wall of the stall and lifting it from the purse shelf or door hook. By the time the victim could react and exit the restroom, the purse and belongings were long gone.

The men in the criminal team were victimizing the men in the restrooms in a much more dangerous manner. These two thugs would wait for a man to walk into a stall and wait to see his pants around his ankles. One would then keep watch while the other reached under the stall, grabbed the belt and pants from between the victim's ankles, and pulled as hard as he could, which would cause the victim to fall off the toilet and he would then remove the man's wallet while he was obviously distracted. The police eventually caught this group in a well-organized sting operation through the cooperation of several casinos and law enforcement.

Drugs are commonly used in a restroom stall because of the privacy it affords. Smells and sounds will usually prompt the security officer to suspect drug use. Another good indication of drug use inside of restrooms is the tops of the toilet paper dispensers or other level surfaces will have tarnished areas. A close look at these areas will produce many cut marks from razor blades or other sharp devices that are commonly used in drug preparation and abuse. Looking for other drug-related evidence is also helpful to deter the activity.

Looking for multiple people in one stall can be an indicator of something illegal or just wrong. There are many legitimate reasons for two sets of legs in a toilet stall, such as minor children assisted by their parents or handicapped persons assisted in various ways. There is an expectation of privacy inside a restroom stall, and officers should always respect that privacy whenever possible. There are circumstances when two sets of feet are observed and certain sounds are emanating from the stall for which security needs to take some action.

The subcultures involving casual same-sex encounters also occur inside restroom facilities and should be stopped whenever observed or suspected. Private locations inside restrooms will become regular hotspots for this activity and will quickly become sites for this type of activity if not deterred immediately. Any officer who has worked vice will tell you this occurs in the most unlikely environments. "Cruising" restrooms is common for this subculture, and taking a little time and effort will reduce this activity. Your local police can assist in preventing this type of unwanted activity.

Then there are the heterosexual encounters that occur in the same manner. People become aroused and use a public restroom to have sexual relations in a semipublic location. There are some people who must have this type of environment to complete the sex act and will merely use a bathroom stall in a men's or lady's restroom. This is more common in nightclub or bar environments but does occur in casino bathrooms as well.

Safety hazards are also prevalent in restroom facilities. Water on the tile floor, broken fixtures or walls, and general cleanliness issues should be reported to prevent a serious accident. Every time an officer checks a restroom, it can be logged by the dispatcher to demonstrate that the location has been patrolled at various times during a particular shift.

11.10 SECURING PARKING LOTS AND GARAGES

Other vulnerable areas of any facility are the parking lots and garages that are attached for customers and employees to use while inside the casino. A parking area should always have someone assigned to monitor or patrol it to provide a reasonable level of protection. The size, shape, design, and environmental conditions will dictate the level of security required in the parking area and the number of security officers that should be assigned to patrol it.

Parking lots and garages are typically open and have multiple access points, making it difficult to harden this very public and soft target (Figure 11.3). As a result, providing a reasonable level of security in a parking environment should be emphasized by any security manager or director. Typical crimes that might occur in parking areas are robbery, assault, rapes, and larceny crimes, including auto burglaries and theft of autos. Additionally, other crimes that occur in these environments are narcotics use and sale, prostitution, and anything else that can occur inside or outside of a vehicle.

In addition, many activities within the vehicles in a lot or garage are undesirable to a gaming environment. From the casual third-party weary traveler who pulls in to get a few

FIGURE 11.3   Parking lot and garage security is an important consideration.

minutes or hours of sleep to the employee who decides to take a work break in his or her personal vehicle; this location requires security presence and occasional intervention.

Because parking lots create many visual obstacles for security personnel, patrol on foot, on bicycle, or in some form of vehicle is the desirable method. The larger the area of patrol, the more security personnel are required to accomplish a regular presence of obvious security. In small neighborhood casinos, the inside security officers will typically walk outside and patrol the lot on foot at frequent intervals. In any event, the physical presence of a uniformed security officer is desired to deter undesirable or criminal behavior and displace it from the property.

Employees will go to vehicles for many reasons during their work shift if not controlled by policy and procedure or department supervisors. The reasons could be as innocent as they forgot their name tag to drinking alcohol or taking illegal drugs or narcotics. Whenever a person is observed inside a vehicle in a parking lot, the security officer should take note and observe to determine the reason that person is sitting or moving inside a parked car.

The patrolling officer may also come upon two or more people who decide that this is a location for various sex acts. This behavior must be stopped as soon as possible and the parties identified if possible. These situations can result in sexual assault allegations at a later time or the property might be blamed for inadequate security and litigation because the activity occurred in your casino parking lot.

Leaving children alone inside a vehicle is also more common than most people believe. Many citations and prosecutions have occurred across the United States after a child was left in a vehicle for hours while the parents drank and gambled inside. When this occurs, the first priority should be the safety and comfort of the children and to make sure they are hydrated and taken to a safe place without scaring them. Careful consideration should be given when making comments in front of children who have become separated from their parents. Comments about the irresponsibility of the parents can have a long-lasting effect on young ears. In these cases the local law enforcement should be called as soon as possible and a search by security personnel for the parents or guardians should be carried out.

The most common vehicle-related crime will typically be auto burglary. These crimes occur in virtually every environment, including police department parking areas. The crime is typically one of opportunity where a suspect will observe an item inside a vehicle and break in to take it. People become victims when the vehicle doors are unlocked, thereby making it easy for the criminal. In most situations, there is some form of forced entry, and it typically involves a smashed window.

The officers patrolling the parking areas can be trained to look for the telltale sign of a burglary, which includes broken window glass in the parking lot. Even if there is no victim and glass is observed, it is more likely than not that a crime has occurred but was not reported. There may be circumstances that involve rightful owners breaking a window out of impatience when they locked their keys inside, but that would be rare. Broken glass usually indicates negative activity.

As the electronics sold to consumers become more portable, the items stored or mounted inside a vehicle become primary targets for the burglar. Collecting a few GPS devices or satellite receivers will bring decent cash at a local pawn shop, especially if the owner does not report the theft to the police. Vehicles with the windshield suction cup mounts for their electronics almost always say "take me" to a vehicle burglary suspect. In many tourist destinations where this occurs, the police have implemented an awareness program warning customers as they park to put those items out of sight. Significant reductions of crimes have been observed where these programs are implemented.

Motor homes become a nuisance if they are allowed to be parked at a gaming facility. In some gaming properties the use of an official recreational vehicle (RV) area helps reduce security issues with these vehicles. In other environments, they are required to be registered with parking permits. A fee can be charged (or waived for premium customers) as a deterrent. The property can make sure that sitting on lawn chairs, using barbecues, and other camping activities are not occurring as a result of allowing RVs to park in the lots. The obvious transient in the older motor home who sets up permanent residency in your lot should be immediately discouraged.

Assistance in parking environments comes with customer use, and it starts the first day you let people park their vehicles. Calling locksmiths, tow trucks, and jumpstarts of dead batteries will be the normal requests. The most common will be when a person cannot find his or her vehicle and will tell security that it has been stolen. Security then assists the customer in finding the vehicle, which is typically parked somewhere in the area. In the event it is actually missing, then the process of looking for the vehicle has already been accomplished.

There are instances where a spouse or relative may have taken the car, parked it at another casino, and then walked back to your casino or it may have been repossessed for lack of payments. All of these questions should be asked as you are driving around with the customer looking for the vehicle. In most environments, the local police are required to be notified prior to a repossession. A call to them may save time and manpower if the vehicle was repossessed. Not all repossession companies comply with these local laws, so the question should still be politely asked of the customer who is frantically looking for a missing car.

Security personnel need to be aware that a vehicle is the personal property of another and is protected by the law. The security officer cannot search a vehicle or seize property from it even if it is considered illegal. This is the job of law enforcement. The security officer should point the items out to the responding law enforcement professional who will take the appropriate and legal actions. The key is to provide a reasonable level of security for the customers and employees who park at your facility

Understanding that the parking areas in any environment are private allows for simple solutions to deter the undesirables by asking them to leave and advising them of the trespass law. Making sure that there are appropriate signs posted throughout the lots and garage as well as warning guests to lock cars and stow away valuables will assist in the enforcement of the trespass law. Obvious security presence has proven to be a valuable tool in deterring undesirable and criminal behavior in public access parking lots.

11.11 PLAIN-CLOTHES SECURITY

In most gaming security environments, supervisors do not wear uniforms and wear business casual clothing. They will perform the simple tasks involved in plain-clothes security and can make casual observations. There are other circumstances where plain-clothes security assignments can be used to enhance special investigations or targeted patrol areas, as described later. The primary function of gaming security is to be obvious and be seen as a deterrent. In certain circumstances where this approach does not deter incidents or crime, a different solution may be required other than hidden CCTV cameras and specialized investigations.

I always found that using a plain-clothes team was not only productive in catching people in the act of crimes, but also was a huge morale booster to the staff when they could dress down and do some exciting work rather than just running fills and credits. It also became apparent that word would get out that your property has uniformed security and plain-clothes security wandering around, even though it is, in actuality, infrequently implemented. As a result of the benefits, I would occasionally set up a team of two officers to a surprise package check at the employee ingress/egress points for maximum effect.

Surprise inspections of employee packages, bags, and backpacks always revealed theft of some form from office supplies to items of significant value. The plain-clothes team working a detail would be assigned a random time to do inspections at various locations, even if only for a portion of an hour at a time. This was quite effective in keeping internal theft at a minimum and was a motivation for security personnel when you would assign them a task that was sure to get results and where they might catch an employee removing property of some type without permission or stealing it outright.

I always tried to make sure that I used two officers as a team for safety and, in the event they were in a position to effect an arrest, there would be adequate control of a suspect. I liked to use this as training and it would help the officers learn to dress so that the radio and handcuffs they were carrying would not be visible, even when they moved naturally. It also taught them how to blend in rather than have the look of a security officer by the way they made obvious observations. Teaching them how to use casino mirrors to watch someone and to anticipate criminal moves was always appreciated by the staff and made them feel a sense of accomplishment that they were chosen for a plain-clothes detail.

Requiring a report at the end of the shift gives officers the opportunity to state what they accomplished on their shift, which, in itself, is a training motivator and it documents the detail as a proactive security measure for future use in demonstrating a proactive security department.

11.12 TARGET AREA SECURITY

Even when all areas of a casino property are covered by patrolling personnel and CCTV cameras, incidents or hotspots will require some form of security response for a proactive security department. I have coined the targeted security presence as *target area security* (TAS), which is a flexible patrol system that works without the hiring of additional security personnel to solve a temporary issue. Any seasoned security director should have a similar program.

Not all departments are large enough to create "power shifts" where a shift of officers is scheduled outside the normal shifts to address problems at the busier times of the casino. Power shifts are useful when incident occurrence rates are obvious and manpower adjustments are warranted to solve the problem. There will still be hotspots that will flare up in the property and creative solutions will be required if the desired result is to reduce or eliminate incidents.

The objective of the TAS program is to provide a reasonable response to a problem to include increased security presence, documentation of increased patrols, and of course deterrence of criminal or undesirable behavior. The program is flexible to the needs of the property and is a desirable solution in the economic conditions of the twenty-first century based on manpower limitations.

The results of this simple program will be the flood of security personnel into an affected area, which will create the illusion to the outside observer that there are many more security personnel than there actually are. The results are immediate, but these measures obviously cannot be sustained for long periods of time. The concept is not new and has been used in law enforcement applications for decades. The technique is typically referred to as *directed patrol activity*, where an administrator or supervisor directs the police to complete drive-through patrols of a neighborhood or location whenever they are in the area.

The normal security patrols still need to be maintained and the TAS is implemented as an enhancement to the environment rather than as a replacement. It is important that all security staff on duty be aware of the targeted area and support the program in all aspects for it to have a successful outcome.

At the beginning of each shift, the oncoming security supervisor identifies two areas to be targeted by the security officers. The decision is based on activities of the previous shifts, directives from the security director, or coverage of an area that has not received appropriate attention. One area selected can be for the protection of people and the other can be selected for protection of an asset. The areas are designated and announced to the security officers during the preshift briefing along with particulars of what to watch for or what actions should be taken. As an example, if there are purse thefts occurring in a particular area of a slot section and a suspect has been identified from a neighboring property, that information is disseminated to security personnel. For illustrative purposes, the following examples are offered.

Target Area: Slot sections four and five, main casino (TAS-1): A series of purse thefts and lost reports have been filed in areas four and five of the main casino during the past several days. One event at a neighboring casino was an actual purse snatching and the victim was injured. Coats, purses, wallets, and various personal items are reported lost or stolen. Wallets and purses, empty of cash and valuables, have been located in trash cans.

Target Area: Garbage compactor area (TAS-2): The executive chef has reported that an employee was observed by an anonymous employee placing a package of lobster tails next to the garbage compactor the previous day. The value of the lobsters was $1,200. During the preshift briefing, the supervisor tells all security personnel and surveillance of the targets and the details. The security dispatcher sets up a log that identifies the areas and a simple method to document the particular officer and the time that each check is made (Figure 11.4).

Once personnel are on duty and patrolling, these two designated areas get emphasis throughout the shift. Personnel are well aware that they must pass through this area each time they return from a work break and any time they are within the general area. At the conclusion of each check, all personnel including the supervisor are required to call on the radio that the area is secured and has been checked. The dispatcher is charged with making sure all personnel have made additional checks each hour from the log. The surveillance personnel can also do a camera patrol of the affected area at designated and random times to document the customers and possible suspects, which will aid in the investigation. They can also assist and covertly watch for activity in conjunction with the security staff in a high-profile patrol mode.

Additional personnel can be assigned on special duties or more serious problem areas to enhance the program. Plain-clothes details by security officers or investigators can also be very effective to flood the particular area with security presence. In example TAS-1, the trash cans will need to be checked in each area to narrow times in the event an empty

Target Area Security Log							

TAS-1	Slot Sections 4 and 5 including south exit doors, trash cans, storage room.						
Time:	16:20	S/O	B-4	Time: 16:40	S/O	B-2	
	16:22		S-1	16:45		S-1	
	16:31		B-7	16:41		B-4	

TAS-2	Garbage Compactor area: Inside and outside check of packages hidden in and around compactor.						
Time:	16:18	S/O	M-1	Time: 16:50	S/O	B-9	
	16:28		S-1	16:51		M-1	
	16:31		B-6	17:00		B-6	

FIGURE 11.4 Sample target area security log.

wallet is located. The cleaning department is involved and must also closely examine the trash before it is disposed of.

Any person in the slot area who is not gambling, appears suspicious, or displays any unusual behavior should be identified if possible and asked to leave if necessary. Field interrogation cards are useful in these situations and will document the contact. The outside mobile officer can pay particular attention to ingress and egress into that portion of the casino and check outside trash receptacles or the trash compactor frequently.

The results are amazing when you review the documented presence of the security personnel. This log can be invaluable if a lawsuit is filed for inadequate security and you need to prove that you had effective response to crimes against persons.

In TAS-2 the trash compactor is an area where theft occurs regularly in any environment. Some employees will take dishes, silverware, lobsters, steaks, or anything else out through the area because it is typically not thoroughly checked. Security personnel are not usually posted at the trash dumping area to check each load. The employee who is motivated to steal will place the casino's property inside the trash then place the can somewhere near the compactor fence area where a gap is located, and he or she can either pick it up later or another person will grab the goods for the employee.

In the trash compactor area, the immediate presence will certainly cause a stir in the employees working there, but the primary objective is to deter the activity and not necessarily catch the thief. A special investigation with covert cameras or surveillance would be desirable if the objective is to catch the thief rather than deter him or her. Combine this with the other area (TAS-1) and you have the cleaning personnel also aware that security is watching trash, and this action will further let employees know something is happening and that they can never be sure when those security officers might be checking their trash.

The employee population will also take note of the activity within the security department and will certainly be aware that at any time security could flood their area of work. These other employees will also start getting into the act and become more observant in the future as a result of the activity. Regulators and law enforcement will also take notice and the logs will demonstrate a proactive security presence.

Care should be given to make sure the normal security functions remain unchanged. Piling up too many target areas will diminish the effect on solving problems. Strategic thinking by the management staff will only increase the effectiveness of security as a whole. This is a good tool to utilize in response to major events, including robbery, assaults, fights, or other crimes against people.

12

Alcohol and the Gaming Environment

12.1 RESPONSIBLE ALCOHOL SERVICE

Alcohol and gambling are typically enjoyed by almost any gaming patron. Selling or providing complimentary alcohol to customers is a practice that has been around since legalized gambling began in 1931 in Nevada. The courts have established, on numerous occasions, that this combination creates a fertile environment for some criminal activity, which includes alcohol-related crimes such as driving while intoxicated and being drunk in public. Along with the service of alcohol comes a certain amount of responsibility or legal duty that a casino has to its patrons (Figure 12.1).

When a casino allows a customer to become intoxicated and then has him or her arrested for being drunk in public or ejects the customer from the casino, the incident creates negative customer relations and the perception that the casino does not care about its customers. That perception includes the premise that casinos will get customers drunk and then summarily eject or arrest them after they become intoxicated.

In most states and jurisdictions, there are liquor liability (dram shop) laws that specifically assign liability to anyone who serves an intoxicated person. The specific laws of each jurisdiction will dictate the minimum standard (statutory law) and the measures a gaming property should put in place. In those states where there is no specific liquor liability, laws are typically ordinances in specific counties or cities that deal with serving intoxicated individuals.

The dram shop concept comes from a historical reference to taverns in England. *Dram* was a unit of measure of ale, and *shop* referred to the bar or tavern from which you could obtain liquor. Over time, the overintoxication of certain people proved problematic to even a tavern owner who would typically put an inebriated man on his horse and deliver him to his wife at the end of the night because he felt obligated to make sure he got the man home safe after getting him drunk.

With the repeal of prohibition in 1933 and with the passing of the Twenty-First Amendment to the U.S. Constitution, state alcohol liability laws began surfacing to control the social drinking of customers who paid for alcohol in a bar. These laws, along with the local ordinances, may include mandatory alcohol management training, cutting

Figure 12.1 With the service of alcohol comes a certain amount of legal responsibility that a casino has to its patrons.

off intoxicated patrons, and prohibiting serving an obviously intoxicated individual. The industry as a whole has an obligation to manage alcohol service and consumption in a responsible manner.

12.2 MANAGING INTOXICATION

Each gaming establishment will normally have a procedure in place to deal with intoxicated patrons. In most cases, the procedure is in writing and follows the local laws regarding alcohol. First and foremost the important thing to remember is that, regardless of the amount of alcohol a person has consumed, after the first drink, the intoxication process has begun. Different people have different intoxication thresholds, but there are certain symptoms of intoxication that will be exhibited by almost everyone.

Every state has what it has determined is the legal intoxication level to operate a motor vehicle, and in some cases, states have established the same limits for pedestrians. You should be aware of your jurisdiction's level of intoxication. In almost all areas of the country, the blood alcohol concentration (BAC) of 0.08 is the level to be considered legally intoxicated to operate any type of vehicle and in some jurisdictions to be eligible for public intoxication arrest.

One of the most difficult and challenging functions of a security officer is to deal with an intoxicated person. Since judgment and loss of inhibitions are two of the early symptoms, most intoxicated persons are already past normal reasoning when the security officer is called to handle a situation or personally makes the observation. The individuals typically perceive that they are not intoxicated and argue the point to the extreme. The first step in dealing with them is to engage them and conduct a brief field investigation. Determining if they are with friends, family, or a spouse would be a good start to establish any potential outside assistance. Another initial step is to determine if they are staying at your hotel facility.

Once the security officer has determined these facts, then the process of delivering them to friends, who are hopefully not intoxicated, is a simple one. In the event the person is alone, lives alone, or has no one to help him or her, the process becomes more complicated. After determining whether the person has a vehicle the next step would be to prohibit the person from driving.

If valet parking is the location of the person's vehicle, this would be a relatively simple process of not allowing the person to receive the keys. If the vehicle is self-parked, it may become necessary to obtain the person's keys from him or her. There are certain people who have and carry an extra set of car keys somewhere on their person and the vehicle should be closely monitored by outside security personnel regardless of where it is located. In some properties, the vehicle is actually reparked when this occurs.

In those circumstances where the patron becomes obnoxious or insistent that he or she will drive and you cannot stop him or her, the local police or sheriff should be called immediately and requested to help deal with the incident. Most law enforcement agencies have laws that allow them to take a person for civil protective custody where he or she is taken to a jail and allowed to become sober without fear of a criminal record. Law enforcement officers do not enjoy dealing with a drunk either and sometimes are resistant to this solution.

Getting the person home would be the next step in the process. Merely dumping the person out the doors or into another facility is not a desired option. If the person leaves on his or her own accord, the local law enforcement should be notified. This records the incident and that you took the necessary steps in the event that same person wanders onto a busy street and is injured or killed. Again, what is reasonable is the question that should be asked when ejecting an intoxicated patron.

A common practice is to establish an account with a local taxi company for the purposes of getting those intoxicated patrons safely home. Shuttle buses and other vehicles can also be used in unusual circumstances. There are circumstances that may even require that a security employee go in the taxi and be returned to the casino to ensure the person gets home safely. If the person is in medical distress as a result of overintoxication, emergency personnel should be called immediately to evaluate his or her condition for possible alcohol poisoning or severe intoxication that could lead to serious injury or death. The key is to do what is reasonable under all the circumstances. It is not expected that you should babysit the person for hours and tie up one or more officers.

Certainly, the primary objective should be to prevent people from becoming overintoxicated in the first place. This is not an easy task and involves many employees in the process. All servers should be trained, supervised, and diligent at evaluating customers for level of intoxication. A bartender, for instance, should not serve alcohol to anyone who is exhibiting signs of overintoxication, even if the person came into the establishment in that condition. Surveillance should monitor bars and service areas to prevent "overpouring" and violations to the alcohol policy for the property. Security officers can be alert for these customers in outside parking areas, restrooms, and sitting areas throughout the facility.

The outside security officer is an important component in monitoring intoxication of customers who are arriving and attempting to leave the facility. The vehicle patrol log should note any actions taken or observations made regarding intoxication. Sometimes allowing a person to sleep inside his or her vehicle is the best solution if you remove the keys and leave a note that tells the person where to obtain the keys once he or she becomes sober. Each situation will need to be evaluated for a proper response by security and not all events have the same blanket solution.

Documenting contact in these situations will prove beneficial in several ways. If a person has been "cut off" from receiving additional alcohol, a system should be in place to identify this person and communicate it to the appropriate employees. A log for those incidents could be maintained by security, surveillance, or beverage supervisors. The facility should make every attempt to stop serving alcohol to an intoxicated person. The easiest method for reporting this is for the server to notify the beverage supervisor who would confirm it, then that supervisor notifies security and surveillance who document the observation and action. The beverage supervisor is also in the best position to ensure that all servers are made aware of the person and the fact he or she has been cut off from alcohol. It also will be good for the supervisor to be able to monitor the servers to determine if they are complying with the alcohol management policy and procedure. Recurring incidents of intoxication of customers from the same server can be managed effectively in this scenario.

Only time, along with no alcohol consumption, will remedy the intoxication level of an individual. Although food does not sober up a person, it does slow down the intoxication process and allows for alcohol to be eliminated from the body without continued drinking. There are circumstances where getting the person into a restaurant and getting him or her some food can be helpful in dealing with a prolonged incident. Since alcohol is eliminated by the average person at a rate of approximately one ounce per hour, it may take many hours for the person to become sober. It should also be remembered that alcohol will continue the intoxication process for some time after the last drink has been consumed. In some cases the intoxication level continues to rise and peaks several hours later.

The proactive security department will have a policy and procedure for dealing with alcohol in all of the areas I have indicated. Training is an important component and all security personnel should be trained not only in alcohol management but also in methods to deal with intoxicated individuals. Having tools for the security officer to use in these situations will prove invaluable in investigating alcohol-related incidents.

Creative solutions to dealing with an intoxicated guest will be used to safely handle the person that cannot handle him- or herself. It will involve much patience and understanding to ultimately protect the customer and the casino. Security personnel should know that part of their job is to deal with intoxication, and proper training in effective techniques will go a long way in solving each individual instance they will encounter.

Customers are typically just looking for a good time and somehow had too much to drink. In most cases they most likely became intoxicated at your facility. Care should be given in dealing with these customers to include support, compassion, and mostly patience. The key will be that you provide reasonable care to intoxicated persons and document that you have a proactive program in the event of an alcohol-related accident or other negative alcohol-related event.

FIGURE 12.2   Nightclubs present dynamic environments and unique security challenges.

12.3 NIGHTCLUBS, ULTRA LOUNGES, AND LARGE BARS

Nightclub attendance has become an increasingly popular social event in the twenty-first century. As gaming properties became larger in size and more competitive, the nightclub business has became a desirable part of the facility (Figure 12.2). This cash-rich environment comes with certain risks and inherent problems that require management's attention at all times. The numerous venues with catchy one-syllable names became prevalent in gaming properties in the late 1990s and continued into the 2000s. These clubs became larger and highly competitive to attract the growing market. Nightclubs became a valuable source of revenue to the gaming operation. Revenues were either generated directly by proprietary personnel or leases were generated with entertainment companies to run the operations with rents based on collected revenues.

The social interactions of younger generations will typically dictate the needs and wants of the customers who desire a nightclub as a form of entertainment. The nightclub marketing gurus will make the venue exciting and a "must see" attraction by offering new and trendy décor, quality music and entertainment, professional lighting and sound equipment, and a comfortable atmosphere. The demand that this creates will generate substantial revenues and gratuities that must be responsibly managed.

A professionally prepared policy and procedure manual for nightclub security is a foundation for the security function. These should be prepared and reviewed by executive level management, risk management, and a company attorney. Known incidents or actions that will most likely occur in a nightclub should be documented to create a consistent application of the security function. If the security employees are left to their own decision process in an incident, they will do what they think is the right thing rather than what the company wants them to do. A well-prepared security manual for a nightclub will also assist in consistency, enforcement of rules, and conduct of security personnel.

In the larger and more popular nightclubs there is usually a long line waiting to enter the nightclub. At the entrance there will typically be several roped-off areas that allow the door hosts or security officers to separate out the regular paying guests from the various types of VIPs. The first thing that is important to know is that everyone who comes to a nightclub thinks he or she is a VIP and knows someone who will let him or her ahead of the line.

Part of the social process in a nightclub is that you must give the appearance that you are important and know someone important to bypass these often long and uncomfortable lines. There are numerous types of "VIPs" that will approach security to get inside quicker and easier. The most common method is of course to attempt to slip the door host or security a cash gratuity to instantly become a VIP. This is a dangerous process that must be watched and managed by competent managers to ensure that rules, regulations, and applicable local laws are complied with.

Tipping employees is a practice that is considered acceptable in nightclub environments. Management should have a distinct and clear gratuity policy that includes when a security employee can and cannot accept a gratuity. Cash is certainly a motivator to violate policy and procedure for many people. The risk of losing employment and the subsequent income from authorized tips will also motivate compliance with the house rules. The gratuity issues always start at the door and permeate through the venue and the process of enjoying a nightclub.

Typical gratuity issues will include heavy tipping by underage persons to attempt entry, line passes and bypassing of long waits, reentry into the venue, requests by females to watch personal belongings such as purses, guarding of tables or couches, and many other unusual circumstances. Whatever the house policy is, it should be well documented and reasonably enforced to ensure that laws and ordinances are followed and customers are treated fairly in the process.

Most people who enter a large nightclub for the first time are unaware of the rules of the club. Customers cannot be expected to know the rules unless those rules are repeatedly communicated prior to entry. This can be done through posted signs and verbally by personnel. Some operations hand the waiting patrons a small brochure of upcoming events and a list of rules and prohibited conduct on the back that they can read during those long waits in line. Many incidents occur after a group of people enter a nightclub and pay a "cover charge" for the pleasure of entering. There is typically no first drink free, no seats to sit down at, a line at the bar, and heavy drink prices once you are able to order. This creates misunderstandings that can quickly escalate into major incidents.

Another typical communication problem in nightclubs is when a group of friends enters and one hands over a credit card to another to buy their friend a few drinks. They are not told the prices or service charges involved, and after a couple hours they are presented a bill for hundreds of dollars. They are charged for the privilege of the couch they are sitting at, a bottle service charge, and other fees they had no idea were part of the process. They balk at the charge, refuse to pay, and an incident occurs where the cardholder is sometimes arrested. This is not a positive experience for the customer and does little for future business. Redundant communication of prices and rules before customers enter can limit these types of incidents.

As each customer finds his or her way to the cashier that is taking in the cover charge or "comping" guests for various reasons (after a long wait in line), the customer finally gets to the front door of the nightclub. To control ingress and egress, some form of marking is required to identify that the customer has paid for entry or that he or she is a VIP of some type. Typically a wristband or rubber-inked stamp is used. Colors, types, and locations (right or left wrist) should be varied to limit those who attempt to bypass the process. This is also important when the customer exits the nightclub to gamble or do other things and returns at a later time.

People can get very creative in a variety of ways and for various reasons in attempting to enter a nightclub. A wrist band can be easily duplicated and a busy door host or security will not necessarily examine it closely at the reentry line. The high prices of some of these venues will motivate creativity in duplicated or forged wristbands or stamps. Controlling minors is critical at nightclub environments and persons who appear young should be rechecked for identification (ID) at reentry points.

Another issue that should be monitored is the misconception by all nightclub personnel that if customers got by the door once, they had their IDs checked and they are of legal age to be inside. Just because the ingress/egress system at the main entrance is designed well does not mean that a person cannot enter the venue at some other location, slip in while security is handling a disruption, or use a fake wristband. If a person appears underage, he or she should be checked regardless of whether the person was checked when first entering.

The marking should be well defined and as highly visible as possible for security personnel to quickly ascertain that the customer has permission to enter and has either paid or has been invited. Ink stamps that wash off easily or wristbands that slide off easily can create issues when a person attempts to reenter or is confronted inside the venue without the clear entry device.

The cover charge in most venues is a large source of income. Originally cover charges were established to keep undesirables from entering a nightclub. People with bad hygiene, inappropriately attired, drink stealers, and those with no funds who merely wanted to socialize were unwanted. The cover charge evolved over the past thirty years into a method to create a revenue source and record the number of people who were legitimately considered customers.

Room capacities became an issue as the popularity of nightclub venues increased. The local fire department will dictate the maximum number of people in any environment and a specific exiting plan will be approved to evacuate that room in the event of an emergency. The room capacity includes employees and vendors and should be considered the base number when making room counts.

There are several reasons that room counts are important in the security and safety of a nightclub. First and foremost should be that the room should not exceed the legal capacity in the event of an emergency. Second is that the more overcrowded a nightclub becomes, the higher the chance of fights or shoving matches will occur as a result. With the exception of the actual dance floor area, a customer or employee should be able to navigate through any other area with ease. Third is that management is able to monitor the heavy business times and more efficiently manage the people and revenues. Last is that the safety of the customers and employees requires that capacities be maintained under the threshold or occupancy load. The recent fires in nightclubs that were overcrowded—the Station nightclub in West Warwick, Rhode Island, and the E2 club in Chicago, Illinois, both in 2003, come to mind—demonstrate the importance of maintaining approved occupancy levels.

A record of the counts becomes a valuable document in litigation, and for demonstrating compliance of laws and regulations to local law enforcement or fire department officials. In today's technology there are automated systems that can count as each person enters or exits a particular venue. I always recommend an actual head count by a designated security officer who then logs the count at specific intervals. The minimum increment of time should be one hour and every half hour during peak business periods if necessary. Nightclubs can fill up quickly and busy employees may not notice overcrowding until it is too late.

The maximum capacity of the room must be managed and monitored at all times. The number of people who exit should dictate the number of new people who can be allowed inside. When the capacity of the room is met or the room appears overcrowded, the quickest and easiest method is to "hold the door," which merely means that no new customers be allowed in until a certain number of existing customers have exited. Reentry points are slowed down until the room returns to the desired occupancy level.

At the end of the night the count log will reflect the number of people who were inside the room at various times throughout the night. If you compare this to the cashier customer counts you should be able to determine the base number of customers in an evening. It is not unusual for a successful nightclub to have three times the capacity in a five- or six-hour period without overcrowding. The phenomenon of "nightclub hopping" or going to various venues in a single evening allows this to occur. Managing the number of people will also help reduce incidents within the actual venue.

Security managers can and should make operational decisions with the other managers when it is prudent to close down early or reduce the number of customers. The temptation to stay open longer than the posted hours will, more likely than not, create more problems than the extra revenue will compensate for.

Lighting and music also play a significant role in the security management of a nightclub type venue. Music disc jockeys and entertainers require management and enforcement of any sound decibel limits, music types, and unusual lighting. The character of the music can agitate a crowded dance floor and therefore escalate incidents that may require security intervention. Certain hip-hop and rap-type music requires special considerations for security. In the event this type of entertainment is mandated, the security director should enlist the assistance of local law enforcement or a security consultant.

Security management should have the authority to make music and lighting requests should the "mood" of the room require it for the safety of the guests and employees. A disc jockey can get a dance floor crowd excited and agitated in a matter of a couple songs depending on which customers are in attendance. Too many lighting effects can also have the same effect and make it more difficult for employees to focus on the customers. The security manager should not overreact, shut off the music, and change the dynamic of the nightclub unless necessary to restore order in unusual circumstances or events. This sudden change can also exacerbate an upset crowd of customers.

12.3.1 Nightclub Staffing Levels

There are no magic ratios or standards that dictate how many security staff should be in an active nightclub venue. Some law enforcement jurisdictions will mandate a ratio of security officers to customers when recurring problems are experienced at a single location. I have seen anywhere from one officer for every twenty-five customers to one officer for every one hundred customers under mandated conditions. Some jurisdictions will actually codify the ratio and therefore mandate how many security officers are to be present at a particular nightclub. You should always check local laws that must be followed.

Staffing levels have many variables that must be considered. If security is to also perform the duties of "door hosts," then the number of security personnel needs to increase to include that function. Security personnel need to efficiently and carefully check IDs of all persons who enter a nightclub. Even those who appear to obviously be of age should have a valid form of identification. If a person is not carrying any form of ID, he or she should not be granted access. Exceptions should only be made by executive level managers.

If a person gets into an altercation, that person should have the means to identify him- or herself. If a person does not carry identification, he or she is either too young to enter or lacks the social responsibility to carry proper identification. These individuals could also be criminals who prey on the customers or undesirables who are not of value to the nightclub. In many cases that I have reviewed, a lawsuit filed years later for an event that seemingly was minor to the security personnel turns ugly during litigation where either party was never identified or no report was taken. Even a short paragraph in the door log would assist in these situations if a report is not filed.

Security at the ingress/egress points should be at a level to efficiently check each ID, check for exiting and returning guests, monitor customers and counts, and respond to any typical door incident. These same officers should be evaluating the customers waiting in line for attitude, appearance, and demeanor and prevent undesirable patrons from even paying the cover charge and entering.

In the event an obviously intoxicated woman is escorted out by one or more men, they can be stopped and identified to deter sexual assaults especially if the individuals just met. Again, the door log is a good place to document this information to include names, addresses, and driver's license numbers. This will not only deter sexual assault incidents but will also allow intervention to keep patrons from hurting themselves or others if they are too intoxicated by drugs or alcohol. It also allows law enforcement to adequately investigate crimes where drugs were introduced to allow sexual assaults or robbery. A suspect will think twice before sexually assaulting an intoxicated female if security at the nightclub has copied his vital information.

Security should also be strategically placed at "choke points" or main pedestrian crossroads. The number of these locations will vary depending on the overall design, number of rooms, and dance floor location. These officers should consider this the primary post and respond as needed in their immediate areas. One of the important functions of these officers is to keep the aisles clear and allow beverage service personnel clear access to customers and to allow for free flowing movement of customers.

The dance floor is another area that should have officers posted. The number of officers will typically be dictated by the size of the dance floor and its proximity to bars or other areas. In a large, crowded dance floor, there should be at least two officers highly visible to customers on the dance floor. Ideally one security officer would be at each side or corner with the ability to respond to any incident. Typical dance floor incidents involve intentional bumping, unwanted intimate advances toward another customer, or domestic squabbling. Hormones and jealousy are strong motivators for a person with a propensity for fighting.

Restrooms inside a nightclub should always have attendants to keep them clean and to report any unusual activity to security. In larger venues, having a security officer posted at the entrance to the restrooms is a worthwhile assignment. Many incidents will occur near the entrance to the restrooms where customers will interact. The restroom will always require patrol by security throughout the night. Drug use, sex, and other unwanted behaviors will occur inside a restroom stall and security should be vigilant in monitoring this area. Privacy laws do not allow for closed-circuit television (CCTV) cameras inside a restroom, but that expectation of privacy creates a location for unwanted behavior. Inside a nightclub, two or more sets of feet in a bathroom stall usually mean more than someone helping a handicapped person.

12.3.2 Club Drugs and Room Checks

With popularity comes the social use of narcotics in any nightclub venue. Security personnel should always take a no-nonsense, zero tolerance attitude toward illegal drugs (Figure 12.3). There are no known ways to absolutely keep drugs out of a public environment. There is no magic electronic detector that tells security that a customer with drugs is present.

The only way I know of to limit the drug activity inside a nightclub is to train the security and service staff in what to watch for. Local law enforcement agencies can be very helpful in this regard and will typically train the staff at no charge in what club drugs are and what is popular in your particular area. Many incidents of sexual assault occur every year in nightclubs that result from some form of drug given to a female patronizing a nightclub or bar. What starts as a social interaction or "hook up" turns ugly and sometimes results in illness, injury, or death after a woman is drugged, taken out of a nightclub, and sexually assaulted. If she wakes up, she will typically find herself in a strange place, often outdoors in a remote area and showing evidence of sexual assault.

A positive method to determine what drug activity is occurring inside of a nightclub is to do a "room check" before the venue opens and immediately after it closes. Security personnel should look under every table and chair, behind every seat cushion, in every trash can, and any place where the public is allowed. They are to check for and collect any items left by the public. The concept is to start the evening with a full room check to establish a clear venue. Items left over from the previous evening or when other events have occurred between shifts of nighttime operation are collected.

At the end of the evening the security staff then makes a full and detailed sweep of the entire room and collects all items that are found including trash. I always recommend the items be brought to the middle of the dance floor. Officers should always wear rubber gloves and exercise care during these checks. Items will be located that have been legiti-

FIGURE 12.3 Drugs should never be tolerated in a club (or any) environment—ecstasy pills are shown here.

mately lost by customers throughout the evening such as wallets, purses, jewelry, and other personal items. Items that are considered contraband or dangerous will also be located.

From an intelligence perspective, the information gathered will tell security and club management what has occurred during the evening. From a club drug perspective, containers, paper bundles, needles, razor blades, roaches, and other paraphernalia will indicate what is occurring that staff has not detected during the operational hours. People drop these items on the floor or in a trash can after the drugs have been consumed. Items such as pacifiers, pixie sticks, empty candy wrappers, pipes, foil, and small liquid bottles are all possible indicators of illegal drug use. Local narcotics officers from law enforcement will be able to assist in identifying what drugs are involved. My staff found several ounces of marijuana, full prescription bottles of narcotics, and full-sized bongs during these checks.

There are other items that demonstrate that unwanted behavior is occurring in the nightclub. Small bottles will indicate that alcohol is brought inside a nightclub. Energy drinks and small water bottles will also indicate problems and that door controls need to be increased. Underwear, condoms, and sex toys will of course indicate sexual conduct in dark corners of a room, which could be driven by local prostitutes or prostitutes who fly into large cities on weekends. On rare occasions, even weapons will be hidden away. The intelligence gathered during these room checks is invaluable and is an eye-opener to management and should be practiced in any nightclub environment.

12.3.3 Use of Local Promoters

Local nightclub promoters should be carefully screened. In larger cities, where competition is fierce, a group of people always shows up who profess to be promoters and can bring customers from competitors' venues to be your new customers. They will typically charge the customer a fee to get the VIP treatment and educate the customer to also tip the employees on the way in. The nightclub will gladly grant such customers entrance, along with the promoter, without paying a cover charge and sometimes comp the first drink. Promoters will sometimes be given cash for bringing in the customers. Typically, a promoter will rent a limousine and collect attractive women who are looking to have a night out and bring them to your nightclub using the age-old concept that where the pretty girls are, the boys with money will follow.

Nightclub promoters should be closely managed, if utilized, and should be monitored by security once they are inside the club. Local law enforcement will tell you that many of these promoters are also suspected in narcotics sales and distribution or other illegal activity. Because of their VIP status, they can enter and exit easily and have unlimited access for illegal activity. These promoters are valuable to management for their ability to generate instantaneous revenues by bringing customers to the venue, but they can also be dangerous to the continued success of any operation. Closely working with local police who handle vice and narcotics will be helpful to ferret out those undesirable promoters and retain the legitimate ones.

The more popular a nightclub venue inside of a casino property is, the more probable that the spillover of incidents and people into the gaming areas will be affected. Long lines through slot areas and intoxicated patrons entering occur more frequently. "Dumping" is a phenomenon that occurs when nightclub security takes an intoxicated patron out of the venue and places him or her in the casino for the casino security to deal with. Incidents at the valet, restaurants, or other bars will develop as a result of nightclub operations, especially when the venue closes.

Being reactive in nightclubs will usually just temporarily quell an individual incident. Proactive security in nightclub operations will ensure a long and successful operation for customers and employees to enjoy.

13

Table Game Fills, Credits, Drops, and Money

13.1 PROTECTION OF CURRENCY AND NEGOTIABLE CHIPS

The secondary function of any gaming security officer is to protect the assets of the entity he or she is employed by. It is important to understand that the protection of people (guests and employees) is the first priority in a gaming property and asset protection is the second priority. When confronted with a choice between assets and people, the gaming security officer should always protect life and safety before property.

A gaming operation has many nuances and characteristics regarding cash and negotiable chips that are based on local regulatory conditions, ergonomic design, and ownership priorities. We will discuss very basic functions to protect the industry from a security perspective and will not delve into specific security measures beyond what serves as public record in various regulatory environments.

I have always wondered how much value a security officer secures over one year. When I first started as a uniformed security officer, I recall just one shift where I kept track during a heavy evening of baccarat and craps play with our high-end customers attending a casino sponsored golf tournament. In that eight-hour shift, I carried over half a million dollars back and forth across the casino floor.

Security officers will be requested to perform tasks that are routine and will involve chips or cash transactions. Regardless of the circumstances, the safety of the employees (including security) is the primary focus when escorting negotiable chips or cash. If a robbery occurs, the money is insured; the people are not. The security officer still needs to be aware of the surroundings and follow the property procedures regarding these important escorts.

The money flow inside a casino is designed to be in constant flux so all the money is never at one location at any given time. In table games, the cash is dropped into boxes, collected and stored, counted, and given back to the cage over a period of time. The chips are bought by customers with cash or markers and that cash is dropped into those boxes.

Figure 13.1 A gaming operation has many nuances; there is always a constant movement of chips.

Security takes away and replenishes the chip inventory, and, as a result, the movement makes it difficult for criminals to get their hands on any measurable amount.

As an example, we can discuss a typical table game where a person comes in and gambles (Figure 13.1). There is an opening bankroll of chips in the tray, which is part of the total bank that the dealer works with and pays or collects with each hand of play. Then there is a drop box where cash, markers (credit slips), and other negotiable items are dropped at the conclusion of each hand of play. This drop box is locked and secured to the table. As customers leave the table and go to the cashier's cage, they hand their chips to the cashier who then exchanges the chips for currency. The table is supplied with chips or chips are removed throughout the shift by using the fill or credit process described earlier.

Revenues from outlets such as restaurants, bars, and shops will also be in constant flow. Banks containing a starting amount will be issued to employees who will go off to their locations and collect money for goods or services and turn it in at required intervals and at the end of their shifts. As a result, there is a constant movement of cash and chips in any casino environment and security plays an important role in making sure cash and chips are delivered to the appropriate destination.

13.2 FILLS AND CREDITS: UNDERSTANDING THE FLOW OF CHIPS

Every customer who enters a casino quickly learns the rules of cash and chip transactions when gambling. It is important for all security personnel to understand that some customers who enter casinos every day have never been inside one and are ignorant of these seemingly basic rules. Security officers need to keep this in mind when the simple inquiries test their patience. When a customer sees a security officer carrying chips back and forth across a casino floor, they become curious, tend to watch, and sometimes will even ask questions. Be sure to respond professionally and do not give them sensitive information.

Table game fills and credits are merely the method in which a gaming table is stocked and leveled off at a certain amount in the "bank" that the dealer works with. Regardless of the type of game the money is taken to or away from, the process remains the same. Strict regulations require multiple signatures and verifications from the point of issuing the money through its final deposit at the intended location.

When a table game has depleted a portion of its par level chip bank, the pit supervisors will call the cashier cage and order a fill or certain amount of chips. The cashier fills this order and completes the fill slip with each requested denomination and corresponding amount. These amounts are stored in chip racks that have specific capacities. The amounts are ordered by the pit to fill each row of twenty chips and each rack will typically have five rows. As an example, a full rack of $1 chips would contain $100 or one hundred chips. Conversely a full rack of $500 chips would contain $50,000.

Regardless of the amount, the fill slip is completed, verified, and signed by the initiating cashier. In some instances larger fills are then verified by a cage supervisor and signed again. The security officer is called and requested to bring this rack of chips to a specific table game in the casino. The security officer will then visually verify the amounts of each denomination and compare them to the fill slip. The security officer will then sign this same slip in the appropriate location, will typically place the chips in a carrying case to protect them from outside interference while transporting, and bring the container to the waiting pit supervisor.

Once inside the pit, appropriate protocols are followed and the pit supervisor checks the fill amount and signs the fill slip. The chips are placed on the table once the current hand is played out. The dealer then takes the slip and the chips and incorporates them into the table bank. The dealer verifies that all of the chips are the proper denomination and amounts and places them into the bank according to the house policies and procedures. The dealer is then the last person to sign the fill slip and one of the copies is dropped into the table game drop box. The final slip with all of the signatures, including the pit boss's, is returned to the originating cashier cage employee and retained for the audit.

As mentioned earlier, the casino will constantly move the chips and cash in various directions, and there is no time when all of the cash and chips are in one specific location. Operationally, this works well and, from a security perspective, this minimizes cash exposures. The surveillance department will monitor or "follow the money" through all of the fill steps and processes to ensure that all employees are complying with the set rules and regulations set forth by the authorities or the gaming establishment.

Those chips that are placed on the tables will be used by employees and customers and will make the rounds of the games and cashiers sometimes several times an hour. Customers will win certain chips and then take them to the cashier cage where they will redeem them for cash and the chips are then stored in the cashier cage. The process merely repeats itself constantly and the security officer typically transports the chips for the casino.

A credit is the reverse process, when a particular table game takes in more chips than the established bank for that particular game. In this instance, the pit supervisor will call security and advise of the credit. The security officer responds to the pit supervisor where the dealer and pit boss will then go to the table game and take a certain total of chips off the game and document the denominations and amounts to be credited.

Credits are completed when there are excess chips in the table game bankroll or at the end of each operating shift to level off each bank to the impress amount for accounting purposes. In the credit process, after all of the signatures are obtained and the chips are taken in by the cashier, a credit slip is completed and a copy is returned to the table and inserted in the drop box. The chip carrying process by security protects the funds while they are in transit back to the cashier's cage.

Most gaming operations will have strict regulations regarding fills and credits, and compliance is strictly monitored by the regulating body. Self-imposed rules and regulations regarding security's role in this process are common, and internal, external, and regulatory auditors will check these records regularly. In instances of procedural deficiencies, security officers will be disciplined if they have not followed the process and completed the required functions in exact order.

13.3 ESCORTING EMPLOYEES WITH CASH DRAWERS

Another common function is the escort of various employees from a point of sale, bank, or other venue to the cashier's cage or from the cashier's cage to their work areas. Although this is a simple process, the security officer should be alert and never be distracted by outside incidents. The process usually involves the escort of funds as the opening bank amount to the work area and at the end of their shift an escort to the cashier's cage with shift revenues and receipts, which can sometimes be thousands of dollars.

Keeping in mind that the main objective is to protect the employee who is carrying the negotiable cash, the security officer should be prepared for the worst case scenario when completing this task, which would be a robber armed with a gun. The traditional approach to this type of event is to cooperate, give the person the bank, and pay close attention to the details of his or her appearance and demeanor if possible. As in any robbery event, the mind will not always function as you want it to, but the safety of the employee and yourself is the first priority.

During these escorts, the security officer should instruct the employee not to expose any currency by placing a cover over the drawer and to follow instructions. In most cash register environments, a cash drawer has a lid to cover the currency and to assist in this process. Another important function of the escort is to make sure that the employee does not make any stops during the walk to the cashier's cage with the company funds. Historically, the cash drawer would sometimes, although rarely, disappear with the employee who does not have an escort. Even emergency restroom stops should be prohibited.

In addition, one of the periods most important for fraud prevention is when an employee is done with a particular assignment and he or she has unobserved access to cash and negotiable items. If an employee has pilfered cash or has converted coupons or other instruments into an excess amount that is contained in his or her drawer, the time from when he or she finishes until he or she turns his or her bank into the main bank is a particularly vulnerable time. Having a security officer present during this process will minimize this temptation.

There have been various Hollywood movies that dramatize the casino as a place where piles of cash are stored and the creative mind can figure out a way to obtain it. In reality the typical casino never has all of the cash in one spot at any given time. The only time that I have ever seen that occur is when the cash is delivered to a brand new casino about to open or in rare cases such as a bombing in Lake Tahoe in 1980. In that historical event, security was charged with evacuating the main floor, which included the casino. All funds that were not contained inside slot machines were brought to the cashier's cage, where they were secured. The only problem was that there was not enough storage room inside the safe to store the funds. The only answer was to pile it onto the floor in bank bags.

In the casino environment, there are typically enough funds to pay any house jackpot or gaming activity at any time, including the number of gaming chips on hand. The exceptions would be those progressive interlinked jackpots where millions of dollars are involved. The cash on hand is always in movement or at a temporary location during the operation.

The money is cycled and this makes it difficult for the criminal when you combine the crowd of people, security, and closed-circuit television as deterrents. Each location where funds are stored must have its own security system that protects it and is typically controlled by more than one employee and as prescribed by strict regulatory procedures.

13.4 THE SLOT MACHINE DROP

Slot machines produced today do not accept coins or tokens. In past years, the process of collecting, counting, wrapping, and managing coin drops was burdensome and time-consuming. Workers' compensation claims, equipment maintenance, and employee payrolls were expended for this process. In today's slot world, TITO, or ticket in, ticket out slips are controlled with bar codes for optimum security. This eliminates the coin or token process, the machine mechanics involving coins such as hoppers, and all of the associated processes.

There are still some casinos that use coin machines, although they are being quickly replaced. The coin drop is still in effect in these older operations. The process is quite simple in that the slot machine contains a hopper where a coin is cycled through and any excess coin drops down a chute into some form of bucket or container. At some point, the slot drop occurs where security and coin room personnel remove these coins to the hard count room.

This coin drop typically involves multiple employees and one or two security officers. Security's function is to watch the buckets of coin and the employees during this process and make sure the coin makes its way to the hard count room where it is processed into rolls for later distribution into the casino. Security officers control the area to make sure they can view all employees and the process. Coin room personnel will want to jump ahead to the next aisle, which will create an inability to properly complete this security function.

The security officer escorting the funds from the slot machines to the coin room is watching the employees who have a drop key, which they use to access the doors of the machines. The key is very important and must be observed during the process. The loss of these keys either by accident or intentionally will cause great concern and, in some juris-dictions, cause the gaming area to be closed. Each lock will have to be replaced and new keys made, which is an expensive and time-consuming process. These keys are critical and are controlled with multiple signatures.

Historically, there are numerous incidents where money or tokens have been taken during the coin drop, which is one of the reasons that TITO technology is a security plus. The typical scam would involve collusion with another employee or an outside person. A simple process of distracting the security officer into leaving a full bucket of dollar tokens would occur. The outside person would walk along, cover the bucket with clothing or some other cloaking device, and carry the bucket out of the casino. Cashing in the tokens was simple as long as it was not done at one specific time.

Another method would be for one of the employees to defeat the lock on the machine by removing or altering the cam on the lock, which would allow someone to come in and merely open the door and take what was inside. Although these methods were open and obvious, the surveillance operator was the final security measure to oversee the process. Momentary distractions allowed for breakdowns in the security and procedures.

The importance of the security officer to ensure that procedures are followed cannot be overemphasized. Procedure violations cause slot drop thefts to occur. Managing the focus of the employees to a defined area, key controls, surveillance monitoring, and sound management of employees are critical to any cash handling area.

Conversion of slot machines to the TITO method eliminated many operational and security concerns and expense. Without coins, the process became one of tickets with value rather than buckets of coins handled by numerous employees. Additionally the entire hard count operation was closed, and what coin was necessary for banks is purchased or a very small part-time coin room operation is in place.

Some customers complain that they prefer the old-fashioned coin machines. The noise that was generated by the intentional metal pans that the coins would drop into was all part of the gambling experience. When a jackpot was paid, anyone within a dozen rows could hear it along with the screaming and celebration. Slot machine manufacturers have creatively duplicated this sound whenever a jackpot is won by a customer through an audio device on the machine that sounds just like the coins hitting the tray.

13.5 TABLE GAMES AND VALIDATOR BOX DROPS

I will not go into specific details of box drops in this book, but I will discuss the general process. Those table game boxes we talked about earlier are removed by security with a highly controlled key and replaced with an empty one at some point during a shift. These drop boxes are unlocked from the table game and a replacement box is secured into the table. The boxes are transported to the soft count room and security area where they are opened, counted, inventoried, and the contents recorded.

Box drops occur differently at each property. In some properties, the boxes are only dropped from the games once every twenty-four hours. In other casinos, they are dropped by each eight-hour shift that corresponds with the scheduled shifts in the pits. It is a mat-ter of financial preference at what interval the boxes are dropped. If a financial officer wishes to have more accounting detail in determining when and how revenues and play are occurring, the more frequent per-shift method is used. Accounting of the boxes by shift will make it easier to record and forecast revenues at various times of the day or night.

The box drop is completed with multiple security officers and should be accomplished as quickly, safely, and efficiently as possible to minimize the exposure of the box cart on the casino floor. The drop is always under the scrutiny of the surveillance department. Specific procedures, routes, and security measures during the drop are designed by the security, surveillance, and financial executives of a property.

Scams that involve drop boxes are elaborate and always involve multiple employees. Actual drop box incidents of theft are very rare but do occur as a result of procedural violations of some sort that are exploited by the employees involved. Storage, repair, and collection procedures are all areas that require security evaluation and procedure implementation.

Bill validators are attached to, or inside of, slot machines that accept currency or TITO jackpot slips as payment. As a customer inserts currency or TITO tickets, they are stored inside a receptacle. The validator at each machine has to be emptied and the containers are handled much like a box drop. These boxes need to be secured with the same importance as the table games drop boxes.

With the drop of validators occurring in the slot areas, the same basic principles of a slot coin drop are followed in order to maintain security and minimize exposure during the drop. There are locations where carts will not go, and the carts are parked at the ends of aisles while assigned employees accomplish the removal of full boxes and place empty ones in their place. The larger the casino, the longer this drop takes or is accomplished by more than one team. A casino with 3,000 slot machines requires more than one drop team.

Also, in many environments an auditor or accounting representative will be assigned to follow the drop process and record certain information. This is a method of verification used so that all of the procedures set by regulators or internally are complied with before, during, and after the particular drop.

Other money drops include vending machines, money exchange kiosks, and anywhere cash is used to dispense items of value. Certain machines will be managed by an outside company, and drops are completed by their proprietary employees. In those circumstances, a casino security officer can be assigned to their drop depending on the facility and the arrangement between the casino and that particular vendor.

14

Managing and Controlling Incidents

14.1 CALLS FOR SERVICE: RESPONDING TO INCIDENTS

The casino is designed to be an exciting and fun place for legal-aged people to go. Inside of the basic casino are various venues that allow admittance for under-aged persons accompanied by adults. Casinos include many different options for guests to spend their disposable income. In most casinos, the presence of alcohol has a direct effect on the attitudes and the social behavior of the patrons. The objective of management should be to keep this flow of revenue constant and to make sure that the guests have a good enough time to return on a regular basis and tell all of their friends to do so also.

A casino has certain legal responsibilities to ensure that guests are protected from unreasonable harm. The legal duty they have varies between jurisdictions but generally requires that they do what is reasonable under the circumstances and that they operate within the standard of care for the casino environment. Maintaining a reasonably safe environment will accomplish and meet this duty as well as ensure the success of your facility.

The gaming security officer will have to respond to numerous incidents during the course of employment that will often challenge his or her patience and professionalism. Each situation is different and the responding security will have to quickly evaluate and respond to accordingly. In many incidents, there will be no specific written procedure and the security officer will need to make common sense decisions.

The basic structure of casino management and the chain of command allow for easy access to persons who have the authority to make decisions in these circumstances. The security officer will normally notify the shift supervisor who will take over the incident if immediately available or radio instructions to the responding officer. Another authority who can assist is the casino shift manager, who is the overall manager in charge in the absence of the casino manager or general manager. We will address the most common incidents in an attempt to convey the desired outcomes for any gaming property.

14.2 INTOXICATION AND INCIDENT CONTROL

We previously discussed the issues regarding the sales and management of alcohol in a gaming establishment. Alcohol regularly contributes to incidents and is often a factor when dealing with or managing incidents. In many situations where altercations or medical incidents are involved, the alcohol factor needs to be evaluated before decisions regarding actions are made.

Since alcohol will affect a person's logic, inhibitions, and judgment, the typical responses to an incident do not always work on an intoxicated patron. Security personnel seem to forget that when a person is intoxicated he or she does not necessarily hear, or understand, what the requests for action are by the security officer. As a result, many security personnel will react too swiftly and not exert enough patience or empathy.

Intoxicated individuals typically cannot function at a normal level and have to be treated almost like children to manage their immediate social behavior. It is also important not to talk to the person in a derogatory, demeaning, or sarcastic manner as their emotional feelings are also affected and may be exaggerated. When responding to incidents, the officers should make a determination other than the initial observations of the main offender. A field investigation to establish the alcohol consumption history of the people involved will determine how the incident will be handled. A simple inquiry to the servers or customers in the immediate vicinity will reveal interesting results.

Dealing with the drunken patron will be the most challenging task an officer will endure. The patron most likely got to that level of intoxication at your casino and now he or she has become a problem that will require action and a solution. Many customers will be quick to remind you of this. Separating two people who have had too much and have engaged in an altercation demonstrates that they have a propensity for physical aggression and you need to minimize the risk to other people. Taking these customers to the security office will also be challenging in that often they will pass out, vomit, and sometimes lose control of bodily functions in the process.

Many casinos are attempting to train personnel in the same methods that police or highway patrol officers use to determine the approximate level of intoxication in an attempt to manage alcohol-related incidents. With operations that have the luxury of implementing that training, it will prove beneficial in the officers' ability to handle intoxicated patrons.

14.3 CLOSED-CIRCUIT TELEVISION AND DOCUMENTING INCIDENTS

Regardless of the perceived seriousness of the incident, the surveillance department can and should become involved prior to a security response whenever possible. This allows for a method of documentation of the events as they unfold and will allow for a forensic review at a later time should allegations of misconduct be made. Security personnel will quickly become aware that they are being watched on recordable video when they respond to an incident and will be subconsciously reminded to follow proper procedures or protocols.

Whenever possible, security can notify the surveillance department as officers are responding to allow closed-circuit television coverage of the event from more than one camera angle if possible. The most compelling evidence in a criminal or civil trial will always be the video of the event. These video clips can also be a very effective tool in evaluating an officer's performance under stressful conditions. A composite disc or tape of numerous incidents is also a useful training tool to demonstrate to security personnel what the desired response is to these incidents. Surveillance agents can also fine tune their skills of forensic analysis and camera locations.

As an example, when time permits, security can call a specific predesigned code to notify surveillance that they are escorting a person out and advising that person of trespass. A code can also be communicated back that the incident is now monitored by surveillance to let the officers and supervisors know that all documentation processes are being accomplished.

The video will also show what circumstances or events are occurring that the initial responding personnel are not focused on. Surveillance also should start a video review of the entire incident once it is contained and under control. Any cameras that may have captured events leading up to the subject incident will be of importance in the field investigation, potential prosecution for a criminal event, or should a lawsuit be filed in the future. A simple thing like seeing a security officer patrolling the exact same location ten or fifteen minutes prior to an event could be significant in an inadequate security allegation in civil court.

14.4 VERBAL AND PHYSICAL ALTERCATIONS

One of the most common disruptions in a casino is an altercation between third parties or customers. It can be verbal or physical and can change in a matter of seconds. There are many different methods that will work in response to aggression, and there are also numerous professional training programs that deal with deescalation skills and nonviolent crisis intervention. These companies offer formal certifications after security personnel are competent in the skills and have completed the required training.

The first step in responding to any altercation is to safely separate the parties from each other and from any perceived audience. Once the immediate situation is calmed, the security officer should make sure that both parties are clearly identified through legitimate identification regardless of their age. First aid for any injuries that require immediate care is then administered. This will accomplish several things. First and foremost, you will identify who the primary persons in the incident are and allow for investigation. Second, you will be getting the first indication from each person of his or her willingness to cooperate and comply with your requests, and third, you will be giving the parties a chance to calm down and allow other responding officers to assist in collecting information as to the cause and whether other people are involved, have been hurt, or are independent witnesses.

Simply responding to a fight between two individuals, separating them, and telling them to go in different directions can create more problems even though it may seem to be the easiest decision at the time. As previously indicated, since they have demonstrated a propensity for aggressive or violent behavior, you now have the obligation to remove at least one if not both from the property. This becomes challenging if they are hotel guests and rooms at your facility. The decision to evict them from the hotel or to allow them to remain should first consider the overall circumstances and whether they are a danger to other people.

If they are not identified or a report is not completed, you will run the risk of one or both of them filing a claim, complaint, or lawsuit and the casino will not have any proof of your actions. In addition, if a third party claims injury as a result of an incident and there is no documentation or persons identified, it will be almost impossible to find that information or the officer at a later time.

In the event a fight between two individuals is broken up, after the parties have been identified and it has been determined that they will not be charged with a crime and they will not be pressing charges against each other, they should be asked to leave the premises. Both offenders are asked to leave and this is done carefully to make sure the physical altercation does not continue. In some rare instances, only one person is requested to leave the premises.

I worked on a legal case where security personnel broke up a fight and immediately put both parties out the same door at the same time while they were still agitated. Security then walked them off the property to another casino and then watched as they reengaged in the fight. That case settled for a confidential amount.

People who have been in a fight or verbal argument should be ejected from the premises and trespassed according to the casino's procedures. After separating the combatants, they should be placed so neither can see the other. After collecting identity information and conducting a field investigation, one of the two can be released out a door away from the other party. As security officers continue the field investigation with the other party, the first one will have ample time to exit. After he is gone, then the second party is released out a different door. The concept is to basically not allow the two people who were fighting to see each other or be in close proximity to reengage in a fight.

14.5 PUBLIC DOMESTIC FIGHTS

Domestic altercations are by far the most difficult and challenging to solve (Figure 14.1). When responding to a domestic fight, whether verbal or physical, the officer still needs to accomplish the goal of separation and field investigation. The responding officer is unaware of the history or conditions that gave rise to the domestic disturbance. There are always very high emotions and visible displays of those emotions. Drugs or alcohol will often be combined with the emotional turmoil, which will magnify the perceptions of the offenders.

Security officers should exert patience and compassion in these situations and attempt to quell the disturbance without taking sides. Whenever possible, the local police should be called to deal with the problem when it has become physical in any manner. The police will have access to reports of any off-property incidents or history of the participants that are on public record and can assist. They will also be able to document the incident, which may prevent a domestic violence sequel.

As an example, a security officer may respond to a call of a report of a couple fighting and, when he arrives, the woman says that the man just hit her. She will say that she wants to press charges against him and tells the officer he is her husband. A common mistake is

Figure 14.1 Domestic altercations are often the most challenging incidents.

that the security will handcuff the husband and take him into custody in the security office or holding room. This all seems appropriate at the time and the objective is to keep the woman safe. Then the woman has second thoughts and says she now does not wish to press charges and that he really did not hit her. This situation now poses various issues that have to be dealt with. Calling in the police in these cases will certainly help. The man in the meantime has been physically restrained and escorted through the casino yelling he did nothing wrong. These scenarios will typically be resolved as disturbing the peace charges, elements of which are obviously present if witnesses say both parties were loud and fighting.

Careful consideration should be given in these situations. If a customer wants another customer arrested for any reason, the local police should be immediately called to deal with the process. The only time that security should get involved is to maintain the peace and make attempts to keep the parties from battering each other until the police arrive. Keep in mind that you have no direct authority to detain them if they both decide to leave unless they have committed a crime that you are willing to place them under arrest for. In those circumstances where a significant disturbance has been made, a disorderly conduct or disturbing the peace arrest may be warranted.

Domestic altercations can change instantly and the security officer needs to be aware that he or she could get caught in the middle of an incident and may be subpoenaed during a heated divorce action later. Notifying your local police will be the most efficient method in dealing with domestic altercations whenever possible.

All incidents involving an altercation, regardless of the perceived severity by the security officer, should be reported and identification of the persons involved should be retained. This will prove to be quite important years later when a civil lawsuit is served regarding allegations of negligence or some other tortious action. Security officers will want to take the easy way out and not report the incident. Constant reinforcement by supervisors will be required.

15

Removing Undesirables

15.1 EJECT, EVICT, TRESPASS, AND EIGHTY-SIXING

Once a security professional understands the concept of the legal duties a casino has to its patrons, it becomes clear that something must be done to keep undesirable persons, especially those who have historically created problems, from coming back (Figure 15.1). There is a well-established procedure or common practice followed for decades in the gaming industry. That process is designed to ban the person from coming back to the property. This proactive procedure is commonly known as the trespass or eighty-sixing process.

After all the dust has settled in any situation, a determination needs to be made in regard to allowing the person you are dealing with to return as a customer, employee, or even an employee of a vendor. This decision should not be taken lightly and can affect the person and the casino. The incident or the perceived propensity for harm to a future guest should be weighed before making this recommendation.

Procedures will vary from property to property and depending on the jurisdiction. Local and state laws should always be consulted before developing a procedure for this important task. A written and formal procedure should be in place to allow consistent application and to document the facility's desire to maintain a reasonably safe environment for its customers. Included in the procedure should also be the authorization levels for eighty-sixing and the required documentation that should be completed.

15.2 UNDERAGED PEOPLE

Minors who are not of legal age to gamble should not be excluded from a casino as a matter of routine unless the local regulations require it. Keep in mind that the young people who you speak with, deal with, and occasionally have involvement with in incidents are the future customers of your casino. By placing a young adult on the eighty-six list, you will also create issues related to the parents who may be well-established customers. The first consideration should always be that the law must be followed to protect the casino from regulatory action that could involve fines or in the extreme the revocation of the gaming

187

Figure 15.1 There are well-established procedures for removing undesirables from casino premises.

license. I would recommend that minors be treated with certain respect and be asked to leave the premises when found in areas where they do not belong.

In the past ten years, some gaming jurisdictions, including Nevada, have levied large fines on gaming properties for not enforcing the law and ejecting minors from gambling areas and bars. As a result, properties began to log and count the number of persons security personnel encountered in these areas, including how many they ejected, and statistically analyse these data. Every time minors were found in the casino, at the bars, or any other area where they were not allowed, the security officer would ask for identification (ID) and, if they were too young, they were asked to leave. Some properties even began collecting basic ID information and logging it into the dispatch record.

This relatively easy procedure involves the security officer calling the dispatcher, who logs the officer, location, and how many minors were ejected or warned. Logs as described in Chapter 11 allow for simple and expedient recording of the occurrences. The dispatcher can then total these figures and have a shift tally that can be added to the total daily, weekly, and monthly (or whatever increment of time is desired) tally to measure effectiveness of the security function.

This logging process allows managers to evaluate whether personnel are checking for minors in prohibited areas and at what level as compared to other officers and shifts. It also becomes a very effective document to prove to regulators that the age law is enforced by security personnel on a sustained basis.

15.3 THE FUNCTION OF EIGHTY-SIXING

The trespass function should be applied to people who are truly undesirable and who may create problems to guests or employees in the future. Many security directors believe that anyone who gets into a fight, regardless of severity, should be eighty-sixed. They also take the position that if the original incident that drew patrons into a fight was exaggerated or not proven, the ban can be lifted.

Larger gaming corporations and tribal operations with multiple locations will also formally trespass a person from all of the properties they manage. This can also create issues in the future especially if trespass is for a reason that is minor and may be considered an excessive measure. In larger locations like Las Vegas, a company can own numerous casinos and in a relatively short time can gain or lose several properties due to mergers and acquisitions.

The other thing that should be considered is that adding the names of half a dozen people per day makes a list difficult to manage and enforce based on the sheer numbers. Trespassing people in excess can also have a reverse effect and be a negative indication of too many problems. The process, like any security procedure, should be watched, managed, and changed as conditions and demographics change. Eighty-sixing is essentially taking customers away from the property permanently, so this should be for a good reason and not out of frustration or other emotions.

The surveillance department as well as the director of security must receive a copy of the eighty-six card or document with a report accompanying the document that adequately describes the reason for the action to permanently ban the person. Many departments will first consult the hotel register, employee list, premium players lists, and the cashier's cage before completing an eighty-six. This allows for any historical data that might be helpful and will let the decisionmaker know whether the person is a hotel guest or a customer with a premium player rating. By checking with the cashier's cage, any bad checks or negative history may indicate opportunity for collection of a debt or criminal prosecution.

The concept is to ban the person from returning to your property in a formal, documented manner that will allow you to arrest the person, if necessary, should he or she return at a later time and create problems or endanger the safety of the guests and employees. The prevailing laws must still be adhered to and the person should be treated firmly but professionally.

15.4 THE FORMAL EIGHTY-SIXING PROCESS

Recording the process of trespassing or telling a person he or she is no longer welcome at your property should be well documented. Typically cards or reports with a picture, a written warning, and a procedure that is to be followed are required. There are very specific instructions in certain jurisdictions as to the process mandated by the regulators. Consulting your specific regulations is crucial. In larger jurisdictions the local district attorney may invoke a procedure whereby the person must have been warned in the previous six months in order for a casino to prosecute offenders.

First, the person has to be told and warned as the particular law demands. One of the most common mistakes that security personnel will make in this process is that they believe they can force a person to the security office to complete the formal process. Based on the Constitution and the various statutory and common laws in place in the United States, this is not the case. Security personnel cannot handcuff or force a person to go to a security office merely for the purpose of placing him or her on the eighty-six list. Obviously, this may not be the case internationally.

It is acceptable to ask the person if he or she is willing to go to the security office to discuss the incident, whereupon the security officer can accomplish the formal process. The request is purely voluntary by the person and he or she can merely walk away. At any time, if that person asks to leave, he or she must be allowed to leave unless there is an overwhelming reason, such as the high probability he or she had committed a felony or if the person is an obvious danger to him- or herself or others. In those instances, the police most likely have already been called.

If a person refuses to let the security officer take his or her picture, the security officer cannot force a person to submit or forcefully take his or her picture with a handheld camera. What is acceptable is that the surveillance department can take a still picture from video to place in the report and on the eighty-six card.

Certain equipment and devices inside a security office can be used to ease the process of formally trespassing an individual. A height marker and clock and date on the wall where the holding bench or seat is located can be helpful when a camera is used to assist in the documentation process. Reading the person the formal warning not to return with camera and audio recording will be helpful in the event he or she returns in the near future.

Instances where a person is handcuffed, taken to a security office, picture taken without consent, pockets emptied and searched, trespass warning issued, unhandcuffed, and escorted off of the property will certainly open up your facility and all of the officers involved to claims and litigation that may include punitive damages. The key is that if you just want to give the person a trespass warning, then keep it in perspective. If a person is being arrested for a particular crime, then certain protocols need to be followed.

15.5 CONVERTING INCIDENTS INTO TRESPASS WARNINGS

There are certain things that can be done when responding to an incident or a person who needs to be told to leave without invoking the formal trespass process. That objective should be to get the person to leave and not arrest him or her. The person is asked to leave the premises and is not permanently barred from coming back as a solution to an immediate issue.

Almost any behavioral situation can and should be converted to a basic trespass warning. If a person is acting out, obnoxious, or exhibits unwanted behavior, he or she should be asked to leave the premises. The exception would be if a crime has been committed against a person or property or if the behavior is extreme. Arresting people for disorderly conduct, disturbing the peace, and related crimes can create many unnecessary issues and circumstances during the criminal and possible civil processes. There are instances where disturbing and disorderly arrests are appropriate, but they should be rare.

Keep in mind that the actions you take, which may involve an arrest, will stay with that person for a long time. Future employment, background checks, and even financial applications will require him or her to list any arrests or convictions. It is an easier process to explain a simple trespass arrest as opposed to a disorderly conduct arrest when applying for a job. In many jurisdictions, the trespass arrest can be removed from official records if the person complies with a judge's order of staying out of trouble for three to four months.

Also important are the criminal process and the associated fines. A person can merely pay the fine associated with a trespass arrest and be done with the matter. People will tend to want to fight the disorderly type charges and the process begins. First, the prosecutor looks at the reports and the charge and makes the initial decision of whether to prosecute or drop the charges. In a majority of disorderly cases the charges are routinely dropped because the basic elements of the crime have not clearly been documented in the reports and statements. The judge also looks at the basic concept of how it is possible for a person to disturb the peace in a place where loud music, people screaming, and bells and whistles are always present.

When approaching a loud and obnoxious customer, the first thing that should be done is to warn the person that he or she is on private property and no longer wanted there. The specific trespass law should be used for the particular location. This warning is typically one of the basic elements of any trespass law in any jurisdiction. If you do not warn a person to leave and give him or her a chance to leave and then arrest the person for trespass, you have not complied with the basic element required.

There are certain instances where the converting of a disturbance to trespass may not be the desired objective. Theft, embezzlement, or major incidents may require that other charges be filed depending on the circumstances and the desired prosecution by the management. These should be exceptions rather than the rule and be the decision of the director of security or executive level manager.

Converting any behavioral outburst into a request to leave allows for a simple and direct solution to the incident and does not require complex scenarios for procedures and training. Personnel will quickly learn that it becomes a simpler process, from the actual warning all the way through the report writing process, for a trespass arrest as opposed to a disorderly conduct arrest. It becomes an easy task for the responding police and becomes hard to argue to a judge later.

15.6 "THREE FINGERS"

The technique used in a routine trespass warning will come in play many times in a security officer's career. Security personnel will tend to get lazy and impatient if not managed properly, which may create problems in the relatively simple process of trespassing undesirables. I developed a process many years ago that worked well for my properties that one of my officers called "three fingers" method and it stuck.

By way of illustration, the security officer responds to a complaint of a person who is loud and obnoxious in the slot area. As the officer is approaching, she observes the individual and sizes the person up as her backup officers are responding. She will observe the individual pending backup arrival and approaches when safe. The first thing that occurs is she requests identification from the person. This establishes several things at the onset.

The first thing that this will establish is the authority the security officer has to the offender. If the person does not have ID or he or she is refusing to leave the casino, the first indicator is made. If the person presents an ID, the officer now knows the person's name. She may take the name, date of birth, and other information from the ID while engaged in conversation. This preliminary conversation will show whether the person is a hotel guest, regular customer, or if he or she has recently escaped from a mental institution. These issues will become very important if you jump ahead and just throw the person out.

In many circumstances, an important customer or local dignitary may very well be the person you are now confronting. Once you have made this initial field investigation and it is determined this is a local who has an attitude, the next step would be to advise the person he or she is on private property, that he or she is trespassing, and that if he or she does not leave immediately you will arrest the person for trespassing. Having a card with the formal, specific trespass language to be read to an offender is helpful in ensuring the appropriate legal warning has been made and the important elements of the crime have been met.

First warning: After you have advised the person of the law and that he or she must leave, I recommend that the security officer ask the person "Are you refusing to leave?" This will make the person think about the question and respond accordingly. If the person responds that he or she will leave but wants to argue about it, this will give the officer an indication that the person is willing to leave. Once you have advised the person of the law, asked the person to leave, and asked the person if he or she is refusing to leave, the officer then holds up one finger high into the air.

The first finger is an indication that the officer has issued the first trespass warning to the individual. If the officer is alone and backup is tied up or has not arrived yet, this will let the suspect know that you have just sent a signal to someone. The officer should still be strategically placed in such a manner as to defend herself and to also send the signal to the person he or she is speaking with that she is trained and professional and will take the necessary action if required. Calling the first warning in, using a property radio code, on the security radio will alert security staff and surveillance of an impending trespass. In many instances the person will leave without incident.

Second warning: The process is repeated verbatim in the second warning of trespass. This will reinforce the requests that the officer wants the person to leave the premises. The same exact warning should be given, trespass law elements covered, and the person should be asked the second time if he or she is refusing to leave. If the person says he or she is refusing to leave, this will certainly change the dynamics of the situation. The officer then raises two fingers into the air and makes a quick call on the radio to alert the rest of the security staff.

Surrounding employees, managers, and responding backup officers will now be aware that the person is being trespassed and that he or she has just been given the second warning and has again been asked if he or she is refusing to leave. The surveillance department should also have been notified to ensure closed-circuit television coverage hopefully prior to the first warning and at least at the point of the second warning.

The person being trespassed will most likely start sensing that an impending situation is about to happen if he or she does not leave as requested. In most situations, this is enough and the person will exit. Many times the exit will be noisy and obnoxious. Officers should maintain composure during this phase of the process, which will most likely involve profanities and possibly insults about the officer's mother or something else to invoke emotion.

Typical responses can include taunting the security officers, yelling as the person leaves, and displaying hand gestures that will attempt to provoke the officer into chasing the person. It is not unusual for offenders to "moon" security by dropping their pants and waving their buttocks at them. If the objective is to get them to leave the premises and they are leaving, there is no reason to escalate the situation by allowing these provocations to elevate to an arrest. If the offender is leaving the casino, you have certainly accomplished your objective. A call to the local police advising them you have just trespassed an obnoxious person who is trying to get into a fight can be made to warn them of a potential problem.

Third and final warning: Obviously, it is now important to strictly follow the previous two warnings and make sure to follow the elements of the law and ask again if the person is refusing to leave. Once this last and final warning has been given, the officer can make the statement that this is the last warning, raise three fingers into the air, and call on the radio that the third and final warning has been issued (Figure 15.2). Certainly more warnings can be given, but the process will just tend to delay the most likely outcome and possibly disrupt the gaming area for a prolonged time.

By the time the third warning has been made, there will be plenty of security personnel present to take the appropriate action. There will also be potential independent witnesses, a security supervisor, possibly a casino shift manager, and other employees who will serve as witnesses to the professional behavior of the officer and the offensive behavior of the offender. There will be circumstances when a supervisor may warn an offender a dozen times and that decision should be respected. Every situation will present varying challenges and the supervisor is charged with solving the problem.

15.7 ESCORTS TO THE NEAREST DOOR

Many security officers and managers believe that they should always tell the person which door to leave from, which is typically the nearest door, when requesting someone to leave the premises. This is not always a wise decision in that a person may have his or her car parked on the opposite side of the casino, be meeting people at a specific location, or need to go elsewhere for some other legitimate reason.

If the security officer is hard-lined about the specific door, this will most likely force the arrest to occur in many circumstances. A careful evaluation of the circumstances should be made to include the attitude of the person asked to leave. There may be, in rare circumstances, a viable reason to demand the person exit through a specific door.

Figure 15.2 The "three fingers" method is a good way to put a patron on notice and to alert security and surveillance of any escalating situation.

The nearest door concept was a common practice at one time when it was believed that security should remove a person as quickly and firmly as possible and he or she should be forced out the nearest door to prevent problems. Softer approaches proved beneficial over time to keep the customer from becoming further agitated and breaking things as he or she left the premises, damaging cars, or calling in a false bomb threat to get even for the ejection.

Again, the objective is to get the person to leave calmly and without further incident. Playing "hardball" about which exit to leave from, when they are actually complying, will also be problematic in the event of a complaint or legal action.

15.8 MAKING THE DECISION TO EFFECT A CITIZEN'S ARREST

Another positive aspect of the three fingers approach is that the process will allow the shift security supervisor to respond and take over the decision process from the officer. If the procedure is followed, the supervisor will already know that there has been a field investigation and that this person needs to leave or be arrested. Regardless of the circumstances that lead up to the officer's first warning, the trespass process has been accomplished and the authority for arrest is present. All of the elements of the misdemeanor crime have been met. The supervisor may choose to issue a fourth warning, which will allow him or her to make the citizen's arrest based on personally witnessing the crime.

Every property has specific arrest procedures and the actual arrest must be made by the person who witnessed the misdemeanor crime (the officer). I rarely had to grab a person to effect an arrest which generally resulted in prolonged periods of handcuffing. I started merely by asking the person to turn around or assume the position and I would snap the handcuffs on. I was shocked that the majority of people complied. Of course, there was always that person who wanted to fight and resist and the more difficult arrests would then occur.

Another important factor is the number of security personnel that are required to control a person until the person is in restraints. In several training textbooks and other printed matter, it indicates that one person is sufficient to arrest. In law enforcement environments, where authority is greater and lethal weapons are carried, this is an easier process but subjects are difficult to handcuff. If you watch the numerous television programs that document police arrests, even they have difficulty.

Each property has a procedure that the chief security officer has approved and should be utilized. In most cases, there should be two security officers that are the primary team charged with handcuffing a combative person. There will be times when only one person is available to accomplish the task. The backup officers, if available, should keep a short distance and control the people in the area and start canvassing for independent witnesses as soon as the situation is secured.

It is not desirable to have more than two security officers attempting to place handcuffs on a combative person, although there are circumstances where the person is exerting more force than the two officers can respond to with opposing force. In those cases, one person on each arm and one with the handcuffs may be necessary.

If five or six security officers respond and all of them take on the process of handcuffing, there is an uncoordinated effort to contain the situation. There is also an unwanted display of unprofessional actions being viewed by the customers in the immediate area. Responding to help a fellow officer is commendable. Getting in the way and prolonging the process is not wise. It will be on the video that management watches the following morning and also by courtroom participants in the event of a lawsuit is brought against the property.

15.9 PROSECUTING THE TRESPASSER

Once the person has been either taken away by the police or issued a misdemeanor citation, the local prosecutor makes the decision of whether to prosecute the person or to drop the charges. This decision is very important to the security department and is a much misunderstood legal process. The prosecutor will look at the person being charged, any criminal history, the circumstances of the arrest, and whether the elements of the crime have been met.

Every prosecutor I have ever dealt with has told me that there are two basic reasons they drop charges. The first reason is typically that the written report and accompanying statements do not indicate that the elements of the crime have been met. Each crime has elements, or components, that must occur according to the statutes or ordinances involved. As an example, if a person is told to leave the facility by a cashier, and security arrives and places the person in handcuffs for trespassing and signs the formal complaint, there could be issues. Trespass is usually a misdemeanor crime, which requires that it be witnessed by the person making the arrest. If the cashier did not properly advise the person according to the statute, all of the elements have not been met to be able to charge the person with the crime. In this scenario, the security officer approached and handcuffed the person without giving sufficient warning or a chance to leave once the person was advised. The trespass arrest would most likely be dismissed as a result of a technicality.

As another example, if security responds to an incident that is evolving quickly and does not have time to warn the person to leave, the security officer cannot arrest for trespass unless there is a specific provision in the statute. In this example, it may be a more appropriate to charge the person with disturbing the peace or disorderly conduct depending on the circumstances. Consulting your trespass and other laws will assist in understanding the differences.

The second and most common reason that charges are dropped in large metropolitan jurisdictions is that the witnesses, including the security officers, do not appear for trial. Even though subpoenas are issued, there is not always effective follow-up for arrests. Employee turnover and schedules will interfere with the ability to show up for trial. In larger operations once the arrest has been made, frequently there is little motivation to follow up on the case with the district attorney.

Consider that the prosecutor has the ability to cut a deal for the charges and to dismiss them based on all of the circumstances. Any attorney can argue and deal with a prosecutor and have charges reduced or dismissed. Follow-up on all arrests is an important function of security management to reduce the exposure to claims and litigation.

It would be prudent for every arrest to be followed up with a call to the prosecutor and a discussion of the event that precipitated the arrest. The security manager or a supervisor can be required to attend any trial of persons who have been arrested and are fighting those charges. The prosecutor needs to know that you will push for an acceptable conviction and that you will do whatever you can to ensure charges are not dropped unless there is a compelling reason.

In larger facilities, it would be ideal if the supervisor of the particular shift during which an arrest occurred be charged with follow-up on that arrest. That would include keeping track of all witnesses, including forwarding addresses, and making sure the prosecutor has all of the documents including associated video evidence. This makes that manager responsible for incidents that occurred on his or her shift and responsible to report the final results to the chief. The learning process that supervisors will go through is invaluable. The overall results of arrests on their performance evaluation can be an effective motivator to make arrest a last resort.

15.10 EMPLOYEE MISCONDUCT

Any time employees are at work there is potential for misconduct in many different areas. The security department is typically charged with monitoring employees along with the surveillance department. This monitoring goes beyond the normal supervision by the relevant department. There are many different violations that can constitute employee misconduct and may require security intervention, documentation, and enforcement.

The starting points for managing employee misconduct are the documented employee rules and regulations. These are typically managed by the human resources department with input from operational and administrative departments. It is expected that all employees will comply with these rules that have been established and approved. The rules and regulations established by management are a result of state and federal laws as well as specific corporate policies based in part on the evolution of the property and on historical events. The rules of conduct are typically memorialized in the form of an employee handbook and are numbered and specific about prohibited conduct. They are commonly referred to as rules of conduct and are given to all employees before their first work shift.

In dealing with employee misconduct incidents, the security department should approach these in the same manner as an arrest in that elements of the procedure need to be met before a violation can occur. These rules of conduct are typically vague but do establish unwanted conduct. The following example is used to illustrate:

> Fighting between employees or with a customer is forbidden. Verbal or physical altercations on the premises will not be tolerated unless in the scope of employment as a security officer, or similar position of authority, and according to departmental policy to protect customers and employees.

This policy addresses altercations that involve employees, other than the security officer responding to an incident, and following established guidelines. The language also allows certain intervention by a manager. If two employees get into a loud argument in the public area and the incident is observed, documented, and managed properly, it is a clear violation of this policy. The rules of conduct will typically address the penalties that can be established, up to and including discharge from employment.

The responding security officer should approach these situations with caution and make sure the department supervisor or manager has been notified. Obtaining witness statements from other employees and even customers may be required and desired to document the unwanted behavior. The security officer should never take sides in these incidents and, instead, should make sure each participant has a chance to write a statement of what he or she saw, did, and said during the incident. It is important to obtain this information while it is fresh and it will prove valuable to the decisionmaker later.

Notifying the surveillance department to produce a possible video of the incident, regardless of whether it shows any unwanted behavior or not, is also very important. If one of the employees makes false statements about a location and what occurred and the video does not show the incident, the video could be a deciding factor for the person charged with the final employment decision. If the video does support one employee and not the other, this will also be an important factor to be considered.

The security director or manager should also have input into the rules of conduct whenever they are reviewed for changes. The director should send a memorandum to human resources whenever the need arises to address conduct that should be prohibited. I have found that having certain security-related rules of conduct will go a long way in enforcing and deterring employee misconduct. The following are rules of conduct that can be helpful.

1. Failure to cooperate in a security, surveillance, or management investigation.
2. Failure to report any illegal activity occurring on the property.
3. Failure to report (or having knowledge and not reporting) any employee theft of company funds or inventory.

Documenting employee incidents is critical if the company objective is to manage the behavior of employees on company time. I have found that if the incident report and accompanying statements, video, and other evidence are obtained in a comprehensive and professional manner, the disciplinary process will move swiftly. Supervisors, managers, executives, and, in some cases, union representatives will have the tools and supporting documentation to discharge an employee or apply disciplinary procedures to correct the unwanted behavior. Incomplete documentation may be the cause of reinstating an employee who has obvious attitude problems.

The security officer who is completing the report should have a clear and concise record of what occurred and of what rules were violated. Whenever possible, a copy of the employee's signature on the original rules of conduct and acknowledgment from human resources will be helpful in the management's decision on the disciplinary incident.

There are many different individual acts or failures to act that could constitute employee misconduct in today's gaming environments. The listing of every possible infraction is almost impossible and there would be thousands of individual rules to follow. Careful consideration and review of the rules of conduct should be made with input from the highest level of security management before the rules are set in print. Input from legal counsel is also important to make sure that all current employment laws are followed. An annual review of these is helpful to keep them current, relevant, and enforceable.

Finally, there may be times when an employee is arrested and placed in handcuffs by the security staff or law enforcement. Decades ago, management would have taken the employee out to the waiting patrol car with as many other employees watching as possible. As a result of some operations parading the employee back and forth in the casino and the subsequent defamation lawsuits, this practice is not used in contemporary environments. Executives who still believe this is a good practice will most likely be sued individually, especially if the charges are dropped.

The security department involved in employee misconduct incidents needs to ensure that proper documentation and collection of evidence are accomplished. Security is not responsible for deciding the guilt or innocence of an employee. If a supervisor of a department wants security involvement in what is clearly an operational incident, the security supervisor should intervene. Security reports are usually written on major infractions, including theft, intoxication by alcohol or drugs, fighting or assault, and other criminal behavior.

15.11 INCIDENTS IN HOTEL AREAS

Earlier in Chapter 11 we discussed the functions of the hotel security patrol and the importance of a physical presence in the sleeping rooms section of any gaming operation. The incidents that occur inside a hotel room and in the areas around them can be unusual, and in some cases, illegal and morally challenging. Response to incidents should always be taken seriously and professionally no matter how awkward, humorous, or strange a situation may seem.

Inside of each guest room, the person who is registered and any of his or her guests have certain protections from invasions of privacy. The security officer should always respect this privacy and not regularly or randomly access guest rooms except in emergency or perceived emergency situations. A check of the local laws pertaining to innkeepers will reveal clear rules regarding the rights of innkeepers, their employees, and the people who rent rooms.

15.12 CONDUCTING THE GUEST WELFARE CHECK

Relatives or a close personal friend may present concerns over a registered guest. This can be as simple as checking on an eighty-year-old man who has not called his worried wife to a potential suicide incident. The security officer who responds to a welfare check needs to keep in mind that the safety of the guest and his or her own safety are the first priority. Response to these should always be considered urgent and never delayed.

When a security officer responds to a guest room, he or she must consider there is an expectation of privacy to the individual registered and weigh it against the welfare check reason and circumstances (Figure 15.3). There should be, whenever possible, two security officers who respond to welfare checks. The officers should be prepared to respond with any emergency medical treatment or to quell any potential disturbances.

Many hotel guests refuse maid service and the rooms are not entered by the housekeeping staff, which can also be an indicator of unusual activity. Some properties have housekeeping supervisor staff do room checks to determine if there are any unusual activities there or items that would require security contact.

Once the room is determined to be locked and there is no verbal response from anyone inside, the room must be accessed by using the master keycard. It is important to also call the front desk and determine who is registered and if the person has any physical

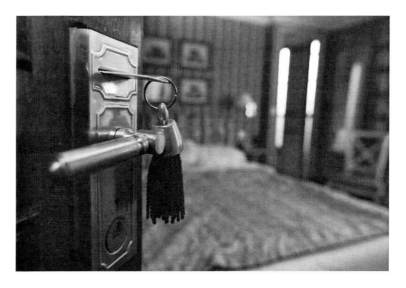

Figure 15.3 Security personnel must be especially prudent regarding guest safety checks, understanding that patrons have a certain expectation of privacy.

199

impairment that might be important, such as being deaf. The officers should announce "security" with clarity before entering.

The keycard, master override keycard, or other room master is then used to unlock the primary mortise lock and the deadbolt on the door. In some hotels the secondary locks may be engaged, which would include a flip lock or door chain. This will create a temporary barrier that will require forced entry. Whenever possible a maintenance employee can assist. In an emergency situation the easiest way may just be to kick or force the door inward.

Obviously, these circumstances should be rare and the end result usually is that a person has passed out, is unconscious, or has expired inside the room. Caution should be exerted when entering to maintain a crime scene if required. In some circumstances, the person may be alert and had earphones or other noise distractions in place and will express surprise that security people are breaking into the room.

My very first incident as a uniformed security officer on a welfare check was for a fifty-two-year-old man who had not called his wife in two days and had requested no maid service. When I finally broke in to the room, he was standing on the outside balcony receiving oral sex from an obviously younger companion. He was also a very good customer of the casino and expressed his displeasure with the general manager. He was no longer a customer after that experience.

In those circumstances where there is a death and you have verified the person is not breathing, there is no heartbeat, and the person is cold to the touch, the room must be secured and the scene protected until the police can respond to determine the cause of death. Identifying any person who enters the room prior to police arriving will help in the investigation. Preparing the lock, if electronic, for interrogation personnel to determine who accessed the room at what times will also prove helpful.

Finding an expired guest will begin a long and sometimes complicated process, especially if there is foul play suspected or criminal activity. You can usually plan on having that room out of order for time, especially if a person had been decomposing for a couple days. Sensitivity to the employees and any relatives will be necessary in these situations.

15.13 DOMESTIC HOTEL INCIDENTS AND EVICTING A GUEST

One of the most common responses to a hotel room will be the domestic call or those that involve personal relationships or relatives. These calls are often unpredictable and have the probability of escalating rapidly. The security officer responding is often unwittingly entering into an argument or incident with no information. The history, dynamics, and personalities are unknown to the responding security officer.

It is important for the responding officer to understand that he or she is not the mediator of the relationship and instead is the mediator of the immediate altercation. The mission should be to keep the peace and quell the disturbance. Again, the notification of local law enforcement can be helpful in these situations if domestic laws have been broken through battery or spousal abuse.

Any experienced law enforcement officer will tell you that domestics are dangerous incidents to respond to and handle. It is the same in the gaming environment and the conditions can escalate quickly and without any warning. At least two initial security officers should respond if available.

The local innkeeper's laws should be consulted to determine if there is a statute or ordinance that allows for removal of undesirable patrons and any laws that govern the process. Many states have specific laws that assist properties with dealing with these incidents. The objective should be to stop the incident and calm the people involved. The outcome could, and often does, result in the eviction of guests from the hotel.

I have been involved in numerous incidents where a person is trespassed out of the casino, based on an incident or unwanted behavior, and the officer never determined whether he or she was a hotel guest. As mentioned earlier, if a person is unwanted in the casino, he or she should also be unwanted in the hotel. However, this may not always be the case. Regardless of the reason a person has been asked to leave the casino, you are now presented with the situation where you as the innkeeper have entered into a contract with someone to provide a room.

In casino trespass incidents, some properties escort the person and his or her party from the security office to the hotel room through the casino and other public areas. Then they stand outside the room and make the patrons pack up their things and check them out of the room. In many instances, the hotel will refuse to refund any of the costs associated with the stay.

The question that needs to be asked is: Is there a compelling reason to evict this patron in this manner? In most circumstances, the answer is "no" and the reason is most likely that it is the policy of the property. These incidents should be handled in this manner when there is an obvious danger to the welfare of other guests and employees and not as a matter of routine.

Taking this action could subject the property to a tort claim for defamation where the plaintiff will demonstrate to a jury that he or she was embarrassed, humiliated, and treated unfairly. The security director or manager will have to testify as to the compelling reason he or she had to physically remove the person from the hotel in the middle of the night because of an incident in the casino.

As corporate environments evolved and multiple gaming facilities have become owned and controlled by one company or tribe, the process of trespassing a person from all owned properties became routine. In cities like Las Vegas, a visitor typically has no clue which properties are owned by which companies, regardless of the expensive marketing campaigns. That customer who got into a minor incident at one casino months earlier and who is later arrested for trespass in another casino for merely entering the doors will certainly have some argument for a legal action.

The decision to evict someone from a hotel room should be made very carefully and all of the circumstances should be weighed by the security supervisor who makes the decision. A bit of investigating to determine who the person is and detailing any personal history will go a long way in avoiding misunderstandings as a result of incidents, arrests, and the eviction of valuable customers. Refunding the night's hotel cost to the customer can never hurt and may prevent claims and complaints.

16

Arrests and Detainments

16.1 AN ARREST AS A LAST RESORT

An arrest is a negative situation for both the person arrested and the security personnel. It should not be envisioned as fun or exciting, although it will certainly energize the security officer with adrenaline and emotions. Any time that a reasonable solution to an incident can be found, the professional security officer should utilize it before resorting to a citizen's arrest. The supervisor then attempts to find the same solution and guide his or her subordinates to creative solutions other than arrest. An arrest by a security officer of an individual at a casino carries no more weight than a private citizen's arrest anyone can make in any jurisdiction.

Although security officers wear uniforms and are perceived by patrons as authority figures, they are not police and therefore do not have police powers or the statutory immunities that come with being a sworn law enforcement officer. With the authority from the private employer comes the permission of the rightful owner to act on the employer's behalf.

Security officers, like ordinary citizens, have certain rights as individuals that they expect to be respected and not intentionally violated. Customers have those same rights and are equal to the security officer. Stopping individuals from free movement or restricting them from leaving is detention and, in most environments, is considered an arrest. Handcuffs or other restraints do not necessarily need to be used to effect an arrest.

In most jurisdictions, it is not necessary, based on the written statutory provisions, to tell a person that he or she is under arrest for a particular crime. It is prudent, however, to advise a person that he or she is under arrest as soon as practical and once any immediate safety issue is resolved. Safety to the person arrested, the general public, and the security personnel involved should be considered. The actual criminal charges may take some time to finalize by the responding and investigating peace officer.

There are situations that require an arrest as a reasonable solution to a disruption in the normal course of business. Some individuals will refuse to comply or cooperate with the lawful requests to leave a property or will create such a disruption that the only legal recourse is to arrest them for the behavior that is prohibited by law. Crimes against property such as larceny or embezzlement will typically not require an immediate arrest action, and involvement of the prosecutor may be desired prior to an arrest. In those circumstances where time is available, reports, statements, and evidence can be presented to a police investigator and then submitted to the district attorney for warrant and prosecution.

Whenever time and circumstances will permit, local law enforcement should be called to handle arrest incidents. They have authority granted to them by the jurisdiction that a security officer (or private citizen) does not have and can be useful in arrest situations. They can also witness the main elements of trespass when the security officer advises a patron that he or she is trespassing and must leave the premises. That same police officer or deputy is then a good witness and can accomplish the custody immediately or, in some cases, make an arrest. This also reduces any potential exposure to liability.

If two neighbors in a residential environment get into a verbal argument and one of them punches the other out of anger, battery has occurred. The person injured calls the police and they respond and investigate. In many instances, the peace officer will tell you to verbally place the offender under arrest and, after you do so, the offender is either issued a citation or taken into police custody. This can work just as efficiently in the gaming environment and can limit exposure for false arrest and other intentional torts.

Police officers can detain a person under general circumstances for up to one hour based on case law (*Terry v. Ohio*, 392 U.S. 1, 1968). Security personnel do not have that same latitude and should be cautious in detaining an individual. A check of the local statutes and ordinances will define the authority to detain under gaming law and under which circumstances. There are also many states that have retail or innkeeper laws that allow for detention, which is usually for the purpose of investigating a criminal act or for the purposes of notifying a peace officer. As an example, in many states a retail grocery store employee has the authority to detain a shoplifter for the purposes of notifying a peace officer.

The local statutes can be consulted for the exact definition and requirements for which a detention of an individual can be legally accomplished. The basic element of most of these laws is the taking of a person into custody in a manner according to law. If the arrest is not made according to law, you subject the property and the owners to intentional torts, negligence torts, and financial liability.

The arrest process will tie up several security officers sometimes for hours and take them away from proactive patrol and other security functions. The smooth operation of security is disrupted, breaks are affected, and the attitudes of the staff change when arrests are occurring. The decision to arrest should be the last resort in a given incident. The exception to this would be dangerous situations, larceny crimes, or felony incidents.

Once a person has been detained and is not allowed to leave, it could be demonstrated that an arrest had been made. Unless there are specific laws that allow for detention for the purpose of notifying a peace officer under specific circumstances, detentions should be avoided. If a person is requested to come to the security office to discuss a problem and he or she complies, the visit is voluntary. As soon as the security personnel block the door by standing in front of it, say, or imply that the person is not free to leave, then it could be considered an arrest or false imprisonment if the person perceives he or she cannot leave.

In circumstances where an arrest has been made or a person is legally detained, the person should be brought to a nonpublic location for the detainment whenever possible. In today's larger gaming security environments, the common industry practice is that a detention area be available that has video and audio recording equipment to protect all parties during detainment. The retention time of this video is different for each jurisdiction. These locations may include a security office, holding room, detention room, or even holding cells. There will be certain circumstances where the person arrested and handcuffed is not moved and a peace officer is requested to the incident location.

Once the person is arrested at some location on the property and is escorted to the security office, holding room, or detention area, the local law enforcement should be immediately notified. The person arrested is seated and restrained using handcuffs if he or she is combative or if the property policy dictates it. If the person has not been arrested, then handcuffs should not be applied unless a compelling safety reason exists.

As discussed earlier, an arrest means that the person held has violated some law that has basic elements to it. All of the elements of the law need to be met in order for the arrest to be within legal authority. The concept of filing multiple charges to see which ones stick is archaic and not professional in the gaming environment for a private citizen making a citizen's arrest. Only those laws clearly violated are important. If the ultimate objective is to get the person out of the facility, then it does not make sense to add numerous misdemeanor charges, which could be interpreted as unnecessarily punitive to the offender.

The responding police officer will most likely review the elements and the evidence to ensure that the requirements have been met. In today's environments, police will request any available video of the incident and will want to review it prior to deciding on action. Having the video ready will not only expedite the process, it will also demonstrate your professionalism. If the elements of the crime have not been met or the arrest is deemed not to be lawful, the peace officer has a duty to release the person from custody, which is typically also a statutory law. Merely requesting a peace officer to take a person into custody does not require an officer to do so if the arrest is deemed unlawful.

Detention can last for hours at a time in some metropolitan areas based on the availability of police and prioritized calls. It can also be lengthy in rural areas where law enforcement has to travel some distance to handle the call. These delays in response can create numerous situations or potential escalation of incidents while a person is waiting for local law enforcement to respond. It is important to understand that if the original reason for the arrest is not valid, or based on legal authority, then all of the subsequent actions can be interpreted by a civil court as additional intentional torts committed against the person in a legal action.

Consideration should be made to ensure that the arrest and detention are the only solutions to the problem that is presented and to ensure that whatever crime you are arresting the person for has clearly been committed. Once that has occurred, then the wait becomes the immediate issue for the security personnel involved.

There are numerous schools of thought regarding this wait between the time that security officers bring a suspect into a detention area and when the police investigate and deal with the arrest. The length of time is the critical issue that must be considered. The security personnel will be unaware in advance of the time they will be tied up watching a suspect in any given arrest situation. Some security professionals require at least two security officers for every one suspect detained. Others require that the suspect be restrained with seat belts or handcuffed to an anchor point and that only one security officer per suspect be present. Regardless of the reason, the presence of security staff should be for the safety of the person detained and the safety of guests and employees.

With every word and action typically recorded inside the detention area, the security personnel should be professional and polite during these situations. In the event of a lawsuit the video will most likely be played numerous times during a trial and especially during closing arguments. A simple comment by a security officer to a suspect can make a huge difference in the outcome. Maintaining a professional demeanor, not arguing or reprimanding the person, not taking sides, and refraining from making humorous comments directed toward the offender will demonstrate that the security personnel are truly professional when the video is played later.

The microphones used in these environments do not always clearly record audio of all that occurs. Multiple people talking, yelling, radio transmissions, and other distracting noises can overpower critical voices and comments in a detention room. Rules regarding talking and use of radios can be maintained to preserve the best record possible during detentions.

Courtesies extended during the detention process should be made or at least considered. If a person is combative and spitting at the officers and demands water it would be reasonable to deny that request until the person has calmed down if a long detention is anticipated. Denying water may not look positive later when the video is played for a jury. Keep in mind that the more water you give a person the more likely the person will need to eliminate it and request the use of a bathroom.

16.2 RESTROOM USE

In some modern security detention areas a bathroom is located inside the detention area. In most casinos bathrooms are located away from the holding area and sometimes in the casino and open to the public. Bathroom breaks are difficult to manage with a person in handcuffs and yet must be addressed. If you deny a person the use of a restroom and he or she urinates or defecates in his or her clothes, you not only have a cleanup problem, but you also are going to irritate the responding police and the denial and detention could be considered inhumane.

In most situations the person will have handcuffs removed to accomplish this. Certainly there should be enough security personnel to restrain the person in the event he or she attempts to escape. The urgency of relieving themselves is sufficient to motivate most people to behave. I have seen some properties utilize a handicap stall where grab bars can be used to secure one hand and still allow for reasonable cleanup with those persons who have demonstrated a propensity for violent behavior. It also allows for plenty of room if closer observation is required. Be sure to allow handicap access if a person requires the stall.

Taking someone to the bathroom can create a host of challenges in an arrest situation. Gender, proximity, escort considerations, and making the determination of how closely the security officer should watch a person performing this bodily function have to be considered. A clear and defined policy regarding this can be developed for security personnel in these situations. Variances for the procedures can be allowed by the security supervisor for unpredictable situations.

The possibility of the person having some item of contraband or something he or she does not wish to be found by the responding peace officer does exist and should be considered. This is a secondary issue to the reason the person has been detained, not a primary one. It is not critical to your arrest that a person was able to flush narcotics down the toilet, for example. Observations and precautions can be taken to watch for it and communicate this observation to the police.

16.3 NOTIFYING LOCAL LAW ENFORCEMENT

For documentation reasons the initial call and all subsequent calls can be made from the place of detention where such calls can be seen and heard on the closed-circuit television recording if possible. The initial call should note that you have the person in custody and you are requesting a police officer as soon as possible. Having the person's name and vital information can help expedite the initial call if the person voluntarily provides it.

The initial call should not be delayed or postponed if you have someone in custody. Getting the local police involved as soon as possible should be the objective. They can assist in the process, investigation, and offer final solutions to resolve the incident.

A status call every thirty minutes during detention can also go a long way to remind the dispatcher you are still waiting and to document the request on that now even more important video recording. Police dispatchers might get irritated about multiple calls, but dispatchers will not be named in a lawsuit or claim later. In the event of a long delay a field supervisor or watch commander might have to be called to assist the process or to explain why the delay in response.

The key is to make the notification as soon as possible and practical and to get police on their way to the situation. Unnecessary delays in this notification can create a host of problems and add liability in certain circumstances. Making sure the person who has been arrested hears you call the police or telling the person that the police are on their way will play well on the video tape in the courtroom.

16.4 CHECKING RESTRAINTS

During detentions the person will most likely be in handcuffs. It is also suggested for safety and documentation reasons that the handcuffs be checked at regular intervals to determine if they are injuring the person in any way (Figure 16.1). Asking the person if they are too tight or requesting if you can check them at regular intervals will also help on that video of the detention and arrest. The time span between checks is dependent on the procedures and training of the security staff. It is difficult to mandate a check every specific number of minutes based on all of the events that might be occurring. It is safer to check the handcuffs more often than not.

Documenting that you checked the handcuffs a certain number of times and specifically the time will also show professionalism and may mitigate any accusations that they were too tight and caused injury. Making sure that the restraints are adequately placed should also be done whenever possible according to your training. During difficult arrests the handcuffs may not be ideally placed on the wrists of a suspect or there was no immedi-

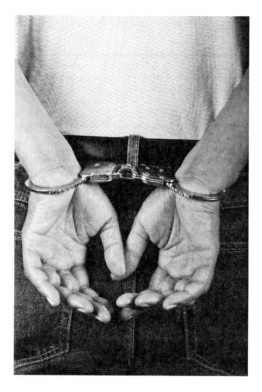

Figure 16.1 It is important, for safety and documentation reasons, to check the patron and hand-cuffs at regular intervals.

ate opportunity to double lock the handcuffs. This should be done as soon as possible and when safe according to the training practices.

An effective training exercise for security officers is to handcuff an officer in training and make him or her sit in the same location where a suspect would be seated. It does not take a long time for the trainee to feel the discomfort associated with handcuffs and sitting calmly and complying with requests for behavior modification.

16.5 DEALING WITH MEDICAL ISSUES

There are legitimate medical issues that can arise during a detention. Whenever a suspect claims or exhibits any medical condition it should be made the priority concern. Medical officers, emergency medical technicians, or local emergency medical responders should be called to make an assessment. Unfortunately many suspects will also falsely claim a medical condition for sympathy or in an attempt to be released. Having professionals assist in the evaluation will screen out these instances.

It is helpful if the security personnel check the person to see if he or she has a medical alert bracelet or necklace that might identify a medical condition. Making sure the person can see, talk, and hear is also important during an arrest.

People with diabetes, mental disabilities, and many other conditions can be problematic during a detention. The objective should be to get the person evaluated by a trained professional as soon as possible and practical. Intentional or accidental overdoses and alcohol poisoning can create a life-threatening situation especially if the wait time is hours during a detention. Heart conditions, pulmonary diseases, and a host of other medical conditions can also present themselves and be challenging to the security staff who must deal with medical issues because the person you have handcuffed cannot.

16.6 CONDUCTING SEARCHES

Security professionals will have varying opinions on when and how a search of a person detained for an arrest should be done. Searching a person who is detained may create civil rights violations based on the basic Constitution and Amendments. Officers who have undergone Peace Officers Standards Training receive extensive training in search and seizure and are more familiar with the process than security personnel. Having them conduct searches whenever possible will prove beneficial.

In arrest situations the search process is normally confined to a search for weapons that may be used in an attempt to escape or take retaliatory action against the arresting officer. This is accomplished with the use of a simple and basic "pat down" to feel for obvious weapons such as guns, knives, pepper spray, stun guns, or similar items. A search to find is not designed to pull everything out of person's pockets and go through every item looking for drugs or other illegal substances. Unless there is a specific law that provides the permission for this, it should be avoided. If you are arresting the person, the responding peace officer will be arriving and can make the discovery of any illegal item and arrest accordingly.

Removing a person's wallet and taking his or her identification out, photocopying it, and looking for other identification without permission can also be problematic. Unless there is a compelling safety reason, this should be avoided and can wait until the peace officer arrives who can then obtain the identification. Conducting comprehensive searches similar to those done in confinement environments are not advised in simple gaming arrests.

There are locations that train security personnel in the process of issuing a summons in lieu of arrest and verifying the identity of a suspect. If the security supervisor wishes to utilize this program, it should be with consent of the person being arrested and the search for the ID done with permission. If the offender is not agreeable, then the wait for a peace officer should be resumed.

17

Theft, Larceny, and Other Property Crimes

17.1 THEFT AND FRAUD: THE SECURITY RESPONSE

Another important function of a gaming security department is the protection of assets. The primary department charged with monitoring the assets in the gaming areas is surveillance, where myriad technology with closed-circuit television (CCTV) views is available. Surveillance will monitor the cash and negotiable items throughout the facility and watch security personnel who may have access.

As mentioned earlier, the process of arresting and prosecuting an employee is sometimes difficult and requires knowledge of the laws and conditions that must be present to accomplish a successful prosecution. Whenever possible security and surveillance should collect as much evidence as possible and present it to the local authority to evaluate whether an arrest should be made and if the crimes involved will be prosecuted. Making an arrest prematurely can result in myriad undesirable results that may undermine the main objective of a conviction. If time and conditions allow, the preparations can be made and a police officer rather than a security officer will come to the property and place the employee under arrest.

If a gaming security officer makes an observation of an employee who is suspicious and possibly committing a larceny, he or she should refrain from overreacting and back away. The security officer's observation can then be communicated to management and surveillance. Surveillance can then start the process of documenting or forensically examining video evidence. There could be a history of other instances that may be captured on video leading up to this observation. That security officer should then immediately write a comprehensive statement of his or her observation to include location, time, date, and all of the basics of who, what, where, and when. The incident should not be discussed by the officer with anyone other than his or her supervisor.

Once it has been determined that a potential crime has been committed, then the pieces can be put together and presented to a police officer who will determine if an arrest should be made or if the case should be referred to the prosecutor who will make a determination.

211

As mentioned earlier when there is no urgency or requirement to arrest, then care and time can be your friend and allow for a comprehensive investigation and the filing of charges later. In some instances the regulators will conduct the investigation and coordinate with security and surveillance.

In the event a security officer observes an employee actually removing company property and it is clear that the property belongs to the company or entity, the person can be detained if all of the elements of the crime have been met. In misdemeanor crimes it typically will require that the person making the arrest must have witnessed the crime (in this case that would be the security officer). Care should also be given to make sure that the item was not given to the employee by a supervisor or manager but the incident should be investigated regardless.

Making sure that all security personnel are aware of the basic elements of larceny crimes and embezzlement will prove to be beneficial in determining severity of the punishment and value of item stolen. Also making sure that the item is the property of the employer will prevent major misunderstandings and claims. An accusation of theft by words or actions that turns out to be unfounded is not only negative employee relations, it can open the company or tribe to claims and litigation.

There will also be circumstances where security personnel will be called to handle accusations of theft or other crimes between customers. These situations require caution and discretion in that secondhand information has not been witnessed. These circumstances are best handled by calling the local law enforcement. They can sort out the details and make a determination of what occurred and what actions should be taken. If security overreacts in these circumstances, it could lead to intentional torts and negligent civil actions. A spiteful customer wanting to get even with an ex-friend can draw security into an uncomfortable situation.

Areas of a casino/hotel that hold guests' property can also create property loss or theft incidents. Bell staff, valet parking attendants, and coat check departments are locations where a guest's property has been entrusted to and has the potential of being taken or damaged by employees or other visitors. In these situations it is important to document the incident in great detail, to include copies of any claim checks, and to gather potential video evidence and collect written statements from all parties including the alleged victim.

17.2 VALET PARKING

In the valet parking department hundreds of cars will be moved and parked by employees in any given shift. As a result there are thousands of opportunities for theft, damage, and rule infractions by employees (Figure 17.1). This department should have very clear and well-defined policies and procedures that the attendants must adhere to. Security and surveillance should be aware of these rules of conduct and monitor and enforce them regularly.

From a safety perspective there should always be a speed limit that valets must comply with when driving customers' vehicles. Prohibitions on reckless driving and other unsafe driving practices should be clearly defined in writing even though driving practices may be deemed "common sense" by management. Violations of these safety rules should be strictly enforced with stiff disciplinary penalties.

Figure 17.1 Valet parking provides employees and other individuals with numerous opportunities for theft.

Once a customer hands an attendant the keys to a vehicle and the attendant in turn hands the customer a claim check, an agreement has been made between the casino and the customer commonly known in most jurisdictions as a "bailee with a duty." Simply stated this means you have a duty to maintain the customer's property in a reasonable manner. Should damage or theft of that property occur while it is entrusted to you, certain responsibility for replacement is placed on the facility. Local laws or ordinances will dictate if there is a limit on the liability (or dollar value) of property removed from an environment where claim checks are utilized.

A common mistake that most gaming operations make is to treat claims for theft and damage in valet operations suspiciously, including suspicion of the victim. This is a concern for managers in that not all claims are suspicious and may very well be genuine where a customer insistently claims that a pair of expensive sunglasses was in his vehicle when he parked it and now they are missing and the only people who had access were the persons who parked and retrieved the car. Treating a customer in a suspicious manner will certainly risk losing his business.

In most circumstances when a vehicle is stolen while in the care of the valet parking area a claim will result. Unless there are mitigating circumstances the casino will be responsible for the vehicle regardless of the language printed on the claim check and signs in the valet area. This then requires security procedures to minimize this risk, which occurs hundreds of times in a given day. Unfortunately valet attendants have a tendency to shortcut the rules in order to please the guests who may offer gratuities for the service they are providing or want to move more cars faster to increase tips by sheer volume of cars parked and retrieved.

An example of a risky security procedure in a valet parking area is where the attendants merely take the keys out of the ignition and throw them on the floorboard or put them on the sun shade above the windshield until they have time to park the vehicle. On a busy valet ramp this provides a great opportunity to a car thief to select which car he or she wants to steal and just wait until the busy attendants do not see him or her getting in and driving away with the car. A luxury car with a value of over $100,000 can be removed in a matter of seconds because the valet department thought it would be okay to leave the keys easily accessible.

Although somewhat time-consuming and considered a hassle by the valet employees, the vehicles and the keys are kept separate at all times while in the custody of valet. In a particular property in Las Vegas that I frequent each car that is accepted by valet has the keys removed and hung on a big ring that is carried by an attendant who is charged with ramp security. As each customer gives the vehicle to an attendant, the vehicle is locked and the keys are placed on this ring. Whenever a car needs to be parked, another attendant merely gets the keys from the ramp security attendant and ultimate control is maintained of the vehicle. In some operations I have seen a security officer posted strictly for the purposes of watching valet cars with keys in the vehicles. As each vehicle is parked in the valet lot the keys and claim check are then hung on the board in a secured room until the customer is ready to claim the vehicle.

Another measure that is commonly overlooked is the locking of vehicles while in the custody of valet. A person hopping a fence or just walking by in those parking lots that do not have a perimeter fence or barrier can access items left inside a vehicle by just opening the door. Expensive sunglasses, satellite radio receivers, GPS navigation devices, and other valuables are often claimed as stolen by valet attendants. It is difficult to investigate if the vehicle had been left unlocked.

When investigating reported stolen vehicles from valet or self-parking, the security officer should first ask questions regarding possession of keys and legal ownership. Repossession employees could merely walk up to a parked vehicle with a set of keys issued by the lender and drive off with it. A simple question of ownership and whether the owner is behind on the payments may solve the mystery. Local law enforcement is typically required to be notified prior to repossession, but a property owner is not. If the person taking the car is not licensed to repossess vehicles, then anything can occur. Asking the customer if anyone else has keys to the vehicle is also important in the event a spouse, acquaintance, or relative may have removed the vehicle for some reason. It could be as simple as the person's spouse who does not want him or her to drive after drinking has removed the car out of concern. Taking a few minutes to ask a few basic questions may solve the immediate issue and not tie up an officer writing an unnecessary report.

Valet parking departments have a wide array of sophistication in security systems to protect the company and to fulfill the obligation for protection of customer vehicles. Although most properties require that an exterior damage check be completed, it is not always done unless management enforces the process. The typical car diagram on the valet ticket should be marked for any obvious damage. I found that having security personnel assigned to the exterior areas with specific instructions regarding valet can assist management in enforcing this important function.

While patrolling the valet area the security officer can make a spot observation of a vehicle with damage. That officer can then document the check on the vehicle log and proceed to the valet office to see if the attendant properly marked the damage on the claim check. The officer then makes a note of the result and the supervisor communicates the results to the valet manager. Repeated violations of the procedure by certain valet attendants can then be addressed with appropriate discipline using the documented log as evidence of the violations.

In recent years and after many risk managers got tired of paying for claimed damage to vehicles while in the custody of the valet, some casinos have installed a video system specifically to thwart fraudulent claims of damage. With digital technology and multiple screen technology CCTV systems that record all sides of a vehicle as it enters a secured valet area have prevented numerous instances of attempted fraudulent claims. Valet attendants drive through or stop at a designated ingress location and the video captures the front, both sides, and the back to include the license plate. People claiming old damage as having occurred while in the care and custody of valet found the police being called for fraud.

The cost of installing this system can be justified by one or two claims involving fraudulent damage reports. This system will also help monitor the driving habits of the valet attendants and keep them from actually damaging cars by scraping or hitting other vehicles, posts, walls, or other obstacles. If a valet attendant delivers damaged a car to a customer that was parked in good condition according to the video, it makes the investigation easier to conduct and limits the number of employees involved and the damage causation possibilities.

17.3 THEFT FROM GUEST ROOMS

The hotel guest who reports to security that he or she misplaced a personal item should be taken seriously, especially if the potential incident occurred inside a hotel room (Figure 17.2). The normal questions should still be asked regarding the last time the person saw the item, whether it could have gotten lost elsewhere, and its value. Unfortunately staff members will take items from guest rooms based on many different factors. In my experience these situations are rare if the housekeeping staff is well managed.

The typical theft by employees inside of guest rooms will be for cash, chips, TITO (ticket in, ticket out) jackpot slips, and prescription or street drugs. Cameras, computers, and similar items can also be taken. The experienced thief, for example, will most likely steal only one of the ten $20 bills inside a room. Greed typically takes over and they take more from other guests as time goes on. Careful tracking of all guest-reported thefts or "lost property" inside of hotel rooms will prove fruitful in investigating these crimes. By only tracking theft reports a true evaluation of potential theft from guest rooms cannot accurately be made. Tracking all reports of missing items needs to be included.

The housekeeper or maintenance worker who takes five Percocet or Vicodin pills out of a prescription bottle in a guest room will be difficult to track and catch and will certainly irritate a guest to the point that he or she may never come back. Removal of illegal items such as marijuana or other narcotics will also most likely never be reported to

Figure 17.2 When theft of a personal item occurs inside a hotel room, security should take particular notice—it may indicate theft by one or more employees.

security or guests will report a legal item stolen in an attempt to find out who took their drugs and get them back. In these situations it is not uncommon for the guest to confront a maid and other staff members and accuse them without involving security. This can become dangerous for the employees and create incidents that will become complicated based on a lack of cooperation from the guest and concern that responding police will arrest him or her.

Working with the executive housekeeper to monitor changes in behavior of staff and tracking employees who work a particular floor or area will be helpful in investigating and catching the employee who steals from the guests. Random checks of staff employees' lockers will also prove beneficial in finding guest or company property that has been deposited during the employee's shift. The employees typically will not carry items stolen from a guest room on their person after the crime. I have also found that spot inspections of' maid carts and storage rooms will disclose interesting items.

In the event that a particular employee becomes a suspect based on location, schedules, proximity, and other factors, there are certain things that can assist apprehension. The first step would be to contact the local law enforcement and speak with a property crimes detective or administrator and request assistance. In many cases they will jump at the chance to legally set up a room and catch a thief.

Leaving marked cash inside of a hotel room and placing a CCTV camera can be done, but require many hours of observation time, the blocking of two hotel rooms for the investigation, and the probability that the staff will observe security entering or exiting the room. It also requires that the rooms not be occupied by a paying guest. These rooms must appear normal since a housekeeper or other employee knows what a typical occupied room looks like. This is not advised absent extreme circumstances and involvement of law enforcement and human resources.

In properties where electronic key systems are used for guest rooms, a proactive method to spot check housekeeping personnel is to take the device known as the "lock interrogator" and spot check various rooms to see if employees are entering rooms when they are not assigned for a specific reason, such as maid service or a maintenance call.

17.4 INVENTORY THEFT BY EMPLOYEES

The surveillance department can be extremely helpful in providing CCTV to combat recurring theft of inventory. Depending on the sophistication of your receiving department, food and beverage auditors, and control procedures, there are numerous places that CCTV can be installed in an overt or covert manner. It always amazes me that a camera can be in plain sight and yet a particular employee will steal merchandise. It is also amazing how many employees can be caught stealing or violating procedures in any environment where supervision is minimal.

The surveillance department is the best group to conduct those investigations involving inventory theft, and they have the ability and expertise to accomplish the project. Cooperation and planning with them will reap great rewards when catching a thief with company property. The methods will vary significantly in how a person steals inventory.

The shrinkage of inventory is monitored by the accounting department, and there are many tools that will assist them in determining if theft is occurring somewhere along the chain of inventory use. These data may appear to indicate theft or may reveal poor management practices or inadequate tracking of inventory within the affected department. Conducting a thorough investigation before interviewing a suspected employee is advised.

The areas that typically have the highest exposure are warehouse, beverage, food, retail, and back of house, including the maintenance and housekeeping departments. The transporting of inventory can also be a target when it is not managed well. The steward pushing a cart of steaks and seafood to a restaurant kitchen stops and leaves his cart in the hallway while he uses the restroom. When he returns he may find a box or two missing. The dishonest employee may have a great barbecue courtesy of his or her employer due to lack of controls on inventory.

17.5 BARTENDERS AND SERVERS

Bars are fertile environments for employee theft and embezzlement. An experienced bartender has the ability to steal up to half of the intended revenues from a casino. There are many ways this can occur. The most obvious is that a bottle of liquor is simply stolen from inventory. The bartender also has the ability to overpour drinks based on the size of a gratuity or other personal gain. In most cases a triple shot is common when a $5 bill is placed as a tip each round. The end result is that the house is down the price of two drinks and the customer is ahead if the drinks cost $7 each.

Some bartenders or servers will also find a way to use the players' incentive programs and convert comps to cash using these marketing programs. The methods will vary but the concept is to sell a drink to a customer, ring it into the register as complimentary, and pocket the cash at some point during the shift. If your property uses employee drink tokens, the process is also simple to obtain these drink tokens and convert them during the shift to cash.

Many bartenders are given the authority to comp drinks if a person is playing a slot machine at the bar. This authority is abused in many bars by ringing the drinks on the register as complimentary and collecting cash from the customers. It becomes easy to collect a series of drink receipts and use them throughout the shift to give to a customer and then pretend to ring the sale on the register while pocketing the cash.

The age-old method still widely in use is to serve a drink and not ring (or underring) the transaction. If a bartender underrings 100 drinks at $1 per drink during the night he has had a good night combined with the great tips he received for overpouring or serving premium liquor and charging for well liquor. Because there are so many opportunities for theft within a bar, this area should be monitored by surveillance regularly. Security observations will assist in detection, and security will be needed to handle the end result after the evidence has been collected on video.

Not all bartenders and servers steal from their employers and care should be given when conducting these types of investigations. If a security officer makes an observation of suspicious activity by a beverage server, he or she should not indicate the observation was made. Instead security should notify the proper chain of command and get the information to surveillance staff who have the tools to apply the technology and expertise to obtain the evidence required.

Close coordination between security and surveillance is required when making an arrest of a bartender for theft. The bankroll needs to be secured along with the trash can next to the register in the event that register slips are needed for evidence. I have always advocated letting a bartender or server finish the shift and have the surveillance department log and document the video and point of sale (POS) records. This allows for multiple counts to reduce the risk of the employee merely saying he or she "made a mistake." A piece of video that shows thirty "mistakes" will be hard for the employee to justify during an interview.

Counting down the register bank will typically reveal a large overage in cash if the employee has not pocketed the cash over the amount that is supposed to be in the register. Having a witness during this process and having the count done under a cashier's cage window is ideal to further collect the evidence to prosecute. Use of the security office where audio and video recording can capture the interview of the employee is also great evidence. Getting to the employee and counting down the register before the employee has a chance to level it off (remove the excess cash) can be helpful if the CCTV cannot obtain a shot of the company money going into an employee's pocket during the shift.

From a proactive standpoint there are things that can be done to minimize beverage theft by employees. Most of them involve basic good management of the employees and enforcement of established rules and procedures. Security can help by completing random, periodic audits of beverage employees during their shifts. This requires a full closing out of the employee register without warning and taking the employee, cash bank, comps and coupons, and tip jar to the cashier's cage and doing a midshift full audit. Although this can be disruptive to operations, it typically will reveal procedural issues or theft and will be proactive in that employees will never know when they might be audited. Every time a security officer comes behind or near the bar, the result just might be an audit and this alone will act as a deterrent and reduce theft.

17.6 FOOD CASHIERS AND SERVERS

Another employee area that requires constant monitoring is the restaurant. Essentially the same issues that affect bartenders typically are of concern. Conversion of comps or marketing coupons is the primary opportunity for a food cashier to steal from an employer. (A list of food and beverage tells is provided in the appendix to this book.)

The marketing department will come up with some pretty unusual promotions that attempt to pull in customers with disposable income. Hopefully they will check with the department heads of security and surveillance before implementing promotions. Buffet or steak specials become tools for theft if not managed correctly.

The restaurant manager will have access to the average cover amounts and can usually tell if an employee is cheating the system in some manner. It could be that procedures are not being followed, which may simply be that the employee is not entering drinks or desserts into the POS system and the company is then not receiving the revenues. These possibilities should be researched before conducting an investigation into theft because the issue may be an operational procedure problem and not an outright theft.

Procedures in these areas are routinely violated, which increases the opportunity for internal theft. A cash drawer that is not closed after each transaction is an indicator of a bad habit or potential theft. When security makes this observation, they should report it to the security supervisor on shift if possible. The security supervisor then reports it to surveillance, who can then observe the employee and make the appropriate documentation and reports to the department head or take immediate action if necessary.

17.7 THE FRIENDS AND FAMILY DISCOUNT

Significant revenues are lost every year to employees who "take care" of friends, roommates, or family members at the expense of an employer. The process is also simple in that the employee somehow creates a complimentary POS or manages to place an order outside the POS system. These losses can add up quickly if a party of five is comped off to a busy executive or an unsuspecting customer's player's incentive account.

The POS system if managed and used properly can assist in catching these incidents. It cannot catch a false report of a major service problem with a party if the supervisor comps the meal as a result. Finding a bug or rat feces are examples. Monitoring of employees' activity on the POS system can assist the security investigator in comparing sales, average cover cost, and incidental sales such as desserts and specialty drinks as compared to the other employees working at the same time.

Servers who get drinks, desserts, or other add-ons and "forget" to enter them on the check may be merely a procedural issue or may be intentional to increase the amounts of gratuities or as a favor to someone. Food managers and supervisors should keep a close watch on this area to maximize revenues. Giving merchandise away is theft and should be treated as theft if it can be proven.

Employees' dining rooms (EDR) should also be monitored. There are a number of employees who will attempt to get more than the traditional one meal per shift or who may bring family, friends, or roommates into the EDR. It becomes an unnecessary cost when this benefit is abused. Although there are identification tracking systems within the payroll system, there are many ways the system can be defeated.

When investigating servers and cashiers in these instances, a pattern can typically be found somewhere in the paperwork or POS documents that will lead to a solution of the problem. Coupon abuses along with other scams will typically be involved in combination with doing a favor for someone. The bottom line is that the company is being taken advantage of through theft and a direct loss of revenue.

17.8 MAINTENANCE STAFF AND ENGINEERS

Much like a construction site, the potential for theft from the maintenance area can also be problematic. Inventories of common parts, bolts, motors, and vehicle parts tend to disappear and no one knows where something went or if it was installed somewhere. Tools are targets if they are owned by the facility and they are not located in a tool room where they must be signed out. Outside contractors who are retained for specialty services, such as heating/ventilation/air conditioning, boilers, elevators, and service equipment, will also lose tools or walk away with company tools if not monitored and controlled.

This area is difficult to investigate if the department head finds that a $4,000 arc welder is missing. A simple report is completed and an investigation could take weeks, which would cost more to implement than the cost of a new welder. It is still important to document the loss and to monitor other equipment, tools, or inventory losses to recommend tighter controls. The outside patrol officer can also be useful in monitoring this type of theft by making observations of engineering employees who make frequent trips to their cars with parcels during a shift.

Any experienced security director will tell you that most theft occurs by employees in various ways and methods. In the current times of economic struggle, a certain percentage of the employee base will become increasingly tempted to take things from their employers. What and how they steal this property will depend on how effective the security program is. This includes the basic security program or inventory controls and not just the presence of the uniformed security officer. A highly motivated thief will simply wait until security is not around to steal from his or her employer. Having good policies and procedures along with adequate controls in each department will reduce the exposures.

Construction projects in casinos are constants. The changes are designed to bring more business in by updating or adding a venue or outlet to the assets. Construction workers are adept at moving through a facility and have the opportunity to steal consumable inventory or products along with materials and equipment.

Security personnel are often befriended by construction workers and caution should be exerted in making sure there are adequate procedures in place to minimize loss. With construction workers wandering around a facility at will, there are many temptations and plenty of opportunities to place an item in a toolbox or trash bin for later retrieval.

18

The Major Security Incident

18.1 GUNS AND GAMING

There are many good publications available on crisis management and recovery that provide detailed programs and procedures that are applicable to the most environments. I will discuss those incidents that are unique to a gaming operation. Fire, flood, bomb threat, evacuations, and major weather-related incidents can occur in any environment, and there are many resources for information and guidance in preparing plans for those events. Your insurance company will also typically have good resources for information and can provide you with basic planning documents.

There are certain additional incidents that can occur on a casino property that should be considered in the emergency operations manual of procedures. Training all employees in the procedures will not only help them survive an event but will also help control the aftermath. Similar to emergency preparedness training, a written plan will prove beneficial. There are many risk managers and insurance or security professionals who can come into a property and make risk or vulnerability assessments based on current trends and available applicable standards. Each property is unique and no single method can be designed as an emergency plan for a specific property.

Having a section in the emergency operations manual that covers the current risks associated with a gaming and similar soft targets allows the gaming entity to preplan for these significant events, for example, a person comes into a casino, pulls out a gun, and robs the cage or another cashier. These events continue to occur and are now foreseeable. From the perspective of liability, having a plan that addresses advance preparation and one that is reasonable and within the standard of care or common practices in a gaming environment will be invaluable in defending claims that will most likely occur.

The times we live in indicate that guns will be the growing concern for security directors. As the perpetrators become more desperate and aggressive in gun use, so too will the incidents that involve them. Terrorism and the significant press coverage of active shooter incidents will encourage those who are bent on killing and being killed to attempt shooting incidents in casinos (Figure 18.1).

Figure 18.1 Guns represent ever-present and growing concerns in gaming environments.

18.2 CASINO ROBBERY

Many security departments in casinos do not have a formal written policy and procedure for dealing with a robbery event. Many directors believe that common knowledge or at least common sense will dictate what should occur or they have verbal procedures. I also find elaborate plans in some facilities with pages of procedures to be followed in a step-by-step process. What is common to all casino properties is that the possibility of someone coming into the property and committing a robbery is very real and should be reasonably anticipated. Robbery in casinos is becoming more frequent as time goes on. Employees should be very aware of the dangers, the "do's and don'ts," and the safety issues involved in this violent crime.

Every casino I have ever been associated with has had some form of procedure, but the procedure varies widely as do documentation and training. Having a written security plan to deal with a robbery event is one thing, but making sure the staff is aware of the procedures is another. The employees who deal with cash should be trained in the process, which usually involves no resistance, giving the person what he or she wants, and not playing hero by trying to take a gun or weapon away from a robber. Local law enforcement will typically have a crime prevention specialist who can supply you with posters and assist in educating employees in what to do.

Other steps include coordinating with local law enforcement on the procedural issues of response, alarm notifications, and where they will position when arriving on the property if an alarm is sounded. A written procedure for surveillance to prepare analytics on the incident and collect evidence is also desirable. Robbery is a serious crime. The protection of employees and guests should be the number one priority and that should be stated in the procedures.

The investigation after the incident is also critical. Closed-circuit television (CCTV) review, protection of the crime scene for potential evidence, and the cooperative effort with local law enforcement are vital to prevent recurring robberies and to catch and prosecute the robber. Outside and inside camera review should also be done for several days prior to the event to determine if the suspect or suspects can be observed collecting intelligence prior to the robbery. Most surveillance operations have a seven-day retention policy for video, so all of the video from the affected areas will prove beneficial. If the evidence has not been saved after a security breach, it will either be overwritten in digital applications or taped over in analog systems after those seven days have passed and lost as evidence.

Security staff will have the immediate responsibility to interview employees and locate any patrons who may have witnessed all or a small portion of the robbery event. Every witness should be treated as valuable and all of the pieces from the witnesses will fall together and assist in solving the crime and locating the perpetrator. Separation of each witness while being interviewed and getting all of their contact information for possible follow up are critical in the event one of the customers or employees files a claim later for injury or emotional distress. The witnesses will have different descriptions of the perpetrator that can vary significantly, and the responding police will decide which description will be broadcast as the official one. This is based on their experience in dealing with crimes.

Coordinating with the law enforcement entity charged with investigating the crime is important and conducting your own investigation while they are still on site can create issues and confusion. After the peace officers identify that they are charged with the investigation, all pertinent information should be turned over to them so that they can adequately do their job. They are in control of the investigation and must be given unlimited access in order to conduct a comprehensive investigation. A report by a supervisor or manager is appropriate nevertheless.

The highest level of security management available responds to the incident. This is not an event that can wait until morning. Interaction by the security director with the law enforcement personnel will benefit the overall outcome and expedience of the investigation. The security director can handle any opening and closing issues with casino managers and can obtain valuable information from the peace officers to allow for a credible in-depth report to the general manager or tribal officials.

Securing the crime scene and protecting evidence from contamination or destruction is also important. Getting employees away from the robbery location immediately is critical in preserving evidence. Employees will want to check their drawers to find out how much money is missing, lock their drawers, or do other tasks they think are important. Getting them away and instructing them not to touch anything will enable the crime scene professionals to look for any evidence that may be helpful such as notes, fingerprints, DNA evidence or items that may have been touched or left behind by the perpetrator.

Taping off the area can be challenging but is very important in controlling the crime scene until the arrival of peace officers, including investigators. Creative solutions may be required if the robbery occurred at the only cashier location in your casino and may require a temporary location for cashier transactions, such as a restaurant cashier booth or customer service booth, until the area where the robbery occurred can be released for normal operation. This allows for customer transactions in an area that will normally still have CCTV coverage. A predesignated alternative location will be helpful in a crisis.

It is normal for entire casinos to be temporarily closed during an investigation of a robbery event. It will be a certainty if someone was shot or killed during the robbery event. Casino managers and executives need to be informed and coordination with law enforcement for release of the area back to normal operations as soon as practical and prudent will be necessary. If the casino shift manager refuses to close a casino after a significant robbery event, the aftermath could be problematic and much more expensive than any anticipated loss of revenues a closure would entail. Calling the highest authority for authorization may be necessary in these situations.

After the dust has settled, the crime scene is released, the evidence has been secured, and the situation has been calmed, there is still work to be done. The employees' welfare is an important factor in the overall success in response to a robbery event. Having a grief counselor available through the human resources department will be beneficial to the employees who faced a catastrophic event when someone almost killed them. Some employees will react severely to robbery events, and compassion in dealing with them is warranted and desired. Others may just shrug it off as no big deal. Having a company-supplied professional immediately available to talk with anyone who needs this help will be appreciated and is the right thing to do.

The security director will have the task of reporting to the executive level what occurred and what was done as a result. A professional recap of the event and the outcomes will be required to answer any claims or reports that the insurance carrier or other entities will require. A library of the video evidence can be assembled and all the video given to law enforcement, along with videos not required. All videos should be copied to hard discs or tapes for further use as these will help in the investigation and any subsequent claims or incidents. Certain video evidence before and after a robbery or any significant event may be of value in claims filed ancillary to the robbery event. It is common for guests and employees who were not even in the immediate area to file some form of claim after a robbery event.

Having a formal plan for robbery events will prove beneficial in the event of an injury or death during this crime. Dealing with the press, as in any emergency incident, will be challenging when the news trucks roll up and block access to the casino to get their best video of the marquee and areas involved. Tight controls to refer the press to the predesignated executive, much like for fire, bomb, or evacuation events, will assist in controlling outbound information to the press.

The key is to have a very basic plan to deal with the event and the aftermath. Training of the security staff and employees who handle cash may save a few lives and let employees know you care enough to inform them on how to be safe.

18.3 ACTIVE SHOOTER

An active shooter incident occurs when a person comes into a facility and starts shooting a gun regardless of the circumstances. It can start as an isolated incident of domestic violence or occur at a social event where a person wishes to kill many people before killing himself or being shot by security or responding police (suicide by cop). An active shooter is engaged in killing or attempting to kill people in a confined and populated area, typically through the use of firearms.

In recent years much attention has been given to shooting incidents around the world. This phenomenon is based partly on an increase in these events, the almost immediate press coverage, and the tenacity of investigative reporters and tabloid-type news programs. As a result of newer technology in communications and social networking environments, video and pictures of an active shooter event on a casino property can be distributed in a matter of minutes. A video clip sent to YouTube and other social network Web sites might contain invaluable information. This instantaneous publicity can actually motivate an active shooter to plan an event.

First and foremost the security professional needs to meet with local law enforcement and be informed as to their procedures for responding to active shooter incidents. Police departments have dealt with these incidents for decades, and they are trained in profes-sional and measured response. With this information the property develops written pro-cedures for its staff to follow. New employees can be trained during their orientation on the basics of surviving an active shooter incident. The Department of Homeland Security (DHS) published a program for educating employees and managers in active shooter incidents in 2009 and also distributes posters and pocket cards to educate and remind employees of the profile, characteristics, and preferred response to an active shooter to increase their chances of staying alive. Incorporating the suggestions will assist security in the planning process. These can be helpful not only to the property but also to the employees who may encounter an active shooter at a mall, theater, or other public event when not on duty.

Security personnel should have basic procedures in place to deal with the incident prior to, during, and after law enforcement arrives to quell the disturbance. Specific lan-guage that instructs employees how to protect themselves and anyone close to them if possible will become a major topic at a civil trial later. Unlike a robbery event, the active shooter event involves someone motivated by something other than obtaining cash and is much more challenging and unpredictable.

The surveillance department plays a critical role in an active shooter incident. They should first be responsible to call 911 and notifying police independently of security or other departments. By having this formal policy, a property ensures that the police have been called. Security and other personnel in the casino are most likely on the floor and busy. Surveillance should have the written instruction that an active shooter incident requires that priority be given to documentation and reporting the activity, live, to the police dispatcher who in turn is communicating to responding police. They need to stay on the phone until the dispatcher releases them. Regular and frequent updates to police can be a matter of life and death to employees and guests. Relaying location and access points available becomes critical for responding police.

Surveillance also is collecting the evidence and positioning multiple camera views of the shooter and the immediate area affected. Once the situation is secured by police action, the arduous task of copying all of the relevant video begins. The surveillance department can also make executive level contact from a predesigned list of key management personnel as soon as practical. This allows the security staff to deal with the immediate safety issues and the aftermath of the incident.

In most active shooter incidents the casino or affected area is required to close, which can create issues from securing employees and cash to blocking or locking doors and posting nonsecurity employees to keep people from entering and attempting to hold any potential witnesses. A predesigned plan that designates employees for these tasks can also be helpful. Utilizing supervisors in other departments helps this process as long as the written plan is clear on what is to be accomplished. Having a beverage supervisor monitor a public entrance may be a better choice than assigning a security officer who may be better utilized elsewhere.

In both robbery and active shooter incidents the CCTV coverage can be proactively designed to camera preset positions. In the new digital world presets can be designed around the most probable targets and with a touch of the keyboard or mouse numerous cameras can swing into play at everything from the interior of a cage to the outside exit doors. Assessing the risks associated with robbery and active shooter events and designing countermeasures will most likely save lives.

19

Training Gaming Security Officers

19.1 TRAINING AS A CONSTANT

Based on history, security personnel require basic forms of training in order to perform the tasks required to protect guests, employees, and assets. Every manager or director of security has a preferred, distinct method of training. The function of physical security in gaming operations is not complex or complicated in most casinos. The department's security personnel should have a basic and consistent method of operating and will typically rely on the basic policies and procedures of the organization they work for and the specific policies and procedures of the security department.

A check with the local and state regulators will reveal if any required training is to be completed. As an example, a security officer in a casino in California has specific licensing and training requirements as does a security guard who patrols the parking lot of a retail store. This basic security training is not specific to the gaming industry. Additional training for the gaming site is required.

Once you know what the state and local laws require (the community standard) for training, then designing a training program can be coordinated and formalized. Security experts also have varying opinions on the subject of training. From a legal perspective a security training program needs to withstand the scrutiny of a lawsuit that alleges inadequate training as a cause of action.

The basis of any training is to indoctrinate the employee to the desired methods of the owner of the enterprise. Without basic security training, as in any environment, an employee will react according to what he or she believes is the right response to any given situation. These responses are based on the employee's childhood, home environment, what he or she has learned, attitude, and personality. A simple problem can evoke a number of different responses from the responding security officer unless there have been clear guidelines established and all employees are aware of and have been trained in the process.

There are many different forms and methods for training. Familiarization with a task is a form of training. Enforcing the required steps through discipline is another form of training. Employees adapt to the routine tasks and respond to discipline when we do not follow the rules. Training methods will vary depending on the instructor. The dynamic trainer will be able to force retention of the valuable information or the key points to any procedure or policy.

This chapter is not meant to propose a design for a training program. It is rather meant to stimulate the thought process when designing the training that the security officers will receive at a casino property. There is a certain basic safety function that security personnel will be required to perform whenever on duty that will typically require specific training. Training can be effective as an "on the job" function as well as academic. The key is to have a formal plan and be able to prove that the training occurred.

During the past two decades much has been written and dissected regarding "on the job training" (OJT). There have been numerous lawsuits that have resulted in plaintiff verdicts based on a failure to train personnel or follow the established training or policies and procedures (self-imposed standards). Many security directors have found themselves in an awkward position on the witness stand in an inadequate security lawsuit when an adept attorney cross-examined them on their training programs and exaggerated the inadequacies in front of a jury. The security experts in a lawsuit will also be critical of the policies, procedures, and the training that is applied. A poorly designed training program will come across in a courtroom and will be displayed on poster board or the big screen to the jury.

OJT systems seem to be criticized routinely and the perception of many people is that all security departments have the ability and should provide an academic training program for all security employees. Logistics, finances, and employee turnover create obstacles in even attempting to design and implement an academic program in most casino operations. There are many OJT programs that are effective and well administered in the gaming environment. The key is to document training. A written program that ensures that the critical functions and responses will be covered during the training process will also reduce the risk of forgetting to include training on a particular topic.

The majority of casinos, especially small to midsized operations, utilize an OJT-type program for the basics or new officer training. The documentation varies widely from property to property. In today's contemporary casino security department there is typically an outline or schedule that the new security officer is to go through during the first one to two weeks of employment while assigned to a training officer, first level supervisor, or a seasoned and experienced preselected officer. The time involved in training a new security officer also varies.

The ASIS International security organization published a guideline in 2004 titled the *Private Security Officer Selection and Training Guideline*, which was the first comprehensive attempt to establish the basics of what a security officer should be trained in and when. It is a guideline, not a standard, and should be treated as one. The guideline has been widely criticized in that ASIS International attempted to begin the process of establishing an industry standard by releasing this guideline, but it did not address the various disciplines where security is applied. As an example, a contract security company that supplies security for a parking area or large convention venue is not comparable to a security operation in a nuclear facility and therefore ASIS's standardized set of training mandates would not be equally applicable. The training required to check a convention badge does not require skill in report writing or many other subjects.

The guideline should, however, be considered as a basic guide when designing a training program for security in a gaming environment. Certain components are important to the gaming security officer's function and others may not be. The guideline is designed for all security disciplines. Certain functions will occur in gaming environments that do not occur in contract security environments or many other proprietary security operations. As an example the ASIS International guideline suggests that a security officer have forty-eight hours of training within the first one hundred days of employment.

The security director is typically charged with designing and implementing training programs for those security officers who will perform the physical security function. That director can research and collect as many policies and procedures from other casino operations as possible and utilize any current guidelines or standards in effect. If that director cannot design or revise of security policies and procedures, the casino can retain the services of a professional security consultant who can assist in the process.

If the department establishes a set of policies, procedures, rules, and regulations that it wishes to use as a guide, the simplistic way to design the training program is to follow those operational policies and procedures in a training program. The easiest way to track and organize a training program is to follow the same outline or table of contents in the security operations manual. This allows the trainee to use that resource for reference.

As an example, it is well known that security personnel in a gaming environment will be required to respond to a medical emergency such as a cardiac event. Procedures written to establish where the automatic electronic defibrillator (AED) unit is located, instructions on its use, care of the equipment, and how to use it in an emergency would be appropriate. The section in the operations manual is mirrored and then detail training information is supplied. The training manual can have a section specifically for this training and certification process. Since this specific training is considered perishable (requires periodic training or certification), certain required training intervals can also be established in the training manual.

The training manual can include many support documents that will assist the trainer in the function. It is important to control this information and all documents approved by the director should be controlled by his or her designee. Another simple example would be for handcuff training: a diagram of the handcuffs with the nomenclature of each piece and function would be useful, and this can be found with a new set of handcuffs. Additionally the proper methods in application, double locking, safety, and when to use them can be organized in the same section.

19.2 NEW HIRE ORIENTATION

The human resources department is typically charged with familiarizing the new employee with the company's rules and regulations and policies and procedures. There is no need to reinvent the wheel by covering the same basic training received in the company's orientation program. The new security officer should arrive at the department ready to be trained and start work armed with the knowledge of the company's mission and guidelines for employment that all employees are expected to know and follow.

When the security officer arrives into the security department there is typically administrative paperwork to be completed, and the officer is issued a uniform and any required equipment. The first person they meet and who guides them though the process will have an effect on the initial impression they get of the department and attitudes of the co-workers and supervisors.

That employee or supervisor should have a positive and professional attitude and project that to the new hires during this impressionable time. Making sure that employees have well-fitting uniforms can go a long way in the employees' work attitude. Introducing them to their first training instructor is just as important. Assigning a new employee to an especially negative or grumpy senior officer will have a lasting effect on how the department operates. If all the employees are trained according to this person's ill-perceived opinion of a particular procedure or policy, the results can prove problematic. A training officer who personally disagrees with a procedure and outwardly displays this to the new hires erodes the procedure over time.

A positive way to determine how the training is perceived as well as its end success is to have the director speak with each new employee after he or she has completed the training. This not only gives the director the feedback that is needed but also establishes with the new employee that the boss is approachable and cares about his or her department and the employees he or she manages. This can be done in written form but is most effective in the one-on-one environment. If the time is taken to speak with each employee in that probationary period and after that initial training program, the staff will become more respectful and responsive to the directives.

19.3 TRAINING OF THE NEW SECURITY OFFICER

Once the new officer is uniformed, equipped, and ready to start the first phase of the training, he or she should meet with the training officer and go over the basics of the security department. Regardless of the experience level of the new employee, each employee should be thoroughly indoctrinated into the new security environment, which may have different components and philosophies from a previous employer. Just because a new employee previously worked in a casino for five years does not necessarily mean that he or she is already trained. In most circumstances those employees can be more difficult to retrain to follow their new employer's mandates.

The department philosophy, guest relations as it pertains to security officers, chain of command, and the mission statement should all be introduced first. I recall my first conversation with my first supervisor as a one-way conversation; it entailed instructions on exactly what he wanted me to do because it was his shift and he did not care what anyone else or what any other shift did. I was to do it his way—period. This type of attitude can also undermine the objective of consistent training of all personnel and consistency between shifts.

The departmental security manual or guide for the security function is introduced and the employee should go through the entire manual chapter by chapter with the training officer to effectively indoctrinate the employee before sending him or her out onto the floor. There are several schools of thought regarding the issuance of the security manual to the employees.

The old-school method in gaming environments was to have one or two complete manuals located where security could have access to them for reference. The more contemporary method is to issue each security officer a copy of the security manual and require a signature on a document stating that he or she received it on a particular date. I personally like the procedure one director used that had this employee record signed as acknowledgment of receiving the security manual and then a second signature and date of when the employee successfully passed the probation and training period. This will reduce apprehensions of new employees as to signing a document that says they will abide by all policies and procedures when they have yet to read them or be trained in them.

It is equally important to require that whenever an employee is terminated or quits the manual must be turned in. Although the manual could have been copied, this rule maintains the importance of the manual to the employees. Placing a high replacement value if it is lost will also be a strong motivator to always know where it is and that it must be eventually returned. When issuing revised or updated manuals the original must be presented and the replacement signed for.

I prefer to train in the use of and issue handcuffs and other equipment during this initial phase of the training. Handcuffs are typically issued to the security officers for consistency in equipment in midsized or smaller casinos. In larger departments, the officers are sometimes required to purchase their own handcuffs. Regardless of your property's position on this, the equipment should be approved to make sure that handcuffs are of quality construction, have common locking hardware, and are properly functioning. Thumb cuffs, shackles, and other forms of restraints should be restricted to confinement settings or special circumstances and are not typical in gaming operations.

When the new security officer is given a set of handcuffs, he or she should be trained in the design, function, and nomenclature of the restraints. Showing the employee how they work by example is an effective way to train. Letting a new employee sit in a chair handcuffed during training for ten or fifteen minutes under supervision is an effective training exercise. Allowing new employees to handcuff the training officer several times can also help familiarize the new hires with the equipment. Policies and procedures regarding locking the handcuffs after application, tightness, checking on a person in handcuffs, and dealing with unusual circumstances such as an extremely large person or a handicapped individual can also be covered. Whatever the policies and procedures are, they should be thoroughly explained, reinforced, and demonstrated to the new employee.

It is fairly common knowledge that casino security personnel will be involved in arrests and will need to use handcuffs at some point. They should be trained before handcuffs are issued to them to ensure they first know the proper use on customers or employees. Whatever the security officer will be expected to do in a casino, there should be some form of training on how to accomplish it.

Specifically recommending a training budget line item is desirable but not always possible. By utilizing a predesigned budget that would include any overtime to cover training makes the process easier and more efficient from a cost perspective. It also helps demonstrate to the executive level that security considers training important enough to budget money toward the process and lets them know the cost of training, which is also important in managing costs and operations. If that is not possible, the director can break out training costs from the actual payroll numbers to forecast the cost of training new personnel.

19.4 FIELD TRAINING

There are various forms of field training in the gaming industry. During the recession period when this book was written, all training programs became a financial challenge for operations where significant revenue decreases created severe cuts in personnel, training, and equipment. The positive result of slow times in the gaming environment is that opportunities to complete one-on-one training with officers are possible, and this can be quite effective for refresher training of officers who demonstrate a lack of proficiency in a particular area.

As mentioned earlier, the most common form of field training is OJT where a new officer is assigned to a training officer, a field training officer (FTO), or a senior officer who has been instructed on the training requirements. Regardless of who does the training, the person instructing impressionable new officers must be consistent with the overall training plan that the director of security has designed.

As an example, if the decision is to train for a full week (five workdays), the training should be outlined for each of those days and include all of the topics contained within the security manual or standard operating procedures. There should be a place for the new officer to initial attesting to his or her understanding of the policy as well as a place for the training officer to sign off that he or she is satisfied that the new officer has received the training.

Short periods of time in the specific position assignments after overall training on the position from the manual can also be very effective. It is important to ensure that the training is not compromised by a negative employee. An example would be assigning a security officer to an outside patrol assignment where a vehicle is used to patrol a parking lot or public parking garage. The training would not need to be extensive as long as the employee is effectively trained in the position requirements, also referred to as post orders in some operations. This training would actually start by filling out a mock vehicle log to include any preshift information like odometer reading, vehicle condition, emergency equipment, and whatever else is required. Then the FTO would allow the new employee to drive the vehicle and guide him or her through the patrol process and what to observe for. Training by doing is again a reinforcement of the academic training process and can accelerate the retention process. Required safety rules for driving company vehicles, guest and employee protection requirements, guest relations, and management of the social behavior of persons entering and exiting the casino can be effectively demonstrated.

Each of the stationary posts and those that require patrol can be physically demonstrated to the new officer and then the person is allowed to perform the functions to include writing any associated logs or reports. Other aspects of training can include specifics in escorts, report writing, and all of the other security officer functions contained in the operations manual.

The most difficult training task is report writing. Since writing a report takes literary skill, and that will vary significantly from one officer to the next, this becomes a challenge for most security officers. Basics in report writing should be given during initial training and throughout the employment of the officer. Review and critique of reports by supervisors and managers will also assist in this process. Having a separate report writing class once or twice a year is helpful in increasing the quality of documentation.

Once the OJT period of five days is complete and the officer is done with orientation and department familiarization, he or she can then be assigned to a shift. Many security departments will assign a new officer to the graveyard or first shift of the day. These are usually the most desirable shifts to start new officers on because they can easily facilitate further training and can establish a protocol that all new hires start from the same place and then can later transfer to another shift if a position opens up. Assignment can create issues with department morale if you place a new officer on a shift that has been requested by an officer who has already worked in the department for some time.

The officer can be tested on his or her knowledge and the success of the OJT program. Although many gaming operations test employees verbally, a written test of retention can be useful in evaluating the employee and determining what topics, if any, need to be reinforced. This test does not have to be extensive and should include questions on key topics that were included in training. The written test is valuable and should be retained in the employee's file to demonstrate training and retention should it be required in the future.

The results of this new officer's progress is then communicated to the shift supervisor or manager who will typically make a determination if more training is required and if the employee is ready to start working alone with guidance. If the officer just does not retain the training or has demonstrated negative traits, retention and the decision to continue the process is typically turned over to the director. This also will allow the director to assess the effectiveness of the training program and the personnel assigned to train new officers.

There are many different field training programs that go beyond the OJT in various casinos that range from two-week formal academy programs to ninety-day or full probation period training with weekly and sometimes daily evaluations completed by the FTO. These are typically seen in larger operations, where ex-law enforcement administrators are directors, and more closely resemble law enforcement training. These are not the standard in training programs when compared to the industry as a whole.

It is also important to remember that you are training security staff for security purposes and that they are not police. Training security officers in the same manner as police will become problematic based on the differences in statutory immunities and the laws that police use. They have very different ramifications when used by private security officers. Police are trained in accordance with Peace Officers Standards and Training, which is much more comprehensive and specialized than casino security and takes much longer.

Training is a very important part of the security department, and the initial training, at whatever level, will be a measure of the success of the department and the director. Whatever initial training is done, it will be closely examined in the event of a major event or litigation where inadequate security is alleged. As a result most operations have documentation that demonstrates that training was completed, what topics and support materials were used, and how the employee responded to the training. Producing a well-documented training record is much easier than testifying about what generally and typically was done.

19.5 SPECIALIZED TRAINING

There are various topics that require specialized training beyond the initial training period. Some operations include these in the initial training. Cardiopulmonary resuscitation

(CPR), AED, safety measures with blood-borne pathogens, and training in confined spaces, defensive tactics, and nonviolent crisis intervention are some of the common specialized training programs. Weapons, including handguns and pepper spray, are also very specialized and should be trained for separately if they are used on the facility. Other topics include certification in bike patrol, laws of arrest, alcohol management.

The casino and security director should evaluate what specialized training should be done and at what intervals to keep the staff certified or refreshed. Outside instructors are commonly used to fulfill regulatory requirements to include any Occupational Safety and Health (OSHA)-related required training. The shift supervisor will usually be charged with ensuring that all officers on the shift have been trained and are current in any required area. Someone should be charged with keeping track of who requires this training.

Many local police departments will assist in training of security personnel. The crime prevention staffs of most law enforcement agencies have the ability to provide officers to assist with training in some functions such as handcuffing, parking lot or bike patrol, and laws of arrest for the jurisdiction. Any free training should be thoroughly researched and used if applicable unless it is not consistent with the operation. You will still need to pay for the trainee's time during training, but you can save direct costs for instruction. Review of the program to make sure that it applies to private security would be beneficial.

Outside consultants can be used if the staff does not have the experience or qualifications to train in a particular topic. These consultants should be evaluated for the appropriate licenses, if required, and to make sure they have the necessary skills before entering into an agreement. Calling other gaming properties they have performed services for can prove beneficial also.

19.6 REFRESHER TRAINING

Refresher training is an effective tool to get the security officers functioning consistently. I have done this or recommended it. This is not only done in the formal sense through the human resources policy, but can also be done in the day-to-day process of managing the security department.

When an officer demonstrates a deficiency in a particular area, he or she might require refresher training. An example might be that report writing is a weakness of a particular officer and he or she consistently turns in unsatisfactory written reports that might include a failure to obtain written statements or filling in the blanks of a report that are required. In this case refresher training can be given to the officer that will reinforce the requirements and provide the information and tools to perform the function better. It may also demonstrate that the employee lacks the ability or motivation to do the required documenting and will help support evaluation or potential disciplinary action.

If you retrain an employee in an area where he or she is not performing well and the employee then grasps the refresher training and becomes a better security officer, you are accomplishing something positive. You might also find out that the officer was never trained properly or that he or she just did not comprehend the initial training. You might also find that the officer just does not have the basic ability to read and write and that this lack was missed in the initial screening and hiring process.

There are also instances where refresher training can be valuable in documenting disciplinary actions. For example, if an officer applied handcuffs too tight on a suspect and did not double lock them, refresher training might be a part of the disciplinary process. The officer, after discipline, can be required to complete refresher training in the proper use of handcuffs and the related procedures before being allowed to use them or return to work.

Refresher training shows that even though there may have been a negative event, the department is willing to retrain the employee in the process. Second, the documentation will prove invaluable in the event of litigation or future disciplinary action, and third, it will send a clear signal to all officers that if they do something similar they will also be required to be retrained. It is amazing how many officers will consult the written procedures after a fellow officer has been disciplined and required to have refresher training.

Refresher training will more often than not improve the professionalism of an officer if used properly. That officer will most likely never forget the training and more importantly will be unlikely to violate the policy or procedure again. In the event he or she does, the document trail will certainly support any termination decision in that the officer was sufficiently warned, retrained, and then violated the procedure again.

20

Common Casino Scams and Crimes

20.1 WHERE THERE ARE PEOPLE WITH MONEY, SCAMS ARE PRESENT

Casinos attract many different types of people as customers. Where customers who have valuables gather, there will always be those undesirables who prey on them (Figure 20.1). There are some scams that are centuries old and others that developed when casinos started their proliferation outside of the state of Nevada. Security officers will typically become aware of these scams and activities quickly, depending on the location, through incidents, writing reports for victims, and observations.

Casino promotions and the constant flow of money create opportunities for criminals to deprive customers and employees of their disposable income and a company of its assets. It is not unusual for a con man to successfully take money from multiple people a dozen times in a few hours.

Petty criminals who are frequently incarcerated in local jails will also talk among themselves and develop new scams to try inside and outside of casinos. Because of the easy public access and the constant activity, casinos are attractive targets for the opportunist and scam artist.

Security personnel are charged with watching for those characters who create a nuisance and affect the perception of a casino by the general public. Security officers, if trained in detection, can be instrumental in deterring scam artists. Many scam artists are very adept and can go on undetected for years.

20.2 THE SHORT CHANGE ARTIST

With the turnover of employees in any gaming operation, the issues related to experience and training when dealing with cash can become problematic. When investigating any cash shortage, one of the first tasks is to eliminate the possibility that a short change artist has taken advantage of an employee. Likewise the possibility of an employee who short changes customers for personal gain can also occur when cash is handled.

Figure 20.1 Where there is lots of money—and many unwitting customers—there will be scam artists and criminals.

The basic technique of the short change artist is to confuse the victim and make him or her think the proper amount of change was received. They will use distraction, confusion, multiple requests, and many other methods that make the victim perceive he or she has been given the correct amount of money. Even experienced cashiers are victimized by these adept criminals who practice their craft regularly.

The cooperation with the surveillance department will be critical in investigating a shortage and should be initiated as soon as possible. Officers can watch the overhead video shots from cameras that are in place in the majority of casinos worldwide. By carefully charting those transactions involving the exchange of cash, they will be able to determine if there has been a crime. By playing the video in slow motion, they can analyze the transaction. Common sense should be applied regarding the amount of loss that requires investigation.

The operational difficulty in these types of investigations is the time that it takes to review and carefully examine a full shift of video that contains hundreds of transactions. In some operations a cage manager can assist in the investigation if he or she is given a copy of the video and can watch the employee's actions and cash handling habits. If a cashier has been shortchanged $20 and the cost of analysis on the video and the investigation will be hundreds of dollars, a management decision should be made whether to proceed with an investigation. In many operations a dollar limit is set that requires an investigation by surveillance or security before formal investigation occurs. In other jurisdictions the regulators will conduct an investigation into shortages regardless of the amount.

I refer operations that desire training in this important area to Michael A. Joseph who produced an exceptional DVD that goes through all of the common scams involving short change artists by demonstrating each one and how they are accomplished. (It can be purchased at www.traininggaming.com and is called *The Professional Short Change Artist by Michael A. Joseph*.) This DVD will enlighten the security professional about this activity that occurs regularly in the cash-rich environment of casinos.

Short change artists practice their trade and are very hard to detect. It is not uncommon for an employee, surveillance agent, and cage manager to miss the theft based on the observable actions on video. Likewise an employee who is adept at shortchanging customers one dollar at a time can go undetected because he or she never comes up short in the cash drawer.

20.3 CHECK CASHING AND THE CASHIER'S CAGE

One of the processes that most casinos perform is check cashing for the customers who frequent the casino. The process is simple and typically will require certain procedures to be followed by the cashiers who work in the cage department of a gaming property. The sheer volume of paychecks, personal checks, and government checks that are processed by a casino cage is huge. The process even involves obtaining a fingerprint on the check in many environments.

A common criminal activity in any casino environment is to attempt to cash a stolen or forged check. Casinos offer relatively easy methods to cash a check and encourage people to do so. There are some safeguards that include centralized credit companies that monitor check cashing crimes or risky customers. If the internal procedures of the cashier's cage are followed, these crimes can be easily managed and a scam attempt will stand out to the employees and supervisors within the cage.

Using false identification (ID) and presenting stolen checks are typical examples of incidents that will occur at a cashier's cage. Creating false IDs has become sophisticated in recent years, and with copying equipment increasing in quality along with availability of specialty paper and watermarking, incidents of fake IDs occur more frequently. There are ID verification books that can be utilized by cage employees. The security department can also be requested to review the ID presented by a customer and check the validity of the ID through the available references.

ID formats change frequently and care should be used when verifying an ID. The decision to cash a check when the person is presenting an ID that is questionable is a business decision that evaluates the risk of payment by the issuer. It is not a security decision but is a cage cashier's decision. The simple decision would be to deny the person the ability to cash a check if the ID is questionable or ask for some other form of ID.

Whenever I had that situation arise and the customer became irate I would typically tell the person that I would be more than happy to call the local police who can verify the ID against the person and if the check and ID proved to be legitimate I would recommend the check be cashed. Many people left rather than have a police officer check the documents.

Stolen or forged checks become much more challenging for security to deal with. A cage employee may look at a check, run it through the centralized credit system, and get a code that states the check is stolen. The employee in turn will tell his or her supervisor who will then call surveillance and security. The process is started, and if the person is attempting to cash a bad check or using what may be a false ID, the next step could be a critical one.

Polite and professional conduct is always recommended. The responding officer needs to be aware that the check may be legitimate and a typical error in the system may have occurred. Whenever possible the check and ID should be held, and local law enforcement should assist you in the process. If the person is in fact attempting to cash a bad check, law enforcement has the ability to cite or arrest the person. If the check turns out to be valid, then law enforcement has assisted you in that process and investigation.

I have investigated instances where security will automatically place the person in handcuffs, which then turns into an arrest, detention, and sometimes other negative events. After further investigation, it is determined that the check was valid and the person cashing it was the correct person. This presents an even more difficult situation and the potential for a lawsuit based on false arrest, false imprisonment, defamation, and negligence.

There are many criminals who obtain stolen checks, IDs, credit cards, and other negotiable items and will attempt to get currency in exchange for what they have. Because a cashier's cage has a constant cash flow, it becomes a target for these scams. The security officer and supervisor should always proceed cautiously and remember that the safest solution may simply be to deny the person the ability to cash the check. If the casino did not complete the transaction, there is only the attempt for fraud.

On those occasions when the suspects see security responding and they take off running, careful consideration should be given before chasing the person down for attempting to cash a bad check. Remember he or she did not accomplish the crime and there is no loss. If anything, concern should be given to those whom the person may knock down in the flight to avoid security. Guests who are elderly, for example, cannot react quickly when a suspect runs past them and knocks them down. What if the guest suffers a broken hip, has surgery, and dies during the surgery? Now this minor incident has become a wrongful death lawsuit where the negligence of the casino is at issue.

Although in many jurisdictions bad check passing is a felony, the risks of taking a person into custody must be weighed against the attempted crime. The zealous or inexperienced security officer will walk into this trap and put the casino in jeopardy of a large jury verdict. Training will also help prevent these types of incidents from escalating.

20.4 DISTRACTION CRIMES

Distraction crime has always been present in the gaming environment. There are many forms that occur every day in every casino. Whenever a suspect takes any action that would distract the attention of a victim from his or her valuables, the result is a distraction crime. These criminals are not easily caught in the act based on the quick time in which the crime occurs.

The most effective ways to deter distraction crimes are to have effective casino patrols, to catch and prosecute the offenders, and to proactively advise patrons to watch their belongings such as purses, bags, coats, and so forth. The security officer, while patrolling the casino, should advise people to watch and keep those personal effects close.

A distraction crime is simple and considered a crime of opportunity even though the perpetrator may plan the event. Keep in mind that in many jurisdictions when a criminal comes into a building with the intent to commit a crime the act is a burglary, which is a felony in many jurisdictions. These perpetrators merely enter a casino and patrol the floor for a victim who might have valuables, including cash or TITO (ticket in, ticket out) slips.

In the TITO distraction crime the criminal will merely look for the inexperienced gambler who does not notice the cash ticket that has real value sticking out of the machine. When a team is working, one of them will implement the distraction by engaging the person in conversation, throwing a small bill on the floor, or anything else that might divert attention away from the TITO slip. The second person will grab the slip and immediately cash it at the cage or a kiosk. The experienced TITO thief will immediately put it into a machine and generate a new ticket, which will be difficult to track back if the person is questioned on the casino floor.

Another scam of TITO slips is when a suspect looks for and collects tickets that have only a few cents on them. These are frequently discarded or merely left in the machines. In some cases the slips are actually claimed by the perpetrators if they observe a credit on a machine that has not been printed and ejected. They will then use these low-value slips as the object to distract the customer by throwing it on the floor or even handing it to the customer and telling the customer that he or she dropped it. The scam is culminated when the perpetrator grabs a purse or coat and quickly walks away.

In days before the TITO jackpot system and in some environments where coins are still used, the coin that is dispensed is used as the bait and the bucket of coins as the target. A few dollar tokens thrown on the floor become too tempting and the customer bends down and away from the bucket and it quickly disappears. This applies to anything of value that the customer has and might be the target of the thief.

These distraction thieves have become quite adept at spotting or "marking" their victims in casino environments. The perpetrators usually watch a customer who wears more expensive clothes or jewelry more closely. These undesirables will typically know one another, become turf oriented in larger gaming environments, and make a good living at distracting customers and taking their property. They will also team up when the targets are plentiful to make sure they are not caught.

When one of these crimes is seen by a customer or security officer, the suspect will flee the casino to keep from being caught. I have seen incidents where the perpetrator is chased through the casino by security, the perpetrator knocks down an elderly patron who breaks a hip, and then the victim files a claim against the casino.

An increase in reports of lost wallets and purses can be an indicator that distraction crimes are occurring, so monitoring the lost and found log can alert a casino there is a distraction criminal at work. The customers will report "losing" items, but these reports should always be taken seriously.

20.5 ABUSING MARKETING PROGRAMS

The marketing department of any gaming environment is under constant pressure from the management to get customers into the establishment and spend disposable income. In locations where there is competition close by, casinos all compete for the same customer base and start a coupon war. Promotion after promotion will be implemented by these marketing gurus in an attempt to lure a small percentage of the market share.

From a security perspective these promotions are challenging to monitor and enforce unless there is a system that includes security and surveillance input prior to implementation. This may sound like a relatively simple task but in reality it becomes difficult to accomplish without the highest level executive requiring that both security and surveillance sign off on the promotion before it is approved.

I have investigated many scams that occur both internally and externally as a result of poor planning or the desire to increase customer volumes without regard for the ramifications. In most cases, the procedures were not enforced, inadequately or poorly designed, or nonexistent and the opportunity became the motivator.

If we examine a few basic promotions we can begin to understand the benefits and drawbacks purely from a security and surveillance perspective.

The first is the "two for one" basic marketing promotion. A casino places a coupon in the local newspaper and posts the coupon on Internet sites in an attempt to drive more covers through the restaurant and hopefully increase other revenues. This promotion says to present the coupon to the cashier at the buffet to get two meal tickets for the price of one. The one-person price is typically elevated slightly for these types of promotions. The promotion is a huge success because the restaurant is showing that one hundred people a night are taking advantage of the promotion. A review of the revenues shows that the buffet is actually making much less revenue than projected and the covers are actually up (total number of people who ate dinner). The initial review is typically done and the determination is made that the promotion has merely displaced revenue and management will wait to determine if overall revenues are increased to include the casino.

The artful employee who is taking in cash at the entrance in reality is converting many comps or coupons into cash throughout the shift, as described in Chapter 17. He or she collects coupons from friends, newpapers, or mass prints them from the Internet because they are not numbered and is collecting payments during her cashier shift for two people and then taking a coupon and ringing it up as one coupon, one cash transaction for a total of two covers. The hostess seats the party after looking at the receipt that shows two people have paid.

The cashier knows how many people she has done this with because she is keeping track using paper clips in a glass next to her register or some other counting method. For each five times she does this, she places one paper clip into the glass. Near the end of her shift when she appears to be clipping her money in preparation of turning in her bank, she calculates how many covers she has converted by counting the paper clips and takes that amount of cash out of the drawer. A restroom break near the end of a shift is a "tell" that should be evaluated.

The promotion could have had a more effective control placed on it which would accomplish the same goal of increasing customer base and revenue and limit the potential for theft. If the same coupons that were mass produced were required to be turned in to a particular location where an employee would verify them and issue two sequentially numbered tickets, a control is established. This employee collects the amount for one person in cash and issues two tickets to the buffet. This insulates the cashiers from the process and the process is done under a more watchful eye. At this same location the employees can also distribute whatever marketing brochure or other promotion is going on as each customer makes the transaction. It also becomes a simple process to monitor and evaluate.

By forcing all customers who have generic coupons deep into the casino, we accomplish the draw. By having an isolated booth or location where the revenue is collected for the one meal and two sequentially numbered tickets are issued along with a receipt, we also accomplish control over the meals and revenue collected. The customer then presents these tickets to the cashier at the restaurant who rings them up according to the marketing code.

In this example we have also created a mechanism that will monitor the success and revenues generated as a result of the promotion by merely tracking the numbers and the revenue. By limiting the number of employees who can accept the mass-printed coupons, we have also closed many locations where the scam could be accomplished by employees who may be tempted. Those nonemployees who attempt to get value from the coupons are forced to the same location where detection is now probable.

An example of a promotion that can go wrong without proper thought or planning is what I called the "bacon promotion." In the early 1980s the property I worked at decided to have a promotion to derive revenues from a metropolitan area one hundred miles away and partnered with a bacon manufacturer that printed $20 coupons on the one-pound packages of sliced bacon.

The marketing gurus convinced the general manager that the promotion would be a huge success for the bacon company and for the casino. There was also a significant deal between the casino and the bacon company for each package of sliced bacon sold. The casino name was right on the bacon package.

During the first week there were very few of these coupons redeemed at the cashier's cage. As the weekend came up, the flood of bacon coupons started pouring in. People were turning in ten or more coupons at a time, and since there was no limitation printed on the coupon and no important rules to follow, this became an obvious problem. The marketing gurus also did not print the disclaimer that stated the promotion could be cancelled at any time.

Hundred of coupons were turned in to the cashier cage during that first weekend, and there were no controls or methods to stop the flow. The bacon company was closed for the weekend. We found out from marketing that only 7,500 packages of bacon had these coupons printed on them (7,500 packages × $20 = $150,000!). By the end of the weekend we had already cashed in a significant number of coupons.

The smell of bacon permeated all of the money, chips, paperwork, and employees in the cage. The cash going over the counter to people, who were obviously not typical customers, was increasing. The telephone calls from various retailers from the city one hundred miles away complaining that people were stealing cases of bacon and customers were cutting off coupons right in the store and discarding the bacon package eventually subsided. The regulators would not allow the promotion to be cancelled. The marketing staff who sold the program resigned shortly after to pursue different employment opportunities and management was required to sign off on all future promotions.

In another major scam a casino decided to give a car a day away as a promotion. Coupons were mass printed and even numbered and distributed through various methods to the desired market. These tickets were placed in a drum inside the casino and every day at the selected time a card was dawn and a winner, who had to be present to win, was announced. During this thirty-day very expensive promotion, a local who did not even gamble won four of the cars because there was no language that prohibited multiple prize claims. This promotion was further complicated as bargaining unit employees were picketing in front of the casino and a row of shiny new cars was parked along the street for show. Mysteriously and slowly the cars received a corrosive splashing of chemicals that stripped paint from them. The perpetrator was never observed, caught, or prosecuted.

A simple approach to marketing promotions should be taken to include a formal signoff by the directors of security and surveillance before a promotion is implemented. Sequentially numbered coupons, rules and regulations, and methods to deal with abuses should all be clear before the promotion is approved and the materials are even printed. Time of drawings, security of completed and blank tickets or coupons, and closed-circuit television (CCTV) coverage should also be reviewed and approved. The "scam factor" should be calculated and evaluated, along with the inherent risks to the property and to the person who will ultimately decide if the promotion should go forward.

Conducting a review of the specific promotion at its conclusion can also be productive in designing future marketing programs and will prevent recurring scams from surfacing when all of the departments reveal the pluses and minuses of the promotion. Revenue auditors, marketing staff, security, and surveillance can all participate in this debriefing process to better manage promotions.

20.6 THE SLIP-AND-FALL ARTIST

The slip-and-fall artist has been working for many years in retail environments. A simple process of taking a wet piece of lettuce from the produce section and pretending to fall on it produces results for these scammers. Many grocery retailers have a store settlement process to merely pay off these nuisance claims. These scam artists are also present in gaming environments and they are constantly looking for a location where a slip and fall can be fabricated.

Escalators were favorite places for fall artists for many years. Today the common practice is to have camera coverage at the top and bottom of each escalator and to record the activities constantly. This, along with the maintenance requirements of the service company and other proactive measures, has decreased the number of escalator mishaps in total and has deterred the scam artist from this vulnerable area. If you do not have CCTV cameras covering the escalators, you should install them as the cameras will prove beneficial in a relatively short period.

The risk manager at each property or the insurance claims representative can assist in identifying locations vulnerable to slips and falls. The one constant location where false claims are filed is the public restrooms. The expectation of privacy and individual federal and state laws prohibit CCTV cameras in restrooms absent a court order. These are typically limited to vice operations where illegal activity is occurring and a sting operation is being conducted.

In the bathroom there are usually no witnesses and it is fairly common to find water on the floor. The security patrols described in Chapter 11 will certainly help deter these fraudulent claims, along with maintenance logs kept by cleaning personnel each time they check the restroom and floors, and will go a long way in trying to prove that employees were constantly checking the restroom and cleaning up spills.

The majority of slips and falls are not scams. There tends to be a greater number of instances where an actual fall will occur and the claimant will exaggerate the events, which still creates a fraudulent act. Security personnel should always portray a sense of urgency and professionalism whenever they respond to a slip and fall, regardless of their suspicions, and take copious notes, collect any evidence, and have the incident thoroughly investigated to include a search for video evidence.

Tracking guest accidents and the time that a guest reports he or she was injured can also be helpful. If a certain area has recurring incidents, it requires further investigation. As an example, if there is a set of two stairs in a casino and there have been multiple falls at the stairs by elderly patrons, there are a few basic investigative measures that could save injury to guests and significant costs for your operation. There may not be a scam occurring but rather an ergonomic condition that requires attention.

Charting the incidents by date, time of day, and basic circumstances is the starting point to determine common denominators. Notify surveillance and attempt to set up a camera to view and record the area during the time frames collected from your analysis. Surveillance can position a camera to view this area as a documentation tool and save the video. The manager can then look at the video and watch the ergonomics and actions of each patron and see when and where falls occur. In stair locations a simple rubber nose protector on the stair edge, a change in carpet color, or moving a handrail a few inches could solve or significantly reduce the number of patron injuries that occur. In extreme cases the stairs may have to be turned into a ramp or other modification.

Wherever there is potential for a slip-and-fall artist to commit a fraud, the proactive security department can assist in the overall deterrence and will become proficient at investigating and catching scam artists red handed. Scammers will look for those conditions that will lend credibility to their false claims and exploit them.

20.7 PROSTITUTION AND RELATED CRIMES

When men and women who have disposable income wander around a casino, prostitutes will surface and peddle sex for money and sometimes other things of value. Prostitution has been around since well before gaming became legal and will be around long after, if not forever. Prostitution is illegal in every jurisdiction except select counties in Nevada, and a gaming operation can still be fined or closed if prostitution is not addressed.

In Nevada there are counties where legalized prostitution is conducted under the watchful eye of law enforcement and county officials. Legal brothels flourish based on the demand by customers who will fly to those locations purely for the purpose of retaining a legal prostitute. The safety issue comes into play because prostitutes are required to be examined by doctors at frequent intervals for sexually transmitted diseases and always require condoms for all sex acts. Many men, and women, patronize these brothels without worrying about being criminally victimized.

The act of prostitution occurs regularly in gaming environments and needs to be constantly monitored for offenders, who are trespassed and requested to leave the premises.

There is a demand for prostitutes by the public and the perception of many men is that you can go to a casino and get a prostitute anytime. Men and women joke about how many "hookers" they see when they are inside a casino or on the streets of major casino resort areas.

Prostitution primarily involves women, but men can also be prostitutes. They can sell same-sex acts or heterosexual ones. They will sell groups, fetish acts, and just about anything that a person could think of, including abnormal or unusual sexual activity. All that is needed for prostitution is a customer who wants sex and is willing to pay for it, and a prostitute who is willing to sell it. The only way to reduce or prevent prostitution is to have a proactive program to monitor, eject, arrest, and enforce a no solicitation program.

In markets like New Jersey and Las Vegas, prostitutes are so plentiful that a casino can actually catch, trespass, and write reports on up to thirty people per day. The district attorneys in some jurisdictions require that anyone arrested for trespass based on a previous eighty-sixing must have advised the person within the previous six months before the arrest will be prosecuted. This makes it difficult to enforce the removal and arrest of previously eighty-sixed prostitutes since they can just avoid a particular casino for that six months and work another one.

Professional prostitutes change appearance in a matter of seconds inside a semiprivate place by putting on a wig and a change of clothes and walk right by security or other staff to avoid eighty-sixing unless security is keenly aware of the activity and the players. In Las Vegas, there are so many working prostitutes that it becomes almost impossible to totally prevent them from selling sex on or around a property.

Prostitutes also appear in smaller communities and environments and will usually prey on men who are slightly intoxicated, away from spouses or girlfriends, and easily aroused by sexy suggestive clothing. Since men tend to have cash available when they are gambling, they are the perfect targets for a professional prostitute. People also commit prostitution acts out of desperation or for temporary financial benefit.

The cost of buying sex from a prostitute varies significantly based on supply and demand, location, level of experience and sophistication, and reputation. Sex can be sold for as little as $20 or as much as $10,000 or more. A man with unlimited disposable income who is looking for specific women with specific talents is willing to pay significant dollars.

The real professional prostitute will enter a casino and not be dressed in overly revealing clothes or have outlandish hair and makeup. She will be dressed much like the women seen at nightclubs or even appear as a professional businesswoman, which many of them are. They will walk a casino as if looking for someone and will approach a targeted male and start the flirting process. Many times this is done at the bar or at a table game, and there is no mention of a price for sexual pleasures until later.

These professionals will look for their "clients" by watching mannerisms, what kind of clothing they are wearing, the brand of watch they are wearing, and even the type of shoes. When a man with money dresses down, he will change into casual clothing that was not bought at a local discount department store and wear an expensive watch and Italian shoes, which will be observed by the professional prostitute.

A typical, middle-aged man carrying a little extra weight who is approached by a sexy woman in her early twenties who wants to "party" is not a usual social meeting. It is the solicitation act that starts the process of negotiating how much the man will pay for specific sexual acts. Once the deal is made, both will go to a hotel room that is usually the customer's, but sometimes it is the prostitute's room and they will finalize the details. The cash is paid in advance and the man is seduced as he wants. In many instances the man will be so sexually aroused that he will negotiate for additional services and pay additional cash for them.

Since the hotel room rented to either party is private and there is an expectation of privacy, little can be done legally once the couple enters a hotel room. If there is a strong suspicion of solicitation, security can wait for the woman to leave the room and inform her that she is no longer welcome and complete a trespass warning.

Another trait is when the professional prostitute is out to make money and not get inebriated in the process. She will sit at a bar, order nonalcoholic drinks, and watch, approach, and engage in conversations with numerous men or women, eventually leaving the bar with one. Prostitutes come in every size, shape, ethnic origin, demeanor, and appearance. Appearance does not matter because every person has different sexual preferences and the prostitute will find a customer eventually, even if the price has to come down. Prostitutes have no measureable overhead costs except clothing, hair care, and makeup.

Pimps are the brokers and supervisors of organized prostitution and can be found where there are collections of prostitutes. Dealing with them is much more difficult and requires planning with law enforcement. They are controlling, abusive, and often dangerous. They must project the image to the public that they have a stable of girls, or boys, who can make others sexually happy for a fee. They are not typically hard to spot but are difficult to catch. Law enforcement involvement is a key component in getting these undesirables out of a casino property and into the local jail.

Regulators will be watching to make sure that security and all departments monitor activity and take a measured response to reduce or prevent it from occurring. Local police departments can be contacted and vice officers can assist in identifying known and dangerous prostitutes and implement a program to arrest them in your facility. It is always preferable to have professionals help eradicate as many prostitutes from your property as possible by arresting them.

With prostitution come the crimes that occur as a result of the actual act and payment. The most common crime is the "trick roll," where a victim is robbed or a theft occurs before, during, or after the sexual act. Since this occurs in the privacy of a hotel room, there are no cameras that can depict the criminal act. In some hotels CCTV cameras in the elevators and hotel hallways will capture the suspect entering and exiting the room, but will not have sufficient clarity to identify the prostitute.

A trick roll usually involves the victim being drugged or just getting so intoxicated that he or she passes out. The suspect will then search the room for any valuables, primarily cash, and exit the room. An experienced pro will even get into the room safe and take cameras, credit cards, and any valuables while the victim sleeps it off, sometimes for hours. When the victim finally wakes up and discovers his or her valuables are gone, he or she is faced with a dilemma. If the victim is married, on business in the hotel, or has a political or high-profile career, he or she will not file a police report. Sometimes the victim will contact security, but not always. As a result the crime does not get investigated. An average customer who is victimized may come to security but insist that security not call the police for any number of reasons. This becomes a problem because the customer has been victimized and there is no follow up. The security director needs to keep in touch with the operation and address these issues head on before they spin out of control.

In many public environments there is a theft crime that occurs and typically involves the lower end prostitutes. Many peace officers have nicknamed this the "grope and grab." It is a variation on the age-old "pick-pocket" crime and once again it involves a distraction. These men and women will inject themselves into a nightclub, bar, or crowded casino and look for a potential target.

As an example, a man is inside a crowded bar and is approached by a woman who says hello. The woman then feels the man's genitals through his pants while distracting him with looks, facial expressions, and suggestive comments. While the man cannot believe his good fortune and becomes instantly aroused, the woman continues her massage while simply removing his wallet from his back pocket, tells the man to meet her somewhere in a few minutes, and slips away never to be seen again.

The same situation occurs with women as the victim where a particularly adept con man will flirt heavily and will work his way to sexual petting while unzipping her purse and removing whatever he can find. In both circumstances the perpetrator makes the person sexually aroused and takes advantage of that arousal to steal. These thieves are difficult to catch in the act and will most likely be reported long after the suspect has left the building.

Security can put together an intelligence file that details each occurrence, when known, and suspects' descriptions can enable security and surveillance to watch the area and attempt to catch the person using plain-clothes officers and surveillance and evict the probable suspect.

21

Managing Casino Security

21.1 THE SECURITY INDUSTRY IN GENERAL AND GAMING SECURITY

A security department cannot be managed from a desk by merely delegating tasks (Figure 21.1). The gaming security professional is always on the move and is highly visible to the security staff, employee population, and management. The motivated manager will seek out department heads and communicate with them on a regular basis. He or she will be approachable and professional and have the confidence of the security staff and the employee population of the facility.

In the current age of the mega resort, there are facilities that are just too large for any one manager to be able to visit every day and still do the other duties of a professional director. In these cases operation managers are assigned to accomplish the basic security functions. It is imperative in these environments that the operations manager for security be a professional manager able to take on this important function.

There are many different publications that address managing in general and managing security operations. One of the most comprehensive publications is *Effective Security Management* by Charles Sennewald, an early pioneer in security management, noted author and international lecturer, founder of the International Association of Professional Security Consultants, and now retired. This excellent publication, currently in its fourth edition, is used by almost all college-level courses in security management and is required reading in many security programs and certification courses. It contains many applications of security in general that are useful and relevant in the casino environment.

There is, however, little that is written specific to gaming operations that have unique circumstances that involve many different functions inside one building. The director of security for a gaming property gains experience in the general security fields of hotels, banking, retail, bar and nightclub, investigations, closed-circuit television systems, parking lot and garages, entertainment, and others. These environments package all the basic entities you would find in a small town or city in one location under the control of a privately owned casino complex.

251

Figure 21.1   Ensuring security is not as easy as the push of a button.

21.2 KNOW YOUR FACILITY

Casinos change constantly and the professional gaming security manager will be aware of changes well before they occur rather than be surprised to hear that a change has occurred. By moving through the property regularly and talking with staff, employees, and management, the effective manager will always be aware of the facility and any changes that do occur.

Mandating that certain things cannot occur without notification to security, who in turn notify the appropriate supervisor or manager, will also help. Whenever the basic footprint of a gaming facility is changed it should require advance communication. Notification involving any moving of alarms or sensitive equipment, ingress or egress points, and money handling areas are just a few changes that require advance warning to security and surveillance.

The contemporary security professionals will know exactly how many table games are currently on the casino floor as well as slot machines, cash ATMs and cashier banks, kiosks for cash and TITO (ticket in, ticket out) redemption, and the impress amounts of cash held at various locations. They will know how many parking spaces are on the facility; the number of hotel rooms, restaurants, and retail operations; occupancy capacities; and how many employees work for the company. Knowledge of these components is required to effectively manage the security of the facility.

By reviewing the security reports and logs on a daily basis the manager will know what issues are occurring, where they are occurring, and what changes may have occurred over the past twenty-four hours. Implementing 24/7 notification of specific events also allows for immediate management of difficult or sensitive incidents (Figure 21.2).

When I was promoted to my first job as a security director I already knew what the first thing on my list was to accomplish. The casino was arresting far too many people and not using tact and diplomacy. I initiated the immediate requirement that I was to be notified on every arrest incident as soon as the person was inside the security office and was to be briefed on the circumstances. I required the shift supervisor to fax a report and statements to me as soon as they were completed. Today the proactive director receives e-mail reports as they are completed and is well aware of the activity even when away from the property.

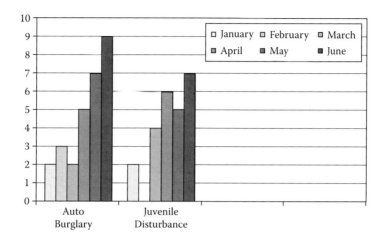

Figure 21.2   Tracking incident reports.

The purpose of this new procedure was to reduce the number of arrests by forcing the staff to manage them rather than just accomplish routine arrests. After several weeks of minor arrests, the number of incidents started decreasing rapidly. The staff did not want to have to wake the chief and tell him someone had been arrested who could have instead been warned to leave just one more time. Eventually arrest incidents became rare rather than routine. Because I knew my facility, I knew that the procedure would work.

21.3 MONITORING POLICE CALLS TO YOUR FACILITY

In the past thirty years, the emergence of recorded logs of police calls for service has been presented by experts in civil trials to establish the likely anticipation that a crime would or could occur to help prove liability and obtain verdicts in favor of plaintiffs. By reviewing the logs that most law enforcement agencies maintain, the plaintiff can obtain information of all calls for police and the type of call to any location, including a casino. These are referred to as calls for service (CFS) reports and they are produced by most law enforcement agencies. They are not designed for public use but are used for crime analysis and for the local police to determine manpower and resource allocations. They have evolved into the security operation based on litigation history when a plaintiff's attorney wants to show a jury the amount of police activity on a property.

Obtaining the data absent a subpoena can sometimes be challenging and expensive in some jurisdictions based on the availability and departmental policies. Some jurisdictions resist these requests and a formal letter requesting them will typically be sufficient. The challenge comes into play when you are not able to obtain the data easily. If obtained with a subpoena in a civil trial, it can be used against the property to demonstrate potential criminal activity.

Internally tracking any incident will help, but that will not include instances where a person has gone to the police department to file a report of some type without a property's knowledge. There is always a variance in the number of calls logged by the police in comparison to what the property believes the number should be. This will most certainly be brought up and presented to a jury during a civil litigation. It will also help identify late reports that are false or unfounded.

It is important to understand that these calls are summaries and do not contain details or in many instances the disposition or police response. They cannot be relied upon to analyze criminal activity in any credible manner absent actual police reports and details. They can, however, be useful in determining how many times the police are called or notified regarding your facility and leased operations within the property during a fixed period of time and at least what the initial call was for.

The most effective way to be proactive in obtaining these statistics is to contact your law enforcement agency and request assistance from the Crime Prevention Department. These police professionals can assist in obtaining the information relevant to your property and the surrounding area or neighborhood near the casino. They can also assist in training and analysis of the calls as compared to similar operations. In addition, they can also assist you in the format in which they are printed so you can adequately compare them against another period of time.

The CFS is also a useful tool for the director or manager who wants to demonstrate to his or her boss the number of police calls that occur and a snapshot of the criminal activity that is investigated. By examining these reports the director can justify payrolls, positional assignments, or requests for staff increases if the data support it. Increases or decreases in incident types can be demonstrated through these basic report summaries. If the director perceives that there are too many vehicle burglaries in the parking lot because he recently read a summary report describing them, the report can be consulted and compared to the same prior month or year.

The ideal interval for these statistics is monthly and annually, but that is not always possible. Attempt to obtain them at least quarterly and you will see any trends developing that require attention. Obtaining these reports at least annually may prove helpful to make sure you are aware of, for instance, a robbery that was reported to the police but never reported to the casino by the victim or the police. They will show trends in parking lot crimes, such as auto burglaries or grand theft auto. They can also be helpful in determining what officer-initiated actions have occurred, such as additional patrols or perimeter checks.

Most municipalities also publish an annual report of crimes in the community. These reports can also be helpful to determine what the neighborhood area has experienced in criminal activity as compared to your particular property. Another source is the Uniform Crime Report published by the Federal Bureau of Investigation on an annual basis. This report will compare the activity in your city or county to national averages and as compared to the population. It compares the more serious crimes using a basis of crimes per 1,000 people.

The contemporary security professional will know the activity in and around his or her facility and will know when criminal activity changes so he or she can design countermeasures. The best source for most of this information is your local law enforcement agency. You must be persistent in requesting the data and justify the request as essential for crime prevention at your facility.

21.4 COMMUNICATING WITH LOCAL LAW ENFORCEMENT

Law enforcement communication is also an important task of the proactive security director. There are various ways to develop two-way communication with the agencies that oversee the jurisdiction you are in. In previous decades, buying a meal or offering free coffee to local police was the normal practice. In today's world, law enforcement is sensitive to this process and will routinely resist those offers. You should stay away from this practice, which might embarrass both parties unless it has been deemed permissible by the law enforcement entity.

There are other ways to foster a positive relationship with law enforcement. First, if you and your staff are professional and do not call the police for unnecessary incidents, you will promote a positive relationship. The perceptions of most police officers is that security officers are not always professional based on the negative incidents they encounter with contract security officers, nightclub bouncers, and retail loss prevention personnel. Those isolated incidents create animosity and a perception about security that is incorrect as a whole.

If police respond to a casino every other day for intoxicated patrons, it may be perceived that the casino has issues in alcohol management. For example, police may be called to control a crime scene of a drunk driver who killed a family on vacation. They may determine from the evidence that the drunk driver got intoxicated at your facility, and they will quickly reflect on the numerous calls that police responded to regarding intoxication at your facility. This not only creates an issue with the police and their perception of your operation, it also can be damaging during a civil trial when the remaining family sues the casino.

Being professional and having the evidence and witnesses available is important when calling the police to respond to your facility. Having blank witness forms from the police in your jurisdiction will also be helpful to initiate the process of separating and writing statements, securing evidence, and protecting a crime scene. As police respond to calls at your facility that are handled professionally without the security officers overstepping their authority, the respect from law enforcement will follow.

It can also be very helpful if you invite the police into your facility to monitor typical issues that they are charged with enforcing. Narcotics, alcohol service to minors, minor gambling, and prostitution are a few of the areas in which they can be quite helpful in a proactive manner. You should not be afraid to invite them in because the end result will be a positive one especially if you invite them formally with a letter or e-mail.

Your local police are also typically available to help with training of security officers. Inviting the local vice officers in to help train your security officers on current local drug trends or how to spot prostitutes will go a long way in establishing that important relationship. It will also demonstrate that the casino is interested in combating illegal activity, which is also their ultimate goal.

Meeting with the local watch commander, chief, or sheriff regularly will also foster this relationship. Inviting the command staff for coffee is appropriate and beneficial in building this relationship. Encouraging the security shift managers or supervisors to meet with the patrol sergeant on each shift will also continue this valuable cooperation. By interacting with your local law enforcement staff you will increase your perceived professionalism and gain confidence of the peace officers.

21.5 PROFESSIONAL GROUPS AND ASSOCIATIONS

Networking is a fundamental process that benefits the security professional. One of the most productive ways to network is to attend your local security chiefs' association or security directors' meeting. In most locations there are groups that are informally and formally organized to meet monthly and communicate information with one another, such as lookout bulletins (BOLOs), crime spree information, or wanted suspect information. These meetings are also designed to communicate trends in nuisance crimes, such as auto burglaries and distraction teams.

If your location does not have a group that meets, you should start one as an informal process. Remember that the group members are not just casino chiefs but can be from retail, commercial sectors, or even government entities. Rotating the location of these meetings monthly is typical and affords the various security chiefs the opportunity to see other venues and security operations. It also evenly distributes costs if a meal or refreshments are involved. Then you can invite the local police chief or sheriff to join in the meetings. Make sure you take notes for each meeting and document who attended and what was discussed as this will certainly be helpful in the future. The larger chiefs' associations have elected officers such as the larger gaming markets in Las Vegas and Atlantic City.

Also available as a resource to security professionals is the ASIS International security organization, which is the largest security organization in the world. There are chapters in every state and in most large cities, and they meet monthly to network and provide training and useful information to security professionals. They also provide professional certification and specialized training, and their annual seminar moves around the country and around the world.

The ASIS International Council on Gaming and Wagering Protection is comprised of security and surveillance professionals from all over the world and it focuses on gaming operations and the issues that are present in those environments. They regularly conduct sponsored training sessions on security topics relevant to the gaming industry annually.

The important thing to remember is to attend every month unless there is a compelling reason you cannot. In that case send the next highest level of the security staff in your casino. When I conduct a full security audit of a casino, I obtain the attendance record of the head of security at these meetings through some basic investigation. If a director attends only once or twice a year, attendance is a topic for the deficiency list in networking and professional development.

These meeting can become unproductive at times and require everyone to keep the interest and information flowing. I have had directors tell me that they feel the meetings are a waste of time and that they have much more important things to do. Explaining this on the witness stand after someone dies as a result of a crime on your property after the suspect had been discussed at one of these meetings will certainly also be problematic.

21.6 TRACKING, ANALYZING, AND MANAGING INCIDENTS

Analysis of why and how incidents are occurring on your property is a common and well-established method of measuring the effectiveness of the security programs in place. Keeping track in a "look-back" method will help the security professional in planning a proactive department. The mentality of "I know what is occurring on my property every day because I see the reports" can create complacency and a lack of focus in seeing the big picture.

The manager who merely reads the reports for the previous twenty-four hours and takes some action on items that are of concern is typical. The problem with it ending at this point is that there is no overall analysis done until it is too late and an area has already become problematic. Statistical reports should be compiled to compare and chart the activity that may be increasing, decreasing, or remaining constant.

As an example, if a property tracks all of the workers' compensation claims on a property on a calendar-type dry erase board, management has a visual reminder of the number of claims that are occurring. The professional risk manager will tell you that the direct and indirect costs of employee accidents are huge expenses to any organization, and care should be taken to analyze any trends or common denominators that may reduce those costs.

As the security manager and staff come to work each day, they are reminded of the numbers of employee accidents by looking at the visual board and will have a motivation to assist in the goal of reductions. Placing a stack of reports in front of a supervisor of security and requiring him or her to chart the incidents, including time, location, date and day of week, and causation, will also be a motivator to that supervisor to enforce the company safety programs and ultimately reduce the number of incidents and reports.

If there have been burglaries in the parking lot of your facility, the analysis may be as simple as determining that most are occurring within a narrow time frame and when a particular shift of employees is leaving work. The focus on that time frame with special investigation or surveillance will most likely prove beneficial.

If a director compiles, or charges someone else to compile the data each month, they become measurement tools of the security program and can be used to strengthen or reduce payroll and expense to a particular area. The results can then be measured and used when requesting additional manpower or equipment. Reviewing the data with supervisors at regular intervals is also a positive move to invoke a more proactive security program.

The danger of thinking that you know what has occurred, and what to do, is that there is a natural tendency to rationalize that you cannot prevent all crime, and that a particular incident does not happen that often. After a rationalization occurs, an incident tends to be dismissed as an anomaly and quickly forgotten. Because a property will experience numerous incidents each day, they become faded memories as each new incident report is investigated and recorded. Managers and line staff tend to rationalize and minimize incidents based on their perceived experience.

By tracking and reminding the staff of the occurrence rates, locations, and other pertinent data, the staff becomes part of the solution by becoming more attentive or communicating with other employees. Motivating the staff can be accomplished using the statistical data with the end result being the reduction of incidents and exposure to your organization.

21.7 INTERNAL STAFF COMMUNICATION

Communication is another important part of any business environment, and security in a gaming environment is no exception. Communicating to your staff the various items that are important becomes challenging in economic hard times and when business is booming. There are various types of meetings that can be implemented to effectively communicate to a security staff.

In recent years the issue of daily shift briefings has come under scrutiny by regulators when wage-per-hour issues become problematic. Requiring an hourly employee to report to work, in uniform, fifteen minutes before his or her paid shift now becomes an overtime issue rather than a standard as it was twenty years ago. In larger operations where there are overlap shifts, this is easily accomplished and a shift briefing can be conducted. In operations without overlap, it becomes more challenging to brief the security personnel.

Some operations merely budget fifteen minutes of overtime for every officer and consider it an operational necessity. If you have that budgetary luxury, enjoy it while it lasts! It is calculated when the security budgets are submitted and approved and is utilized as a routine. Other operations must become creative in finding a solution to the briefing dilemma when they are prohibited from utilizing overtime for this communication time.

The security briefing has historically been the time when the security personnel are advised of important items to watch for, complete, or attempt to prevent. It has also been the time for short bursts of training or refresher time for a particular rule, policy, or procedure that required a reminder. Briefing logs, or pass-on logs, were developed to maintain a record of what advisements each shift was given during the briefing period and to document the process. This log process still occurs in many operations.

What has become another interesting briefing function is the use of computers to brief the incoming security personnel rather than organize the traditional briefing where everyone from the shift piles into a room, the supervisor talks, and all personnel are required to listen. Each employee is assigned an e-mail account and the information that needs to be relayed is sent to a mass list of employees within the department or a specific shift on what needs to occur.

Some managers have implemented this briefing method and are convinced it is more effective than the traditional briefing. BOLOs from law enforcement agencies are scanned and sent through the electronic system to each officer as well as any directives from the head of security, shift manager, and even the general manager. The information technology (IT) department sets up a log to show when each employee signed on, how long he or she was on line, and essentially whether each one reviewed the material sent.

This method of briefing is more focused and the employee can process the information at his or her own retention speed and not be pressured by fellow officers. It lacks the social interaction that a traditional briefing has but can be used effectively in most operations. Some directors have informed me that e-mail reduces the horseplay associated with the traditional briefing by isolating the employee.

Shift meetings, can be accomplished at infrequent intervals. I have seen this done quarterly, semiannually, or annually with positive results. The human resources approach toward managing personnel promotes a form of communication where line employees can voice concerns or issues that are important to them. In this forum the staff of a particular shift has an opportunity to meet with the supervisor and director to solve recurring issues or clarify a management philosophy or rule.

I discourage meetings of an entire department because they tend to be unproductive and the intentions are lost as one or two officers dominate the meeting because they have an audience and a personal agenda. Meeting the shift staff on a quarterly basis is ideal because it keeps the staff stimulated and the line employees know that they will have an opportunity to voice a concern that is not addressed on their shift.

The shift meetings do not have to be long and should be no more than an hour in duration. Communicating statistical information, calls for service, trends in criminal activity, and personnel-related issues are great topics for these meetings. The shift managers of security will also start to manage their shifts more effectively if they know the director will be meeting with the shift every three months or so. I have found that those supervisors will actually seek out each staff member and solve individual problems before a meeting rather than at a shift meeting in front of the officers and the director.

Another great tool for these shift meetings is to collect incident video clips through the surveillance department and play them. This provides a training dynamic to show what is preferred behavior and to provide appropriate positive compliments to officers who are seen on the videos performing well under pressure. It can also demonstrate those incidents that are not desired or are unprofessional. The mere showing of the videos will send a signal that someone is paying attention to incidents.

Shift supervisor meetings are critical for a successful security operation in a gaming environment. Monthly meetings for the salaried managers and supervisors will address issues head on and prove beneficial in the long run. The security management staff is the backbone to the operation, and communication is the primary tool in accomplishing proactive security. Statistical information should be disseminated and compared by shift at these meetings and staffing and operational issues should be reviewed. Supervisors are typically salaried employees and therefore not subject to the overtime issues.

As an example, if a director, or supervisor, wants to determine what the staff is doing on an hourly basis, the best tool is analyzing the dispatch log to determine how much time each officer is tied up on each call or assignment and how much time is devoted to patrol of the assigned area. The analysis results can be communicated to the supervisors in the monthly meeting.

If, for example, it is determined from the analysis that the swing shift hotel officer is only patrolling the hotel areas 30 percent of the time on the shift, a more detailed analysis may show that the officer is being called out of the hotel by the dispatcher to perform other duties. All of the supervisors can collectively help solve the patrol issue in the meeting by working out any overlap or common issues as well as assist the affected supervisor in solving the patrol deficiency.

If area checks are required and called into dispatch, the logs can be examined to determine if a particular area is neglected in the patrol function so this can be corrected to the desired level.

These meetings can take longer than an hour at times, but the director should be careful not have meetings that regularly last several hours. Long meetings tend to become unproductive and dreaded by the management staff. The key is to have them, keep them brief and to the point, and have meaningful information that affects all of the supervisors. You should not use this meeting to chastise the staff for the errors committed by one or two supervisors. That should be done separately and privately.

It is also important to calculate the costs of meetings in your annual budget and make it an integral part of your operation. The cost of meetings can become managerial issues and should be managed just like any payroll expense.

21.8 POLICIES AND PROCEDURES

I have examined hundreds of security manuals in my career for various reasons and under many different circumstances. In gaming operations no two manuals are the same unless a past director has merely taken someone else's manual and copied it. The security policies and procedures are the foundations of any security department and should be treated as such.

In almost every litigation or claim case that I have worked, the policies and procedures become issues. The security manual is typically required to be produced during a lawsuit to determine if you had a procedure in place for a particular topic, if it was adequately designed and followed, and updated in recent history.

The policies and procedures for the security department are "self-imposed standards" that you should be following. If you or someone before you designed the manual and required each officer to sign for it and be familiar with it, then it also becomes the standard you should be following.

From that general sense, the policies and procedures are the rules that your staff is to fall back on and be trained in as they relate to your specific operation. If you do not have a procedure for dealing with a particular item, then your staff will deal with it in the best way that they think will solve the issue rather than what you and the company want. The employee will rely on his or her own personal feelings, moral issues, and life experiences, which are not always effective.

As a result, most companies will memorialize the policies and procedures in a security manual, standard operating manual (SOP), or other document. Contemporary security departments will have the manual organized by subject matter; it will contain rules of conduct, procedures in handling various incidents, reporting requirements, post orders or position descriptions, and job duties and responsibilities. It is important to make sure that the functions and incidents a security officer will respond to have some form of guidance on what the company desires.

Size is not as important as content when designing a security manual. In Chapter 19 we talked about organizing the training program to follow the manual, which is the base document of the operation. Whatever the security operations manual dictates the training program should follow and ensure that all personnel are trained in the particular topic, policy, procedure, practice, or rule.

There are many different theories on what should be contained in a gaming security manual. Each director has his or her own view of what is important and appropriate to be memorialized in the operational procedures. An issue can surface when a particular director dictates procedures based on his or her own experiences and not necessarily what is in the best interest of the company or tribe.

Keeping the manual up to date is another issue that becomes problematic when disciplining an officer for a rule violation or proving compliance to a regulator or a jury. The theory that nothing changes will not hold up if things have actually changed. A periodic review of the operations manual should be completed. Contemporary experts have recommended that a security operations manual be reviewed at least once every year and any changes be made and documented. If there are changes made between manual updates, then an operational memorandum can be placed in the manual and distributed until the next full revision.

For historical reasons any revision made to an operations manual can also be noted on the policy to include revision date and person authorizing the revision. It is not an easy task to find the time to read, revise, and formally change an operations manual. I found that by dividing the manual among the security management staff and having them review and recommend changes to the director is an effective way to accomplish revisions and keep it up to date. It also develops your management team and allows you the opportunity to see what each supervisor is capable of when considering that next promotion.

The supervisors can talk to line staff and determine why the procedure is in place, if it is being followed, and if it no longer applies because of operational or physical changes. They present the recommended changes to the director who would have the final say and give the supervisor credit for locating and recommending the particular change. All of this will enhance the communication process and the team concept within the security operation. It gives the staff ownership in developing the security manual and promotes the team approach.

The first thing to understand is that whatever document is in place at a particular time is your operations manual and should always be preserved. The procedures in place three or four years prior will be of issue in an inadequate security lawsuit. There should be a location where all versions of manuals are kept. As each manual is revised, a copy of the old manual is dated and filed for future reference. When a request is served on your company to produce the policy and procedure manual in place at the time of an incident that occurred years prior, you will be unable to do so if you have not stored the older versions and this will become a point for closing arguments. With the technology in place today an electronic document can be maintained for ease in revisions using a word processing program, but retaining a hard copy of the document is always advised for as many years as possible

Gaming operations tend to run in cycles and operations revert back to a policy or procedure that had been implemented in the past. If you have all of your past documents, the work will become easier if you do not have to reinvent the wheel and can review the old procedure and make minor modifications.

It is also important to remember that the primary security function for any gaming operation is to protect the people within the boundaries of the facility. The guests and employees should always come first and the operations manual should reflect this in format and presentation. I have seen entire sections of security manuals devoted to guest protection, but this is rare. In many operations there is no mention of guest protection, although it may be implied. Guest protection in a gaming facility is vital yet it is rarely addressed in writing in the manual.

261

Security experts also advise that a formal chain of command chart be included with titles only and be updated whenever there is a change in the command and reporting structure. The chain of command is important and it should be followed by all who are under it. If the chain is jumped by anyone, the person should be instructed to follow the chain as indicated in the formal document. Exceptions should only be made in extreme circumstances. This will also enhance the performance of the operation.

21.9 WRITTEN REPORTS

Security reports are completed every day in the casino environment and are as diverse as the people who complete them. Every security director I come in contact with tells me that he or she wishes the staff could do a better job at writing reports. The problem comes into play when you try to train a person to do a report in a format that you want. You cannot educate employees, or sometimes reeducate them, on how to read and write, how to use proper sentence and structure, and even in spelling and grammar.

The security reports are the form of documentation that the facility requires to process claims, record events, discipline employees, and manage the social behavior of guests and employees. It is important and needs almost constant attention by all of the security management team. A concerted effort of all security personnel needs to be encouraged to get the best possible product available from the existing staff.

Many operations employ a separate officer who is charged with writing incident reports. Medical officers and emergency medical technicians are also charged with completing guest medical incident reports, guest accident reports, and employee accident reports. In these operations the security management believes that they can best train these few security officers to complete satisfactory reports, and they select the personnel for these positions based on their competence as report writers. This can be very helpful in consistent reporting of incidents. Using this method will not promote training of the rest of the security staff, who will then be unaware of how to write a report if the occasion arises. Ideally all security personnel should be trained to complete written reports, although the reports will differ in quality.

Having report writers does have drawbacks. The person most familiar with the incident is not reducing the information to writing the actual report. In these instances it becomes even more important that the written statements be comprehensive in order for the report writer to adequately describe what occurred. It is also difficult to determine if the writer of the report was even involved other than completing the report, which can cause confusion in a courtroom.

Keeping the report process simple will result in less apprehension by the staff who have to complete reports. A complicated report writing procedure will discourage certain staff from completing reports, and they will find excuses not to write one. Basic rules such as making sure each box or line is completed even if it is "N/A" or "None" will at least demonstrate that the question was asked. Having reports with blanks leads one to think that it is incomplete and opens up the possibility of allegations that what occurred was not properly documented.

Having the narrative in a report that is first person in format will also help in describing the events. Following the old school third-person format will confuse the writer unless the report forms are very specific as to who each party is. As an example in the third-person format: "Suspect #1 was approached by this R/O after Victim #2 gave his description to Officer #37" makes the reader have to flip to the names and determine information and disrupts communication. In the first-person format the same can be said more clearly: "Rodriguez was approached by me after I obtained his description from the victim, Mrs. Smith." Plain language in the world of casino security will be much easier to accomplish and easily understandable by the appropriate staff.

Responding to any incident will include locating witnesses who are asked to complete a statement. Locating independent witnesses is crucial in incidents involving assaults, arrests, accidents, or major disruptions. As part of the response the second or third officer on scene can canvass the people to attempt to locate the independent witness who is not an employee and is not part of the incident. In many instances that independent witness will be critical in a criminal or civil trial later.

There are usually several security officers who respond to an incident. Having each security officer complete a statement even if he or she did not actively participate in the incident will also prove beneficial years later. If a backup officer made an observation that might support a fellow officer's statement or if he or she canvassed the people in close proximity for any possible independent witnesses, that will demonstrate professional conduct and will be a positive. If the indications are that there were three or four officers who responded and only one of them completed a statement, it may reflect as careless, incomplete, or unprofessional.

If security personnel first interview a witness and make some basic notes that outline what they saw and collect their contact information, they can then be requested to complete a written statement. Once completed the officers can consult their notes and make sure all of the information relayed verbally is contained in their statements. If the witness forgot to note something in the written statement that he or she told an officer verbally, this is the time the witness can be reminded of that. If the officer realizes that the witness missed a crucial piece of information after he or she left the casino, it is difficult to follow. In criminal incidents witnesses would usually be required to also speak with law enforcement, and using the peace officer's written witness form will prevent security from having to complete two statements.

After collecting all of the evidence involved in an incident including statements, the security officer can then outline the incident on paper. The outline should flow and tell a story of how the incident occurred, the precipitating factors (if any) and the details of location, time, parties involved, and the other basic elements of a report (who, what, where, when, and how). Then the security supervisor or manager can assist in determining what elements of which crime occurred or what company rule may have been breached.

As an example, if the written reports and statements contain all of the elements of the particular crime that may have been violated, then prosecution becomes much easier to accomplish. By reading the statutory law involved in an arrest the officer completing the written report can review his or her report and make sure that it states what action precipitated the arrest of the person.

Experienced officers and managers will resist the outline process and indicate they have written hundreds of reports and do not need an outline. Careful examination of their reports will be a positive argument for the use of outlines. It will be rare if a person has the ability to instantly recall all of the details of an incident especially if he or she handled several calls between the incident and the writing of the report.

Reports can be reviewed and sent back if necessary for addendums that may be required. It is always desirable for the original report to be complete, but it does not always happen that way. The supervisor plays a key role in reviewing the initial report to make sure the content is what is desired, is professionally written, and can be easily read by the target audience.

I found that creating a list of words most commonly misspelled in security reports and a vocabulary list of common terms is helpful to the officers. I kept a notepad on my desk and added words that I found that were misspelled by more than one officer and then make up cards for the officers to keep in their pocket notebooks and in the security office for easy reference. It did not take long for them to learn from repeatedly referring to the list to memorize the words they had misspelled most of their lives.

There are many other reports and logs that are used in the industry as written records of security activity. I have discussed the importance of the dispatch logs throughout this book and some methods that can be used to efficiently use them to prove security presence. The dispatch log is the control document that the security management should use to assess manpower, task efficiency, patrol coverage, breaks, and responses to incidents. There can never be too much information contained in a dispatch log, but it is designed for brief entries, not long narratives.

Position logs or activity reports in parking areas, hotel patrols, and many stationary positions help to monitor the activity and incidents that a particular officer may be involved in. Vehicle logs can be used by a supervisor as an indication of how much patrol is accomplished by simply looking at the starting and ending mileage listed on the report.

Every director has his or her own version of what should be included in the written reports used in a casino, and no one system is right for everyone. Constant review and training through revisions or communication will eventually improve the quality of the individually written reports. The key is to make sure that attention is paid to the reports and that they are reviewed and monitored for compliance with the established guidelines of your operation.

21.10 STANDARDS AND GUIDELINES

Finally, the security industry is moving toward guidelines and standards adopted by various organizations. As these become finalized by professional organizations, including the ASIS, the National Fire Protection Association, the International Association of Chiefs of Police, the National Indian Gaming Association, and the International Association of Professional Security Consultants, they will become the benchmarks for security operations to follow much like Peace Officers Standards Training is for law enforcement.

In some cases these organizations will be in conflict and produce standards and guidelines that will be confusing and sometimes impossible for every casino to follow. It is important to keep informed of these as they are published and make sure that any obvious deficiencies at your facility are corrected to be in reasonable compliance with the professional standards or guidelines. Once they are utilized by the majority of casino operations, they will fast become the standard of care by which courts will instruct juries when they are deliberating on a civil matter.

One of the easiest ways to monitor this is to assign a staff member to keep track of new standards and guidelines and keep the director informed as each one comes into play. Based on the current activity there appears to be a race to see how many security standards and guidelines can be adopted by these organizations and as a result there will be many published on virtually every security topic within the next decade.

If there are standards and guidelines, the management charged with security oversight needs to educate themselves and review them. These guidelines and standards already appear in litigations where a plaintiff's security expert criticizes a casino operation for not following the standard of care.

APPENDIX: ADDITIONAL FORMS AND RESOURCES

AUDIT PLANNING SHEET

		Key Areas and Transactions		
Department	**Location/ Transaction**	**Frequency**	**Resources**	**Key Objectives**
Table games	Fills/credits	Quarterly	TG SOP manual Cage SOP Security SOP MICS	Proper verification Signatures Delivery Receipt Paperwork
Table games	Credit transactions Marker issue/ redemption	Quarterly	TG SOP Cage SOP Security SOP MICS	Verification Signatures Issue Receipt Drop
Slots	Jackpots	Monthly	Slot SOP MICS	Verification Signatures Payment
Slots	TITO kiosk	Monthly	Slot SOP MICS	Review redemptions of $1,000 or more
Marketing	Players club	Monthly	Club SOPs MICS Program/promotion rules Exception reports	Review account merges, name changes, point adjustments

AUDIT MASTER SCHEDULE

Department	Area/Location	Frequency	Duration

AUDIT MONTHLY SCHEDULE

Month/Year: _____

Department	Area/Location	Duration	Shift	Investigator

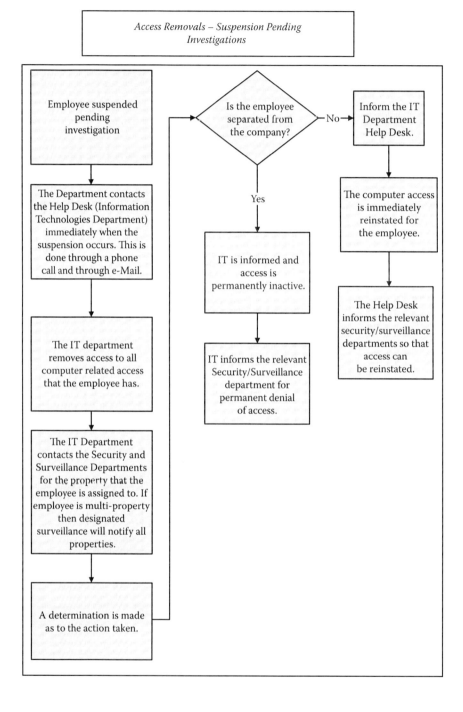

Access Removals – Separations from Company

Employee gives notice for separation from company or employee is terminated and date of separation is predetermined.

The Department Head informs the IT department as to the date and time of separation and the IT department removes access effective that date and time.

The Department Head informs the appropriate security/surveillance departments, who will remove access at the effective date and time.

Surveillance/IOU Patrol Flow Chart

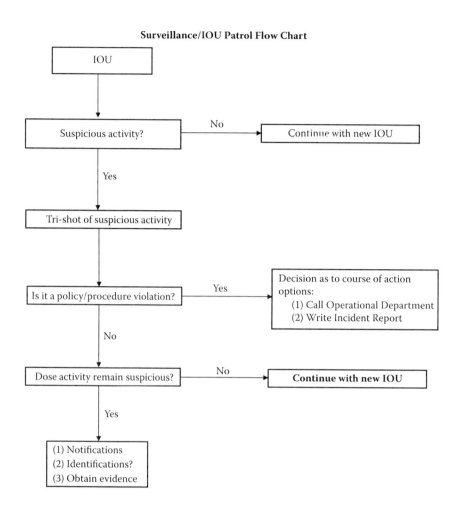

FOOD AND BEVERAGE TELLS

Scams/Indicators/Tells of Theft and Fraud

1. Serves drinks or food and collects money while register is being closed out at end of the shift, or when ribbon is being changed.
2. Phony walk out—keep the cash and claim customer left without playing.
3. Short ring: charge customer actual price, under ring the sale on the register, and keep the difference.
4. No sale: charge the customer actual price but sale is not rung (entered) into register or point of sale (POS). Bartenders may put into toke jar, pocket or cash drawer. If the cash drawer is used, bartender must track the stolen funds using straws, matchbooks, pennies, coasters, etc.
5. Phantom cash register (or satellite register during special events) set up at certain times (happy hour). Sales not recorded normally or on master register tape and can be skimmed by bartender.
6. Voided sales: employee voids transaction or portions of transaction and keeps proceeds.
7. Overrings: employee overrings to reverse sale.
8. Fictitious paid-outs (cash taken from register to pay for deliveries or other miscellaneous items).
9. Altering breakout of tip and check amounts on credit card receipts to overstate tips and understate the check.
10. Employee accumulates guest checks and rings after customer leaves. Checks can be altered or destroyed.
11. Employee steals cash and covers it up by falsifying register readings/totals.
12. Employee provides customer with old check/receipt and does not record current sale.
13. Employee records sales on training key which does not feed into daily receipts or cumulative sales total.
14. Charges customer full price but enters as senior citizen or employee discount.
15. Employee works out of open cash drawer (sales not recorded).
16. Employee does not ring up sale.
17. Bartender claims a drink was returned when in fact it was sold.
18. Bartender gives away drinks to friends, family, and other employees to increase tips.
19. Bartender comps paying customers and keeps cash.
20. Undercharges for premium liquor in anticipation of larger tip.
21. Overpours liquor in anticipation of a larger tip.
22. Bartender brings his or her own bottle and pockets cash from sales.
23. Cocktail waitress and bartender collude: waitress does not input orders into system, bartender makes drinks offline. Cash from sales split between waitress and bartender.
24. Bartender trades free drinks to other employees for food or other services.

25. Complimentary coupons, two-for-one coupons, special offers, etc. are stolen by hotel maids from guest rooms and sold to bartenders or cut from newspapers magazines and brought in by employees to justify missing inventory or to allow theft from cash paying customers.
26. Sales from draft beer/kegs not entered into register.
27. Handwrite bar tabs and ring up amounts less than sales.
28. Collusion between server and cook—server does not input order into system, cook makes food off line. Proceeds from sales are split by server and waitress.
29. Staff claims a meal was returned but was, in fact, served and paid for.
30. Checks from comped guests are altered or split to include meals or portions of meals of cash paying customers. Resulting cash overage is pocketed.
31. Employee has frequent cash variances, over or short.
32. Theft of meat or food from walk-in coolers.
33. Employees claim that missing inventory was returned to bartender, spoiled, or burned.
34. Produce and steal surplus food.
35. Employees do not enter into register "to go" food or coffee, pocket cash received.
36. Wrap food or drink in paper and store in trash for later retrieval.
37. Kickbacks from vendors (generally inferior product or quality is sold, chef gets a commission).
38. Accepting lesser weights (or receiving does not weigh product). Vendors may add ice to cover up missing product.
39. Feed friends, family, other employees for free.
40. Chef purchases specific items not for sale or for employee or personal consumption.
41. Employees at food or beverage kiosks bring their own food or beverage to sell at location.
42. Chef obtains and submits falsified invoices that transfer food purchases to supplies to cover up thefts.
43. Wine steward claims sold bottle was returned or broken.
44. Collusion between person receiving food or beverages and vendor truck driver to provide short weights. Stolen product is often sold on the streets.
45. Employee keeps funds from vending machine.
46. Employees steal silverware, glassware, tablecloths, etc.
47. Employees keep cash from cover charges.
48. Use the manager's swipe card to void transactions or alter register information.

INCIDENT REPORT LOG

Yr-Mo-IR #	Date	Time	Category	Description of Incident	IGC #	Location of Incident	DVR #

BLACKJACK COUNTDOWN SHEET

Player Name: _____   Player Number: _____   Table: _____

Race: _____   Sex: _____   Age: _____   Ht: _____   Wt: _____   Hair: _____   Eyes: _____

Other Features/Clothing: _____   Requested By: _____

Observers: _____   _____   Dealer: _____

Shift: _____   Date: _____   Start time: _____   Stop time: _____   Spot 1 2 3 4 5 6

Comments: _____

	Count	Bet	Aces	Player Cards	Dealer Up Card	Decision	W/L/P
1							
2							
3							
4							
5							
6							
7							
8							
9							
10							
11							
12							
13							
14							
15							
16							
17							
18							
19							
20							
21							

EVALUATING BLACKJACK PLAY

Card Counting

Card counting is done by assigning a value to each card (plus, neutral or minus). Cards 2 through 6 are counted as plus 1. Cards 7, 8, and 9 are neutral and have no value. Cards 10, face, and ace are counted as minus 1.

Money Management

Flat/Hunch/Random

Win Progression—The player will increase wager each time it wins and decrease if it loses.

Loss Progression—The player will increase wager when it loses to attempt to regain previous loss.

Advantage—The player will increase the wager when there is a high plus count. The player will decrease the wager when there is a minus count.

Basic Strategy

Hard Doubles

8 = always hit
9 = double 3 – 6; hit 2, 7 – ace
10 = double 2 – 9; hit 10 and ace
11 = double 2 – 10; hit ace

Hard Totals

12 = stand 4 – 6; hit 2, 3, 7 – ace
13 – 16 = stand 2 – 6; hit 7 – ace
17 = always stand

Pair Split

2s, 3s, & 7s = split 2 – 7; hit 8 – ace
4s = split 5 and 6; hit 2 – 4, 7 – ace
5s = double 2 – 9; hit 10 and ace
6s = split 2 – 6; hit 7 – ace
8s and aces = always split
9s = split 2 – 6, 8 and 9; stand 7, 10 and ace
10s = always stand

Soft Hands

A2 – A3 = double 5 and 6; hit 2 – 4, 7 – ace
A4 – A5 = double 4 – 6; hit 2 and 3, 7 – ace
A6 = double 3 – 6; hit 2, 7 – ace
A7 = double 3 – 6; stand 2, 7 and 8, hit 9 – ace
A8 – A9 = always stand

Short Cuts

Remember to look for patterns most players will play regardless of the deck or how much they have wagered.

Short Cuts—Large Wagers

- Aggressive double downs and splits—11 vs ace, 9 vs 2, 10 vs 10, 10/10 vs 5, 10/10 vs 6.

277

- Standing during possible bust situations—16 vs 10, 15 vs 10, 16 vs 9, 12 vs 3, 12 vs 2.
- Taking insurance with any hand.

Short Cuts—Smaller Wagers
- Passive double downs (hitting instead of doubling)—11 vs 10, 9 vs 3, 10 vs 9.
- Hitting during bust situations—16 vs 10, 15 vs 10, 16 vs 9, 12 vs 4, 12 vs 6.
- Never taking insurance.

Critical Index

When the count becomes favorable to the players, they will change their hit and stand pattern to get the best advantage over the house. Most common deviations used according to the true count:

| | Dealer's Up Card | | | | | | | | | |
Player Cards	**2**	**3**	**4**	**5**	**6**	**7**	**8**	**9**	**10**	**A**
16								5	0	
15									4	
14										
13	−1	−2								
12	3	2	0	−2	−1					
11										1
10									4	4
9	1					3				
10/10				5	4					

Always take for insurance, if the true count is a plus 3 or higher.

| | Dealer's Up Card | | | | | | | | | |
Player Cards	**2**	**3**	**4**	**5**	**6**	**7**	**8**	**9**	**10**	**A**
AA								−9	−10	−5
TT	10	8	6	5	4	13				
99	−3	−5	−6	−7	−8	3	−10	−11		4
88										−13
77	−12	−13	−16	−17			2			
66	−2	−4	−6	−8	−11					
55										
44		8	4	0	−1					
33	−1	−6	−9	−10	−16					
22	−4	−6	−8	−10	−14		6			

				Dealer's Up Card						
Player Cards	**2**	**3**	**4**	**5**	**6**	**7**	**8**	**9**	**10**	**A**
A9	10	9	7	5	5	14				
A8	9	5	3	1	1	16				
A7	1	–3	–7	–9	–11					
A6	1	–5	–8	–11	–14					
A5		4	–4	–8	–14					
A4		6	–1	–6	–10					
A3	14	7	1	–3	–6					
A2	13	7	3	0	–3					

				Dealer's Up Card						
Player Cards	**2**	**3**	**4**	**5**	**6**	**7**	**8**	**9**	**10**	**A**
16	–9	–11	–12	–13	–13					
15	–6	–7	–8	–10	–10					
14	–4	–5	–7	–8	–8					
13	–1	–2	–4	–5	–5					
12	3	2		2	–1					
11	–12	–13	–14	–14	–16	–10	–7	–5	–5	1
10	–9	–10	–11	–12	14	–7	–5	–2	4	4
9	1	–1	–3	–5	–6	3	8			

SURVEILLANCE OPERATION PROCEDURES

Standard Response to Slot Jackpots

Subject: **Surveillance Response to Slot Jackpots**

Issue Date: February 19, 2010

Revision Date:

Number:

Page: 1 of 2

Slot jackpots of $25,000 or more require surveillance response to ensure the jackpot is legitimate, is properly paid as per established controls and procedures, and paid to the correct individual.

1. The agent assigned to slots must monitor the slot terminal for jackpots and/or unusual activity.
2. A radio tuned to slots must be monitored at all times by the assigned agent.
3. Slot jackpots of all amounts should be checked as often as possible during slot patrols, as well as suspicious or unusual activity noted or reported by radio.
4. Slot jackpots of $25,000 or more require the following:
   a. Surveillance will place a tri-shot on the machine/area to observe the verification of the win by slots, gaming authorities, and security. Report any discrepancies or violations of controls or procedure to the on-duty slot shift manager or above.
   b. Surveillance shall review play leading up to the jackpot and check for tells of cheating or suspicious activity. Observed tells or suspicious activity must be immediately reported to the slot shift manager and/or gaming authorities.
   c. Surveillance shall take a photo of the winning player.
   d. The name of the player shall be checked against surveillance databases for criminal or advantage play activity. Information obtained should be reported to the slot shift manager and/or gaming authorities.
   e. An incident report shall be filed by the agent responding to the jackpot. Included within the report shall be:
      i. Name of player
      ii. Date and time of jackpot
      iii. Machine identification/location
      iv. Jackpot type
      v. Employees and others involved in payment and verification of jackpot
      vi. Note whether controls, policies, and procedures were followed
      vii. Results of the review of the play leading up to jackpot
      viii. Photo of the winner placed in the player database and referenced to the incident report number
      ix. Video does not have to be saved but may be held, if necessary

5. Slot jackpots of $100,000 or more.
   a. Perform the above
   b. Alert the director of surveillance
   c. Video shall be saved

GLOSSARY OF GAMING TERMS

ACSM: Assistant casino shift manager.

action: A bet or wager. Amount of money wagered by the player during the playing session.

advantage play: Any legal skill, system, or type of play that takes advantage of a game or game type, or marketing promotion's inherent weakness(s) or uses the poor training or use of game protection procedures of a gaming employee to gain an edge over the casino (i.e., card counting, hole card play, slot teams, etc.).

agent: A player who works in collusion with a dealer or floor person to cheat or steal from the casino. Also surveillance agent: A title for an individual who operates cameras in the surveillance room.

all in: Betting the whole bankroll.

ante: Required wager to get money into the pot before cards are dealt.

audit: A surveillance assignment requiring observation of an area or transaction, department, or employee(s) in order to detect violations of controls, policies, or procedures, or indicators of theft or fraud.

back counting: Counting the game and playing only the count is a plus. Usually jumps into play at such times and can be signaled in by another player on the game.

back of the house: Employee and support areas of the hotel/casino.

bad beat: When a great poker hand is beat by a better hand, such as when a straight flush is beaten by a higher straight flush.

bankroll: What the player has available to wager, which will determine his wager amounts.

basic strategy: The optimum strategy for 21 play. Used by advantage players and cheaters to obtain maximum advantage or utilize card or decision information obtained. Used by surveillance to detect advantage players and cheats.

beard: A player who bets for another player. Someone who does not want his or her identity to be known.

beef: A problem or dispute with a player.

bet spread: The difference between a player's highest and lowest bet.

Biometrica: The company that pioneered facial recognition software used in the gaming industry. Also provides the infrastructure for the a national surveillance information network and database.

BJ Survey: A computer-based 21 analysis program that aids surveillance and table games personnel in the detection of advantage play, accurate evaluation of a players knowledge and skill, and that player's advantage or disadvantage against the casino.

blind: A required bet before the cards are dealt in poker.

blockout work: Cards that are marked by blocking out areas or portions of the design.

break-in dealer: A dealer learning to deal at a particular property but already on the clock, new dealer.

bullet: An ace.

burn card: A card discarded by dealer after cutting the deck.

capping: Adding a check to a wager after game decision is made.

card counting: Keeping track of the cards dealt in an attempt to determine when the advantage lies with the player or with the house. There are many different systems but they are primarily based on assigning values to individual cards as they are dealt from the deck or the shoe. See also advantage play.

card mechanic: A card cheat who manipulates the cards or used sleight of hand.

cheating: Any illegal activity used to alter the course or outcome of a game or to obtain information not available to other players (i.e., marking cards, using a device to obtain hole card information or to cheat a slot machine).

chip cup: A cheating device used to hide higher denomination chips or checks within the hollow center. Cup is made to depict a stack of green or black checks. A dealer working in collusion with a player will insert higher denomination checks during transactions.

chips: Items used to denote amounts of money in gambling. Normally in $1, $5, $25, $100, $500, and $1,000 denominations, although larger casinos use $5,000 and higher denominations. Chips are traditionally used in roulette games. See also checks.

checks: Same as chips. Normally used by surveillance and table games personnel.

close watch: A surveillance observation of an area or subject requiring that the subject is continuously monitored by the surveillance department. Usually initiated by information or a tip.

CM: Casino manager.

c-note: A $100 bill

collusion: Two or more players secretly working together or with an employee to cheat or steal.

cooler: Deck(s) of cards introduced into game normally through collusion with the dealer or floor staff. Decks are stacked and prepared for player wins. So called because they are supposedly cool to the touch as compared to the cards that were in use on the game.

countermeasure: A response by surveillance or the property to a threat or actual incidence of advantage play or crime; may be a policy such as prohibiting mid-shoe entry, or an action such as securing a door to prevent employee theft.

coverage: In surveillance, coverage refers to the video of an incident taken from the cameras recording the event or area.

cover bet: A bet used by advantage players to camouflage their play, usually when a floor person is watching.

critical index: In blackjack, certain strategic plays or adjustments to basic strategy at certain true count totals.

crossroader: An old, traditional term for a cheater. Someone who works or plays legally in one casino but cheats at another when off duty.

CSM: Casino shift manager.

cut card: Normally a colored card used to cut the deck and to protect the bottom of the deck from exposure.

daub: Any substance used to mark cards.

dealer/agent: Usually used to refer to collusion between a player and a dealer to steal (dump the game).

detection: Observation of a crime, advantage play, or policy/procedure violation.

DOS: Director of surveillance.

dump the game: A dealer dumps the game to a confederate by overpaying wagers, pushing losers, not taking losers, etc. See also dealer/agent.

edge: An advantage, as in house advantage.

eighty-six: Remove, trespass from the property, usually permanently.

evaluation: Analysis of a player (normally a 21 player) by the surveillance department. Usually takes into account the player's knowledge of basic strategy, money management, and card counting abilities.

eye in the sky: Surveillance department.

fat: Gambler with a large bankroll.

flashing: Dealer exposing top card or hole card to player, intentionally or unintentionally.

flash work: Marking cards by shading the back of cards except for a small portion to indicate specific values of cards.

flat bet: Countermeasure to advantage players by requiring the player to bet the same amount each hand.

flats: Shaved dice used to hit certain numbers more frequently.

fraud: Theft by deception.

gaff: Anything that is made or altered to cheat at gambling.

George: Big tipper, term used especially by dealers.

Gem-backs: Borderless card back design developed by Gemaco Playing Card Company.

glim: Shiny object used to reflect value/index of card.

G-note: A $1,000 bill.

Griffin: Griffin Investigations, a service that provides an online service reporting individuals or teams of individuals detected cheating or involved in advantage play.

grind: Low action.

hand mucker: A card cheat who specializes in switching cards in and out of a game.

hard hand: A blackjack hand without an ace. Hand has only one value, it is what it is.

high roller: Big player, high action for the casino.

hit: In blackjack, to indicate or request another card from the dealer.

holdout machine: Usually a mechanical device used by a card cheat to aid and hold cards switched in and out of game.

holdout man: Card cheat who switches cards in and out of game as needed.

hold percentage: Percentage of money kept by a casino from the wagers made by the player. Usually refers to slot hold.

hole card: In blackjack or stud poker, the hole card is face down.

hole card play: Using the information provided by an exposed hole card, gained legally or illegally, to make playing decisions in blackjack.

insurance: In blackjack, a side bet offered to players when the dealer's up card is an ace. Pays two to one if the dealer has the blackjack, otherwise the bet loses.

internal theft: Employee theft. Cheating, theft, or fraud committed by a company's own employees.

IOU: An acronym for a surveillance patrol technique: Identify, Observe, Understand.

IOU patrol: A basic surveillance technique. Used to identify individuals, the play or activity in that area, and to determine if the player or activity is a threat to the property, and provides for the gathering of evidence.

juice: Commission charged by a casino. See also vig.

luminous readers: A deck that is marked. Marks are invisible to the eye except when viewed through a red filter (such as the card discard tray located on most table games) or red tinted glasses or contact lenses.

marker: Credit instrument issued in a casino.

mechanic: A cheat who specializes in sleight of hand, can be a card or dice mechanic.

mechanic's grip: A method of holding the deck to allow a variety of card manipulations. Used by card mechanics.

money management: Any method devised and employed for wagering to purportedly allow maximum win or prevent drastic loss.

monitor: The observation of an area or person. Used interchangeably with "observe."

muck: A hand mucking maneuver.

natural: An ace and a ten in blackjack.

observe: The surveillance of an area or person. Used interchangeably with "monitor."

observe and report: The basic function of a surveillance department.

occupational fraud: The clandestine theft of organization's assets by employees of that organization.

off the top: First bet after a shuffle.

overhand run-up: A method used to stack the deck(s).

palm: As in palming a card. Any method used to conceal a card or cards in order to switch it in or out, or steal it.

past posting: Placing a bet after the outcome of the game is known.

pat hand: Hand worth at least seventeen points in blackjack.

patrol: The movement of cameras through an area or activity.

peeking: Techniques used to cheat or in advantage play to see the dealer's hole card or top card.

pivot point: The plus or minus count where a bet or strategic decision is altered.

pressing: A player presses a bet when he or she lets a winning bet ride along with the original bet.

protect the assets: Basic mission of the surveillance department.

push: A tie.

quads: Four of a kind in poker.

rack: A plastic container to carry table fills. Also can refer to the check tray on table games.

rake: Money removed from the pot by the house in poker.

rated play: In table games and slots, rated players are those frequent players whose play is tracked for comping and rebate purposes.

readers: Cards marked for cheating.

reflector: Same as glim.

refused name player: A player who will not identify him- or herself for rating and comping purposes. Usually considered unusual or suspect by surveillance due to its relative rarity.

response: A surveillance reaction to a threat or observation that requires action.

RFB: Free room, food, and beverage. Comped for big players.

riffle stacking: Stacking the deck using a riffle shuffle.

riffle test: Used to test a deck of cards for marks. As the cards are held and riffled, the back design of the cards are observed. If the design has been altered by marks, some (not all) can be detected in this manner.

riffling: A shuffle process. Cards are divided in half and "riffled" together.

RNG: Random number generator, commonly used to generate random numbers in games such as video poker, keno, Pai Gow, etc.

round: In card games a round can be a round of hands (often used in dealer pace audits), or a round of betting.

rubbernecking: The constant looking around by cheats checking to see if someone is on to them.

running count: Counting each card, adding or subtracting as necessary to create a count of the deck or shoe at the end of each round.

scared money: Playing on money you can't afford to lose.

score: A large win.

scout: Used by cheat teams or advantage play teams to locate weak casinos or dealers that can be taken advantage of.

session: A player's period of play.

shill: A player employed by the casino to get and keep the game going.

shiner: Same as glim.

shuffle tracking: Advantage play, used by an individual player or a team of players to track certain cards through a deck or shoe.

shuffle up: Shuffling cards prior to designated time, usually at instruction of pit boss to inhibit or send a message to a suspected advantage player.

silver mining: Looking for coins, credits, or tickets left by another player.

SIN: Surveillance Information Network; a general term used to describe a cooperative network of casinos in a jurisdiction or nationally that share information.

snapper: In blackjack, an ace and a ten-value card.

soft hand: In blackjack, a hand that contains and can be counted as one or eleven.

sorts: Groups of cards that are marked by the same imperfections.

spooking: In blackjack, standing behind a dealer to pick up the hole card and signal the value of the card to a cohort.

stack: A group of cards secretly set in a predetermined order.

stacking: Secretly arranging certain cards inside the deck so that they fall to a certain player.

stiff: In blackjack, a hand that may bust if hit once.

stripping: In card shuffling, reverses the sequential order of the cards.

surrender: In blackjack, to give up half your bet in order to not complete the hand.

surveillance agent: An individual who works the cameras in the surveillance room.

table hold: The amount of money won by a casino during a particular shift or day.

team play: Using two or more players in advantage play such as back counting, hole card, etc.

tell: Any indicator or behavior by a person/player that telegraphs a cheating move or technique, is indicative of advantage play, or provides information of how a player will bet or play in a particular situation.

tell play: Playing the game and adjusting strategic plays based on the observation of other players to detect body language or other behavior or tendencies that give away information.

threat: A potential risk to the property by a employee, player, visitor, or guest as in an advantage player who poses the risk of loss, or a employee who may obtain access to a sensitive area for illicit activity.

toke: A tip for the dealer or any employee in the casino.

tri-shot: A basic and minimum surveillance camera setup used to provide the necessary information and evidence.

true count: An adjusted running count to further determine the balance of cards remaining in the deck or shoe. Calculated by dividing the running count by the number of decks remaining.

true odds: Real odds, actual odds. The ratio of number of times one event will occur to the number of times it will not.

units: Normally refers to betting units, used to denote wager amounts made by individual players. For example, a player betting one $25 check up to four $25 checks can be said to spreading up to four units. The unit in this case equals $25.

upcard: In blackjack the dealer's card that is seen and played to. Used to determine proper play with basic strategy.

vig: Juice, commission charged by the casino.

VIP: Very important person, high roller.

whale: A huge player, often bets the maximum. Can make or break a casino's profit for the year.

white-on-white: Card marking method using some type of white substance on the white border of on the backs of cards. The marks can be seen at certain angles.

wong, wonging: In blackjack, to join play only when the count is advantageous.

x-ray: Often used as the radio call sign for the surveillance department.

z-out: Close out the cash register to determine sales, used in retail.

INDEX